D0261772

GROW UP

GROW UP

AN AUTOBIOGRAPHY

KEITH ALLEN

EBURY
PRESS

1 3 5 7 9 10 8 6 4 2

This edition published 2008

First published in 2007 by Ebury Press, an imprint of Ebury Publishing
A Random House Group Company

The Random House Group Limited Reg. No. 954009

Addresses for companies within the Random House Group can be found at
www.randomhouse.co.uk

A CIP catalogue record for this book is available from the British Library

The Random House Group Limited supports The Forest Stewardship Council
(FSC), the leading international forest certification organisation. All our titles that
are printed on Greenpeace approved FSC certified paper carry the FSC logo. Our
paper procurement policy can be found at www.rbooks.co.uk/environment

Printed in the UK by CPI Cox & Wyman, Reading, RG1 8EX

ISBN 9780091910716

To buy books by your favourite authors and register for offers visit
www.rbooks.co.uk

In memory of
David Williams
Liam Carson
Joe Strummer

'Do what that wilt shall be the whole of the Law'

— Aleister Crowley

CONTENTS

THE NINETIES

THE NOUGHTIES

AFTERWORD

Foreword

DEAR READER

I recently noticed a four-page article in the *Independent* entitled 'When is a person officially a Grown-up?'

Such luminaries as David Lodge, Billy Bragg, Jo Brand, J.G. Ballard and Jenni Murray all gave their definitions of the age at which you are technically Grown Up. Their answers were: eighteen, thirty, never, twenty-five, fifty-six and six, respectively. Which shows that no one can really decide. Others decide for you. With that in mind I present my case in this book – and when you've read it, it is up to you whether to shout: 'Oh grow up! ' or: 'My! Hasn't Keith Allen grown up recently,' or even: 'He'll never grow up.'

And, like me, you'll probably ask yourself why people in the public eye write these books.

I guess the answer would be that memoirs are of interest, though why on earth I would want to know about some mindless footballer's prowess at the age of eleven is quite beyond my ken. But, having said that, I can easily see how the stroking of *my* young cock in a Maltese cellar would be of great interest to *you*.

And I presume the idea is also to invite you into the workings of my mind. Why I am the way I am … A little example for you. When in India recently, I was confronted with the tricky problem of giving alms to the poor.

While being followed round by hordes of urchins might be appealing to the Gary Glitters of this world, it is not to me. If you give them each a penny it encourages them to hound you to death. It also has very little effect on their collective lives. So I hit upon this idea. I would keep as much small change as I could on the bedside table of the penthouse suite of my five-star hotel room. I would then let fate take command. The first beggar who tapped on my cab window on my last day would be the one who got my laundry bag full of money.

On my way to the airport, the cab came to a standstill in one of the many traffic jams that are collectively known as Mumbai, and a beggar tapped on my window. So I wound it down and handed over the bag, which had turned into a considerable sum. Enough to change a beggar's life. So if you are ever in Mumbai, trailing in my emotional wake, remember that you have a choice in life – give a bit to each or a lot to a few. And know that I prefer the latter. I'm not sure the taxi driver that day would agree, having the side panelling of his cab kicked in by a crowd of beggars looking for more out of me.

Sometimes you have to be taken by the mood. I do what I do at the time and hope it's the right decision. Whether this is grown up or not I don't know. To live according to this philosophy requires a certain confidence, though, and I suppose comfort in one's own skin. Some people think I'm a complete arsehole. I don't mind that now. Once upon a time I did. That moment of change from caring what people think of you to not caring is, for me, the defining moment of the 'growing-up' process. With me it was also the realisation, during my various incarcerations in HM prisons, that I wasn't a *criminal*. In a perverse kind of way this gave me the freedom to indulge in my favourite pastime – having as much fun as I possibly could.

So, if you come to the conclusion that I am the arsehole you always thought, it's only because I have omitted the parts that will convince you otherwise, which will be included in Part Two of my memoirs.

A few thank yous to some dear dear friends:

I would like to thank BAFTA and the RTS for their unswerving patience in not giving me any award of any description ever.

Harold Pinter for his undying support and faith.

Dame Judi Dench for her intention to sue (ooh, you naughty girl).

David Furnish for only staying at my fiftieth birthday party for eight minutes.

Bill Clinton for signing an autograph to Osama Bin Laden.

David Williams for making me into an actor.

And, finally, thanks to all the dead people I know. See you soon.

Whether this collection of memories reinforces or changes your opinion is neither here nor there. What is, however, here, is my percentage on the book jacket price, a proportion of which will be used to fight various lawsuits.

THE FIFTIES

Chapter 1

CHRISTMAS ISLAND, 1957. The deck of the HMS *Warrior*. Eddie Allen stared at the land mass in front of him. He was a handsome sailor with a happy smile and a lithe, athletic body. Not blessed with height, he was blessed with charm and good looks. Eddie sniffed the air, hair short, neat and slicked back. The sun was low in the sky and the sea was flat. The crew stood in rows waiting for orders which soon came.

'All ratings turn away from the sun.'

They turned their backs and stared at the horizon. Only the high-ranking officers continued to stare at the island, binoculars trained. Eddie fingered the camera in his hand, checking it was wound on, finger on the button.

Silence.

A blinding white flash was followed by the wind forced outwards, then the sound, a subterranean boom and unearthly rumble. The mushroom cloud from the explosion filled the sky. Eddie and the crew could stand the tension no more and turned to look right into the nuclear fungi. He put the camera to his eye and got the shot.

'Look at that.'

Eddie turned to his mate to get a light for a celebratory cigarette. The crew were now at ease, mingling and talking excitedly in groups, taking photos and waving.

'That's history, that is. Something to tell the kids, eh? We were there when the first H-bomb was detonated.'

It was a momentous event, signalling a new era of death and destruction in the world. A few weeks later, an equally momentous event was about to occur that threatened to bring similar levels of chaos to my world. Eddie Allen came home.

Everything is sketchy. No more than a few frozen images. The door opened with a familiar clunk. Eddie came in and hugged my mother Mary. I remember her being tall but she wasn't, probably five foot three, with dark skin and black hair. She wore neat and tidy skirts and pinnies and moved with quick efficiency when tidying or cleaning (which is what she did all the time). Talking and murmuring went on between them for some time. He was talking excitedly about a photograph he was holding. Stabbing it with stubby digits.

'There you go, Mary, that's me, and behind me, there, that's the H-bomb.'

'It's lovely, Eddie.'

The big shadow turned to me.

'Where's my son? Is that really you? Haven't you grown? How old is he, Mary?'

'Three and a half. He's getting so big.'

'Come here, son. Haven't you grown up?'

Mum put the photo on the mantelpiece and he lifted me up to look at it. Above the mantelpiece was a mirror. In the mirror was me and this strange man, Eddie. We stared at each other reflected in the glass. Then both of us looked at me, a gawky kid with NHS glasses that were patched over one lens. All the other kids had two good eyes. He put me down and walked out of the room. From the off there was no denying I was different, the eye saw to that, which meant Keith Allen was either special or the odd one out. At the front door Mum was waving Eddie off. That was it: as suddenly as he was here he was gone again. Oh, but he left the photo, so that's all right then.

In the garden Billy the boxer dog snarled and pulled at the chain. He didn't seem to realise that he was tethered to the washing post. It fascinated me to see him circling and pulling. He was straining so much he was choking himself. Perhaps it was an autoerotic dog fantasy, but aged four that didn't concern me. What did concern me was poor Billy being tied up, held back, unable to be free. It was the same for me. On the bus into Portsmouth we'd sit on the top deck, me in a child-restrainer and Mum holding the reins. If I tried to go anywhere I'd be yanked backwards.

'For goodness' sake, Keith. STOP PULLING or you'll get a smack.'

A few minutes later I'd try again only to feel the yank and the smack on the legs.

The leftover chocolate melted in my hand and filled the crevices between my fingers. My white shirt seemed as good a place as any to wipe my hands. Billy cocked his head and I offered him a piece.

'You want some chocolate?'

As he strained to reach it, large dollops of slobber fell on the grass. As my hand got near his mouth, his tongue came out to lick the chocolate, but I whipped it away.

'Gently.' If he wanted it, he was going to have to work for it.

He stared at me hatefully, then more submissively.

'Take it gently.'

He opened his mouth like a puppy, delicate and soft. Instead of rewarding him I took the chocolate away and put it in my own mouth, smiling triumphantly. What we're talking about here is a small child demonstrating the kind of psychology a Nazi interrogator would be proud of. Billy's ears fell in disappointment, then the growling started, low and personal.

There followed a staring competition which Billy was in no mood to lose. Which one of us would look away first? Usually the dog had the run of the garden, but that morning he'd decided that the kid next door was better breakfast than Pedigree Chum and had taken a large chunk out of his leg. Consequently Mum had spent a long time finding out how much it would cost to have him put down.

'Mum? Is Billy going to die?' I'd asked.

'No, love, it's too expensive. He'll have to stay tied to that post instead.'

Poor Billy lived because we couldn't afford to kill him. Again I knew how he felt. Even at four years old I had a nagging doubt about how popular I was in our house. So there we were, kindred spirits, kid with dicky eye and dog with anger issues. We continued to stare at each other.

This was one fight neither of us social misfits wanted to lose. His snarling noises made me want to poo myself.

Suddenly he went for me, his large fangs narrowly missing my nose. Mum stuck her head out of the kitchen window.

'Keith, get away from that dog.'

'I'm not near the dog.'

'I know what you're doing.'

'I'm not doing anything.'

'If you get bit it's your own fault.'

'I'm just looking for Bill the Tortoise, that's all.'

This was partly true. I had been conducting a highly scientific experiment involving my tortoise, who was also called Bill. (Not being a very imaginative bunch, the Allen family named all its pets Bill.) The experiment involved the Tortoise and the Mangle but an Aesop's Fable it was not. This was no moral tale expounding the age-old lesson of 'give and you shall receive'. This was another exercise in torture.

When Mum put my clothes through the mangle, they came out all flat. Would Bill do the same? Perhaps getting wind of my plan, Bill had made himself unavailable for comment.

Some days later I was still looking for Bill. He should have been fairly easy to spot because on my insistence Mum had painted 'BILL' on his shell in big white letters. There were voices coming from the garden shed and, being naturally inquisitive, I went to investigate. I was old enough to know that tortoises had not yet developed the power of speech but it was worth checking.

Susan and two of her girlfriends were in there starring in an all-female version of Doctors and Nurses. One of them was prodding a straw up the other one's nunny.

'Well, nurse,' said Susan. 'You appear to have a nasty object up there.'

Susan was my nemesis, my older sister by nearly two years. She was dark like Mum, with Shirley Temple ringlets and long legs. She was already a head-turner, but also well behaved and good at school. But all I saw was the enemy … Anyway, the game continued.

'What is it, doctor?'

'I think it's a penis.'

'A what?'

'A penis. It's what boys have.'

'How did a penis get up there?'

'It must have got stuck. Don't worry, I'll take it out.'

I didn't have the faintest idea what was going on but not unsurprisingly I was hooked. Clearly it was time to join in and offer my services as 'the penis'. The girls weren't very pleased to see me and my entry was greeted with much screaming and rearranging of undergarments.

'GO AWAY. We're playing.'

'I'm gonna tell.'

'Whatcha gonna tell?'

She had a point. This was a new one on me and not an easy thing to explain to my mother. But I'd seen enough to confirm my suspicions that girls were different. They had strange stuff going on up there. Stuff I needed to know more about.

'I want to play.'

'No.'

'Please.' (I never EVER said please. Herein lies a clue to the level of my desperation.)

'Shove OFF, squirt.'

Susan pushed me out and shut the door. It was a meagre existence being the only man in a household of women. My life revolved round being shouted at by Mum and excluded by Susan, who was already looking towards puberty whereas all I had to look forward to was several more years of not knowing what my cock was for. Apart from the shadowy figure who had come and gone there were no men in my life at all.

Maybe it was this world without men that led me to assert my masculinity at every turn so that no one thought I was a woman. (All the women I knew cooked and cleaned and got fat and I didn't want that to happen to me.)

The first way it was expressed was bullying Jeremy, my next-door neighbour. Jeremy was tall and skinny and had big lips (which was not a crime) and wore glasses (fine – I had them as well). The biggest problem was that he rarely took his thumb out of his mouth. Typical conversation between me and Jeremy over the garden wall:

'Why can't you come and play, Jeremy?' (Probably add an appropriate small-child expletive.)

Thumb out of mouth. 'Can't. I'm playing with my sister Maria.'

Thumb back in. Now even at that age I knew that this was the mark of a deviant. He also always wore a collar and tie – but that we must blame his parents for.

He wasn't a proper boy like me and Peter Hardcastle, my best mate. First of all, Pete looked a lot like me, which is why I liked him so much. He was also a good runner. A particularly fine feature, which seemed rebellious and exciting, was his hair, in which he was allowed to wear Brylcreem. And, yes, I liked him because he was called Hardcastle. What a good name. But his most important quality was his everlasting devotion to me.

'Mum? Can I play in the road? All the other boys do.'

'You're not old enough.'

'Why not?'

'Because you're only four and a half.'

'When am I old enough?'

'When you learn how to be a good boy.'

A few weeks later either the nagging had paid off or Mum got so sick of it that she opened the garden gate and let me go over the road to the playground in the square.

'I'm watching you,' she said, wagging her finger. But it was an empty threat. A minute later she was back at the mangle, giving it as good as she had.

I got on the swing and got a good push-off, Peter watching me. I was soon cruising through the air so high that my arse was falling off the seat. The next push propelled me up and over, so that all I could feel was the sensation of falling as my hands somehow kept a grip on the chains and the earth rushed towards me.

Of course, Mum had decided to stop mangling clothes at that very moment and saw the whole thing. She came running out and slapped me for nearly killing myself.

'Don't you dare do anything else dangerous when I'm watching you and don't be disappearing as soon as my back's turned.'

As soon as her back was turned, we disappeared. We were little boys, what else were we going to do? Something dangerous, of course, and nothing was more dangerous or as much FUN as climbing trees. No longer confined to the garden, the world was my oyster.

Peter climbed a tree and sat on the first branch.

'Oi, Keith! This one.'

He offered a hand to pull me up but with one spring I was up past him.

'Where are you going?'

'To the top.'

It was a competition and as usual I'd raised the bar. He gawped up, eating the dirt displaced by my clambering feet, probably half hoping I'd come crashing down past him. At the top of the tree I could see all of Bridgemary and Gosport, all the way to the sea. An infinite horizon that offered endless possibilities.

On our first day in the Infants, me and Pete certainly felt the toughest. Mum let us walk there on our own. No one worried about traffic or perverts or paedophiles then.

In the playground a game of kiss-chase was under way. The older lads pushed each other aside to kiss the prettiest girls. Immediately it was apparent that weakness was punished and cockiness reaped rewards. I made a mental note to misbehave as frequently as possible.

A week later me and Pete were in front of the headmaster for the first time.

'Allen? Hardcastle? You know what you have done is called *stealing*. Do you know what that means?'

We shook our heads. When we'd dismantled all the school photographs in the assembly hall and taken the wooden frames, we hadn't seen it as stealing, simply redistribution of school wealth. But after we tried to sell the frames to the housewives on our estate, Mrs Hardcastle at number 3 decided to redistribute this information in the direction of the headmaster of Bridgemary Infants, who subsequently decided to redistribute his cane on my arse. It was a cruel world for a young entrepreneur.

On our estate nothing spread faster than gossip and nowhere was there a hotbed like the phonebox. In the evenings all the women used to queue up to phone their husbands stationed abroad or on ships. The Second World War still loomed large in everyone's mind and it wasn't uncommon for an impromptu sing-song to break out in the line for the phone.

But this evening there was no singing or jollity, only severe stares in my direction after it had been passed down the queue that I'd been trying to sell stolen goods. It may have been a long way to Tipperary but at that moment I would have quite happily sprinted there.

I could see Mrs Hardcastle talking very fast to my mother while glaring at me. She was possibly the ugliest woman I'd ever seen. Mum came back and without a word took me home and spanked me.

'Ow. What was that for?'

'You think it's funny to dismantle school photo frames that are there for *everybody* to enjoy and then try and sell them?'

'No.'

'You're not going out until you say sorry.'

'Sorry. Can I go out?'

'No.'

No wonder we kids lied if that was the example our mothers set.

It was a Sunday and something was clearly afoot. Levels of housework activity had been stepped up and Mum was wearing a different expression on her face. I decided to mull it over in my 'submarine'. The kitchen floor was my favourite place; it became the sea, and I manoeuvred my way round it on my back. You had to be careful to avoid the multiple underwater hazards, such as the coke-burning stove which even in warm weather burned hot to heat the water for the whole house.

Suddenly the house was full of Mum's friends. I took the opportunity to manoeuvre my submarine north by north-east and up-periscoped under Pat Fraser's skirt. There wasn't another submarine in the world that could slip from one position to another as silently as me. Pat Fraser laughed and her heel dug into my periscope arm. My scream gave my position away to the enemy.

'He's trying to look up our skirts again …'

Mum grabbed me up and as revenge did the thing I hated most. She spat on her hankie and rubbed my face. Grown-up spit stank and was full of stuff that wasn't supposed to go on kids' faces. I struggled and pulled and held my breath.

'You wait till your father gets home.'

'Who?'

'You know, your father. Don't be silly.'

'No I don't.'

I didn't. Apart from the shadowy figure who left a photo on the mantelpiece. She gave a sharp intake of breath to signify she was getting cross.

'Don't try me, Keith.'

I didn't try her and went to ask my sister instead.

'What's he like, my father?'

'Durgh.'

She made a face at me so I hit her. It still didn't get my question answered. Who was my father and where had he been? More to the point, what would he do when he got home? I both wanted and didn't want to know. I stared at the photo on the mantelpiece.

We waited for my 'father' interminably that day. There were inventive ways to pass the time, like running out and staring at my reflection in the hubcaps of cars with my funny eye. If I took off my glasses and closed my right eye, the good one, it all became a blur, like someone had smeared Vaseline across the world.

After an age of waiting I ran back to the house, head down, to see how far I could get before I collided with something. The answer was as far as the kitchen door and the obstruction was – a pair of sturdy male legs. This unidentified object turned out to be Eddie Allen, the missing father. Mum stood behind him, arms crossed, beaming.

'Say hello to your father.'

He chucked my cheeks and patted my head awkwardly. Apparently he'd been away for more than a whole year, which people kept repeating, tutting and sighing and shaking their heads like it was something quite amazing. He smiled at me.

'You been a good lad for your mother?'

My nod and smile were as angelic as humanly possible. Mum looked at me and narrowed her eyes. It was a lie, of course. The house filled up with more of Mum's friends but I couldn't take my eyes off Eddie. He was talking a lot and the gathered crowd hung on his every word and laughed at his jokes. There was a smell in the air that was coming from his clothes, like ingrained oil or petrol. Then he went into his bag and brought out a pair of guns in a holster and called me over.

'These are for you, son. They're from South America. Very advanced replica guns they have there. Very. You could hold a bank up with them.'

He held court while I played with the guns and aimed at his head and fired. A huge SNAP filled the air and Eddie winced and glared at me. Oops … it had taken less than five minutes to piss him off. I stood with the gun behind my back, as if to pretend it hadn't happened. Instinctively I knew this was not the kind of joke he liked.

He managed a tight little smile. 'Why don't you go and play with the guns outside?'

This seemed a good escape plan and once out of the door I ran all the way to Pete's, a gun in each hand, fingers over the trigger like a cowboy desperate to tell his compadre that trouble had just ridden in to town.

'My dad's back.'

'What's he like?'

'Dunno.'

We started shooting each other and then Pete let out an enormous fart, to which I replied with a louder one. We collapsed laughing and kept forcing them out, pretending the guns were special farting machines.

Then out of nowhere Eddie appeared, looming over the gate. Again he didn't find it funny. Maybe he was insulted by the way we were using the guns.

'Come on, Keith. Your mother wants you home.'

I recognised this as another adult lie straightaway because Mum never wanted me home. She always wanted me out from under her feet. As we walked back up the street he put a hand on my neck, as if marking his territory.

'Right, son. Things are going to change. From now on I pick you up from school. Keep you out of trouble.'

There wasn't any protesting on my part. You didn't mess with my dad, I just knew. Everyone knew.

On Monday after school I waited at the gates for him, longingly watching the other lads run off to play in the woods or on the railway bridge. Eddie arrived and stood there, hands in pockets, looking for me. I didn't go towards him immediately, just watched him from the comfort of distance. He spotted me and waved awkwardly, coming over. A woman walked by, laughing and smoking. She was wearing high heels and lipstick. Dad tutted, shaking his head, muttering disapprovingly.

Then a little girl ran over and the woman scooped her up in her arms and gave her a big hug. Eddie stared, then looked at me, and we both walked home in silence.*

If I didn't know who my dad was before, I certainly did now. My freedom was severely curtailed, and if I uttered an iota of protest there was a thwack to contend with. Mum may have been pleased to have him back on a more regular basis, but she also changed as a result. She would be on tenterhooks to his mood, altering hers to suit his, making sure they were both in step.

Dad met Mum when she was waitressing in a café in Plymouth. She'd left Llanelli in order to 'better herself', which presumably meant finding a husband with decent prospects. Eddie had joined the navy and his ship was stationed there; he was working his way up the ladder to becoming a submariner. The first few years of their married life was spent in 'hirings' – a single room in Portsmouth while they waited for the navy to find them a house. They had nothing, no possessions apart from two screaming babies: Susan and me. When they did get a house, Dad was often away from it.

* Years later, Dad told me he'd envied the woman. He didn't know how to be like that with me.

*

On the way to school was a road bridge over the railway that brought the metal muscle of the British army to Portsmouth docks and then out via the warships to some vague corner of what was left of the empire. The steam trains pulled everything from tanks and helicopters to jump boats and aeroplanes with their wings folded in on themselves for easy transport. There was a sense of being in the middle of a huge military machine that was always moving, and somewhere in the back of my mind I knew that my old man was part of it.

On this occasion tanks were passing below. With my hands I made fake guns and took the tanks out one by one. Pete appeared and joined me hanging over the bridge and copied my hand-gun in silence. It was about four o'clock. A few of the older lads from Holbrook Juniors had congregated on the other side of the bridge and were play-fighting.

'Oi, Pete … watch me.'

My latest trick was to climb up on the parapet on the other side of the bridge, where cars passed and pedestrians weren't meant to go, and walk across it that way.

He looked up then away again in boredom. He was right. Though foolhardy and dangerous, it was nothing new. Every kid had done it. I tried to get his attention with a twirl but he didn't bat an eyelid; neither did the older lads on the other side of the bridge. They were the ones I really wanted to impress. Yet again the bar needed to be raised.

'OK, then, what if I do it when a train comes underneath?'

'Don't be stupid. You don't dare.'

'I do. Watch me.'

Pete shook his head and laughed as if it was a bluff, but it wasn't. To walk the parapet when a steam train passed underneath meant walking blind as the bridge would be enveloped in fog. One slip could mean death.

Still, there was no going back now. The dare was there to win and Muggins here had stepped up. A steam train was chugging towards us. The bridge was filling up with mums and kids going back to the estate. I had an audience.

'La la la la la la la laaaaaaaa …'

I did a couple of fancy turns and stood brazenly on the thin ledge of the parapet conducting an imaginary orchestra. It was madness, everyone knew it. The older lads started whispering to each other and nodding in my direction.

'Bet you chicken,' one of the lads shouted.

'Bet I don't.'

Chickening out was not an option, though shitting my pants was. In fact, it was that, rather than the fear of falling, that occupied my mind. The train was a few hundred yards away and coming fast. This was my chance to prove myself to my heroes and in the process become their hero. A couple of women on the pedestrian side of the bridge stopped and gasped, gripping their children more firmly by the hand.

'Keith Allen, get down from there! Or I'll see your mother.'

But they seemed a long way away, too far away to reach me. Everything slowed down. The train approaching, the taunts of the kids, the anxious mothers. All I could feel was the thin width of stone beneath my feet. The train was upon me and I closed my eyes.

'Keith, you could get killed!'

I didn't know what death was. Whatever it was, it was better than failing the dare. As the train went under the bridge the noise became deafening. I inched forward, all pins and needles and a strange buzzing sensation. I must have disappeared from view; I heard someone screaming.

The mist started to clear and I could see the other side and ran for it before my legs buckled. All the lads cheered me and I pumped the air with my fists. This was what it was all about – people adoring me, people loving me.

The crowd started to disperse, the anxious mothers fading away, dragging their kids, no doubt relieved I wasn't their son. The older lads sloped off with peeved looks as they were forced to acknowledge my achievement.

'Keith Allen, King of the Bridge!' Pete shouted and saluted me in return.

I was up where I belonged. From now on this would be all that mattered. And recapturing that buzz would be my aim in life.

Chapter 2

MUM, SUSAN AND me spent our summers at Nan's house in Llanelli. The valleys round Llanelli were mining country and my mum's family were miners for many generations back. She was one of eight: Roy, Alf, Arthur, Ivor, Les, Gwyn, Ethnie and Emma. Mum was Emma, except that at home in Gosport no one called her Emma, they called her Mary. Nanny John was the matriarch, and Nan's was the centre of my universe.

The train journey to Llanelli was one of the best things about the whole holiday. The Great Western Railway went through Gloucester and Stroud, snaked into Monmouthshire to Cardiff where we changed trains to Swansea. It was seven hours filled with excitement and anticipation.

Nanny John had the softest skin of anyone I've met in my life. I never saw her wear make-up. She would stand, broom in one hand, other hand on hip, talking across the fence to Mrs Morgan next door. Her arms were the best arms I'd ever seen or felt. They would envelop me as soon as I arrived. Nothing bad could happen to me there. As to her shape, she was almost a complete square. Her dimensions would impress Pythagoras. But never mind that. Any woman who cooked and cleaned for eight children and thirty-nine grandchildren will always be a hero in my eyes.

Uncle Roy worked on the coal tip. Eager to do anything that involved getting dirty and pissing Mum off, I nagged him to take me with him.

Uncle Roy passed me another lump of coal and together we filled the sack.

'That's right, boy, fill it up full now …'

I'm sure there were rules about child labour and five-years-olds but as the coal soot covered me from head to foot the words 'happy as a pig in shit' applied nicely. Roy stooped to fill his own sack, a fag fixed in the corner of his mouth. His job was to sell the coal around the estates. Hard money in an even harder environment.

At the end of the day we drove back to Nan's, me sitting proudly on top of several bags of coal filled with my own bare hands. As we turned into Lewis Crescent, Mum came running out of the house towards the truck. She saw me and her whole face relaxed, then a split second later calm was replaced with anger and she bawled at Roy.

'You weren't supposed to take him. We didn't know where he was.'

'He's a right little worker that one, Emma, you should be very proud.'

Roy attempted to make things right, though it was my legs that were in danger, not his. Mum grabbed me and pulled me inside, where I received two deft slaps to my calves.

'That's for going off without telling anybody. And look at you! You're black.'

It took an hour in the bath to get the soot off and my clothes were ruined. Mum and Nan had spent the entire day thinking I'd wandered off and fallen into a mineshaft somewhere.

'Now get to bed.'

It was my dubious pleasure to share a bed with my Uncle Gwyn. He was the youngest of my uncles, the only one who didn't have to do National Service, and he was easily the smelliest, still having the whiff of adolescence about him. He was tall and his feet were too long for the bed. On top of that he slept in old baggy Y-fronts and would fart all night. As soon as he joined me in bed my head went under the pillow to escape the stench. The only good thing about sleeping with Gwyn was that he had a cool glow-in-the-dark Timex watch which to me, being a sheltered lad unaccustomed to modern technology, was easily the most exciting thing ever. As Gwyn slept, the watch lit up the room.

Gwyn let out a huge rip, stained with a hint of cabbage and egg. It was a miracle how the force of his own fart didn't wake him from his slumber. On second thoughts it was probably the gas that kept him under. Silently I slipped out of the compost heap called bed and headed for the landing, looking for a place to sleep.

Sometimes I sought refuge in Nan's chest of drawers. The bottom one, where she kept the linen, was big enough to get into. Tonight it was the airing cupboard that found my favour, so I curled up and went to sleep in there. Anything but lie in that stink pit with Gwyn.

In the morning Nan found me and laughed.

'Get out of there, you funny boy! Come and help me bake a cake.'

Nan was up at six every morning to light the stove in the kitchen that heated the water for the men to wash in when they got in from work. The house was the centre of the community, always busy and noisy, especially on Sundays. The entire extended family always dropped in for tea. Although Grandad was the breadwinner, Nan was the head of the family. Grandad was quiet and serious and sensibly let Nan do all the work.

Grandad was the complete opposite of Nan. He would stand over the compost heap in the back garden (on to which would go every conceivable bit of household waste – tea bags, ash, nappies), dark eyes darting, tall and wiry, like a prisoner of war staring through the fence of a camp. I begged him to tell me about the war but he refused to talk about it at all. He was one of those men of whom, as a small boy, you are wary.

I knew something had happened to him in the war. I used to listen intently when people talked about him.

'He was one of the first soldiers into Belsen. That's when his hair went white.'

I had no idea what Belsen was but the idea of something being able to make your hair turn white was beyond scary. Thinking about it kept me occupied for hours.

Once I made him lose his temper and that upset Nan very much, not so much him dragging me out from under the bed where I'd hidden but that I'd managed to drive him to it. Maybe it was because of the war, I don't know, but if there is madness in our family, it came from him. Years later Grandad John was admitted to a lunatic asylum, where he died, which basically finished Nan off too.

Nevertheless, meeting him from work was my favourite occupation, up there with watching Nan baking or cooking, her arms moving rapidly round the pots and pans, her big bum wobbling. So on this occasion, when Nan had got tired of me watching her or just thought I must be bored and sent me off to meet him, I was happy to comply. Down the road through the estate were the gates to the steelworks. I waited for him to come out, singling him out from the other men by his walk. He always wore the same: cap, blue overalls and a grey raincoat. We wandered home, him telling me stories.

'Sometimes we work all through the night.'

'All night?'

'And sometimes we do a continental.'

'Can I come?'

As soon as I knew this involved getting up at 6am I was less keen. He and my uncles had spent their whole lives in heavy industry, pumping the blood round the industrial heart of Britain, leaving only to go and fight the war before returning to the mines and the mills.

Back at home, Grandad went to get washed and I returned to the kitchen where my Auntie Ethnie was helping Nan bake her famous Welsh cakes. Through the day the numbers increased to over thirty as all my uncles and their wives and kids arrived. We piled out into the crescent and the semi-circle of grass where we ran around and played football.

As soon as there was a break from playing, it was back into Nan's kitchen to get sustenance.

'Do you want food, boy?' she boomed, never too busy to make me a butty, even if she was doing about fifty things at once.

'I'm starving.'

She buttered a huge loaf of bread, cut it into triangles and left it on the table. All the kids dived in and pushed each other out of the way to get at the fodder. We all holidayed together and consequently grew up together. Ethnie poured us all some dandelion and burdock and gave me a wink.

'Don't drink it all at once, Keith, it makes you burp something terrible.'

Auntie Ethnie was sexy. She was like Mum, dark hair and dark eyes. She adored me because, like her, I was naughty. She used to blink madly and twitch her head and mouth, which made her look like she'd had some thought, but nothing would come out. Maybe she had a mild form of Tourette's. If I'd been a man then, I would have observed that she had pert tits, large nipples and lovely legs. She was like a tiny storm with a hoover, which she would throw to the floor when she argued with Nan and slam the door behind her, tottering to the pub, cussing backwards like an early version of the girls in *Rita, Sue and Bob Too*. Quite funny that she ended up marrying a very quiet man, a golf-playing, choir-attending steel worker called Cyril; a less likely partner you couldn't imagine for the wild child of the family.

The door bell at Nan's was always going.

'Halloooo? It's the pop man ... anyone at 'ome?'

How he could fail to see the forty-one people crammed into the front room was anybody's guess. The pop man delivered carbonated fizzy drinks to the whole estate with such exotic flavours as pineapple and ice cream, which had less to do with food than chemical concept. There was a delivery man for everything then: coal, milk, bread, veg, even pop got delivered on the estate.

Taking a liberal portion of bread I went and sat in the front room and listened to the banter of the adults. Mum and Ethnie were sitting on two pouffes by the fire with their legs apart, deep in conversation. They didn't see me looking and were both unconsciously fiddling with their fannies. Not knowing what the form was with fanny fiddling and adults, I thought this was normal, because they were doing it in full view of the room. After they'd fiddled they would take away their hands and rub their noses as if checking that it all smelt all right down there. So mesmerised was I by this shared crotch sniffing that I dropped my bread on the floor and in a bid to rescue it knocked my glass of dandelion over. Uncle Gwyn came in and chastised me.

'Trust it to be your Keith spilling everything, Emma ...'

But Mum just laughed and went back to her fanny fiddling with Ethnie. It was as if she was two different people. In Gosport in our little empty house with just me and Susan, with Dad so often absent, she was a mouse, but as soon as we got to Nan's she came alive, laughing and speaking Welsh, all feminine manners out of the window. It was quite apparent to me, even at my young age, that she belonged in Wales with the big loud rambling extended family, not isolated amid the starched conventions of suburban England.

The only uncle who rejected the regular wages and job security of heavy industry was Uncle Les, who went to farm a few miles away in Camarthen. In high summer we'd all go and help him get the hay in. There was great ceremony involved in these trips and numbers could be up to twenty.

While the adults got the hay in, Les took the kids down to the cow sheds to help milk the cows. One day he stopped and pointed one out to me.

'See that one, Keith? What's different about it?'

'Nothing.'

As far as I was concerned, a town boy at heart, the Friesians were one long black and white carpet interrupted only by heads and arses.

'That one is called Keith Allen. I named him after you.'

Well, that was different then. Suddenly that cow was the only cow in town. It was different, special, and I could have recognised him two miles off by his fabulously unique markings.

Les knew every one of his cows by name because he called them all after his nieces and nephews and cousins.

The rest of the family were already picking blackberries and Les gave me a bucket to fill. This was the tradition, once the hay was in. We would leave at dawn to get the bushes before anyone else from the valleys got there, though such was the voracious appetite of the Welsh for their blackberries that we didn't always make it first. For weeks after, whichever auntie's house I pitched up in, it would be blackberry pie for breakfast, lunch and dinner.

Shortly after Dad reappeared in my life in Gosport, we piled into his recently bought Austin Seven and went to visit his parents, Grandma and Grandpa Allen in London. During the three-hour trip to London me and Susan spent the time hitting each other secretly so Dad wouldn't notice or peering out of the window. As we drove through Fulham, Dad pointed out the sights.

'See that house, son? That's where your dad was born. Right in that window there.'

'Oh.'

'And see that? That's Craven Cottage football ground. Me and your grandad stand on the terraces there. If you're good, we'll take you.'

Footie? If my dad liked footie as much as I did, he couldn't be that bad. And the thought of going to an actual game was like a trip to Wales without Gwyn's farts.

We arrived at their flat and I noted the neat and tidy room. Grandma Allen had ornaments everywhere like my nan did. But there the similarity ended. Nanny John lived in a madhouse and let me climb up the Welsh dresser to count the China dogs, whereas here I couldn't even go to the loo without saluting.

Grandpa Allen had a white pencil moustache, cold blue eyes, not very much hair and a vicious temper. Grandma Allen was vivacious, lively, busy. She slipped me a couple of bob when Grandpa wasn't looking.

So there sat Grandpa Allen, upright in his chair, chewing a sandwich while Dad, aping his straight-backed pose, talked to him. I fiddled with a little brass bell on the fireplace but it slipped out of my hands and fell on the floor with a clatter. Grandad looked as if someone had just dropped a shell on his trench hole and Dad snapped at me, clipping air.

'You little idiot. Sit down and don't touch anything else.'

Someone was at the door. Grandma Allen went to get it. It was dad's sister, my Auntie Peg. As soon as she walked in, the tension of the occasion was broken. She addressed me directly, which was something of a novelty in the Allen family. We bonded immediately.

Getting to know my father meant getting to know his rages. But getting to know his rages also meant being able to see them coming and get as far away as possible.

Dad had to go for an operation on the cartilage in his knee. We all went to visit him at the Haslar naval hospital. The best thing about this was the squeaky floors, which got more squeaky if you made a special effort. This is what happened in my thought process (good and bad being very similar):

1) Best thing in world – Annoying adults.
2) Worst thing in world – Adults being annoying.

Mum slapped me for making squeaking noises, and propelled me faster along the corridor towards Dad's ward. He was sitting up in bed and seemed pleased to see me. The tray table in front of him was covered in bits of balsa wood and he was gluing them together.

'See, son? This is how you make a Spitfire.'

I sat on the bed next to him, and watched him in awe as he carved out what would be the propeller. I loved it when my dad made things with his hands. It always made me proud.

'Will it fly?'

'Course it will. When I finish it we'll launch it together.'

He had to stay in a couple of weeks (back then a cartilage operation was a particularly nasty business). Every day we went to see him, the plane had taken shape even more. The wings were made of reinforced tissue paper, with an elastic band round the propeller. When it was finished he put it on the chair by his bed until I arrived. Unfortunately, that day Nan, visiting from Wales, came with us.

'Hello, Eddie! How's the knee then? Painful is it?'

Without looking she pulled out the chair and plonked down her ample behind on it. The Spitfire disappeared from view, disintegrating on impact. She sprang up as part of the undercarriage attempted to make its way up her bum.

'Oh my God, what the bugger is that then?'

We all looked at Eddie. He stared at Nan in silence, colour filling his lily-white face, his mouth tightening. It was like watching a wave rise. His tongue went over his bottom teeth and pushed his lower lip out. (This was the sign I learnt to dread.) Then he unleashed a rage that was like being dragged underneath a car. Shock first then pain later.

'You've bloody wrecked it! Look what you've done!'

'Oh sorree, Eddie, I'm really really sorree.'

Nan cowered on the end of his temper. Several of the other patients looked over, disturbed. Privately I was pleased it wasn't me, this time at least.

You could be excused for thinking that Eddie didn't like children but he obviously did because at the beginning of 1959 Mum had got pregnant again. I didn't know at the time but Mum was frightened of giving birth again because she'd had such a terrible time with me. At over ten pounds I was a big baby and it was a long and excruciatingly painful process – for us both, or so I was told – during which we'd been in danger. We pulled through, alive but subconsciously scarred.

A teacher told me to go home because my mother was 'in labour'. It was only when I got to the end of my street and saw loads of women clucking around that it struck me that that meant the baby was coming.

My father was waiting for me, along with Mrs Simpson from over the road who, although she wasn't 'our type', was allowed to bring a gift. She thrust a tub of Neapolitan ice cream into my hands and winked.

'We don't want your little brother getting all the attention, do we?'

After that she was definitely my type. Dad took the ice cream away and pushed me to the stairs.

'Go up and see your new brother. He's in the cot next door to your mother.'

It was too late. My little brother was already getting all the attention. Still, I was excited to see him.

I peered nervously into the cot. There was nothing there. I ran in to my mother who looked, frankly, dreadful. And worse, fat like she was still pregnant.

'Why are you still fat? I thought you'd had it.'

'It's not an *it*, he's a lovely little boy.'

'Well, somebody's nicked it then cos it's not in the cot.'

'*It's* called Kevin. And nobody's stolen him. Go and have another look.'

Back at the cot I cautiously pulled back the covers. There, under about five blankets, was a tiny pink spot with brown stuff on its head. Mum was right: no one would steal *that*.

It was obvious Kevin was special. Instead of being difficult and noisy like me, he was good-natured and placid. Even his arrival had been easy, with the icing on the cake that epidurals had just become available on the NHS and Mum had floated through the birth on a sea of morphine.

After Kevin was born we went to Wales. Now that Dad was with us, there was much reshuffling of bedrooms in the Llanelli house to accommodate us. We ended up with a bizarre set of sleeping arrangements that no one batted an eyelid about.

Nan unfolded the campbed and tucked in sheets while Dad got another one down from the loft.

'Eddie, you and Susan can have the campbeds and Mary can share the bed with Ethnie and the baby.'

'Right, fair dos.' Eddie erected the other bed.

Hang on ... That meant my dad was sharing a room with Auntie Ethnie. Was this ethically sound? Presumably she got in bed first and turned the lights out before Eddie made his way to the campbed, to preserve her modesty (not that modesty was one of her most obvious qualities – see fanny fiddling paragraph). But this was the working class and if you only had one tiny house you all had to fit into it. The idea of hotels was ridiculous. Why pay for a room when you could all share one? Never mind the stench in the morning like a particularly stuffy sewage works. Or that you might wake up in the night to see somebody's husband, legs akimbo, snoring on a campbed. Privacy was not a word much bandied about at Nan's, or if it was it had a subclause exempting 'family'.

Nan finished making the bed and looked at me.

'And Keith's in with Gwyn as usual.'

My hands covered my face in disappointment. Another few weeks of slow methane poisoning at the hands of the flatulent Gwyn.*

Dad wasn't used to the noise and chaos of Wales and found it strange. He was the outsider. My uncles tried to bring him out of himself by

---

* I got Gwyn back a few years later. My first wank was in his bed (thankfully without him in it). It was a painful process of pulling and forcing the foreskin backwards, akin to tempting a shy tortoise out of its shell. The unnatural action gave way to unnatural joy as thin fluid sprayed all over the sheets. That would serve Gwyn right for years of slow poisoning.

taking him to the pub while the women stayed at home and cooked, but I think he found the huge Welsh family intimidating.

I stand up, make sure everyone is watching me, and holler at the top of my voice (in my best hooligan accent):

'COME ON YOU SUUUPER LILLEEEEEEELY WHIIIIITES ...'

This is the way I support my team, Fulham, *now* – making sure everyone, including the occupants of Harrods, can hear me. But on New Year's Day 1960, it was very different. Eddie and Grandpa took me to watch my first football match.

It was freezing cold, a good day to be wearing a thick wool coat and scarf, the type both Grandpa and Eddie had on. The streets round Craven Cottage were full of people, men mostly, all walking the same direction.

Grandpa said: 'You'd never have made the grade, son.'

Eddie shrugged.

I wondered what they were talking about. In the stadium twenty-odd thousand men sent the air foggy with their breath as the Fulham players shivered and shifted in their starting formation. When the whistle sounded, a roar went up that shook me to the core. I wanted part of this.

Opposition Sheffield United's shirts made a particularly vivid memory for me. Against the monochrome of life, all dull grey, black and white (compounded in the stadium that day by the fact that Fulham played in black and white), their red and white striped jerseys stood out brilliantly.

Fulham had all the early pressure; every man in the crowd was concentrating hard, willing the players on, not much noise at all. Then, after some patient build-up play (praised by my grandad), Fulham put one in the net. I was whipped off my feet and into the air. Dad had thrown me upwards. If the roar at the first whistle shocked me, nothing could have prepared me for the collective male orgasm that happens when twenty thousand home fans hug each other in celebration. Even if more muted in those days, I was fascinated to see the happiness this event released in my normally tighter-than-arsehole male relatives. Grandpa and Eddie slapped each other on the back and gripped each other's arms. After

Eddie had put me down, Grandpa lifted me up so I could see the players celebrating on the pitch.

'See the scorer, Keith? That's Johnny Haynes, and over there, that's Tosh Chamberlain.'

Eddie added: 'He plays in the same position as me.'

I looked at Eddie in shock. 'Were you in the Fulham team, Dad?'

But Eddie didn't get the chance to reply before Grandpa repeated: 'He would never have made the grade.'

A few years later, Dad showed me a Fulham soccer album from 1949. And there he is, in a baggy white vest, long shorts and plimsolls. Just as he didn't get a chance to reply that day, maybe he never got a chance to make the grade because of Grandpa.

Walking to the pub after the game was the best feeling ever, the three of us bonded together with the love of one team. We met up with some of my uncles, and Mum and Nanny Allen. All the kids were left on the street, like little dogs on a leash, waiting for scraps from the adults. From that day on I was a sworn Fulham fan. Even in the darkest times of our relationship, me and Dad could always talk about the football.

Chapter 3

IN 1960, EVERYTHING changed again. Eddie came home with some news.

'Get packed, Mary. We're going to Malta.'

His submarine had been posted to the British naval base in Sliema, and instead of him buggering off on his own again, we were going too. Mum started packing the house into tea chests.

'But what about school?' I said.

'You'll still have to go to school.'

'And what about my friends?'

'You'll make new ones.'

I was pretty happy with the old ones. I slunk off to say goodbye to Pete. I liked him. In fact, I couldn't imagine life without him.

'Don't reckon I'll see you again,' I said, kicking the dirt outside his front door.

'You get to go on a plane!' he replied.

He was right about the plane. We flew out from Brize Norton on an RAF plane. I was so excited it was impossible to keep still and stay in my seat.

'I want to go into the cockpit,' I whined. Mum gave me another thwack.

'Sit still until we've taken off.'

Once we were in the air they did call me to the cockpit and the pilots showed me all the dials and switches. My sadness at leaving everything behind in Gosport was forgotten.

When we stepped off the plane in Malta, the heat wrapped itself round us. It was nothing like hot Britain, which was always tinged with cool wind. The heat seduced me instantly. Me and the sun was an affair waiting to happen.

Malta was everything a small boy could ask for. Firstly, because there wasn't an official naval housing compound in Sliema, we weren't with all the other stuffy English families in some kind of ghetto. We had Maltese neighbours, carpenters who boiled up shark skins to make glue and kindly old peasant women who thought I was cute. (More fool them.) Even the buses were cheerful, painted red and orange and decorated liberally in flowers.

'Can I sit at the back, Mum?'

She shook her head and pushed me up the steps past the bus driver, who was shouting at a friend over the road in a language that sounded like the clack-clack of a football rattle. It seemed that people here prioritised having a good natter above, say, running the country. Often the bus would come to a halt so the driver could lean out and chat to an old lady about the price of goats.

The journey to my new school took forever, which was pleasing, and the town made good eye candy. Well, it did if you were interested in rubble. It was one big bombsite.

The bus left the town behind and headed into the countryside. It was empty and sunburnt apart from the carpeted steps of terrace farming. This mysterious barren existence appealed to me – probably because it was the antithesis of suburban Gosport. No neat trimmed hedgerows here, just women with beards and bountiful supplies of goats.

We came upon an old converted fort that was the school and were offloaded. I stood in line waiting to be allocated and taken to a classroom, but hold up, something wasn't right. It was the windows, they had no glass in them.

Miss Street, apparently my new teacher, pointed out why.

'It's too hot,' she breathed in her thick Irish accent. The kind that still, today, makes any young lad melt. Miss Street smiled through full red lips and even redder lipstick but, best of all, she had red-painted toenails. And even better than the toenails was the way she said, 'Hello, boys …' in that deep husky way only the Irish can.

The good thing, I thought immediately, about having no glass in the windows was that sudden gusts of wind would blow up Miss Street's skirt. Hmmm. Teachers and skirts. Teachers and breasts. Titties and skirts. Keith and Allen. A pattern was starting to form in my head. Things that went together well.

Because of Miss Street, and my other teacher, Mr Wise, school was OK. There was no reason to play up so, funnily enough, I didn't. We were all happy in Malta, and then of course there was Dad. With his sub parked down the road he was around a lot and we all lived under his thumb. Except that he was happier too; he wasn't under so much pressure from himself. We were in a foreign country where English morals and standards didn't apply. Because of the heat it was more relaxed and free. My father, who normally operated to a very strict work ethic, seemed to ease up a little and enjoy life.

Every weekend was a huge social jolly with all the English naval families getting on the boats and heading for the various bays around Gozo for snorkelling and beach parties. Like everyone else we loaded up the picnic basket in the back of the car and headed for the port.

For the first time I saw 'Eddie Allen' in a social context. Up to then it had always been 'Dad' within our four walls, where he was often uncommunicative. In company he was a different person, organising trips and events. My mother was less animated. She shied away from the 'navy wife' thing and stuck with her close girlfriends Mrs Fraser and Mrs Mills from Bridgemary, whose husbands had been billeted here at the same time as us.

A typical day trip went something like this. Eddie makes everyone laugh. Eddie chucks kids overboard. Eddie flirts with all the other women. Eddie is everyone's friend. Eddie ignores me.

To celebrate the engagement of one of the sailors, Dad organised a fishing boat to take us to a secluded beach in one of the outlying bays. The boat chugged through the water, cutting the glassy blue sea. All the kids were up the front, trailing their hands in the water, while the adults sat under the tarpaulin at the rear. Eddie's voice could be heard above all the others, leading the chorus of adult jokes that didn't sound funny but made everybody laugh.

'Go on, Eddie, tell us the one about the naughty waitress.'

'I can't, she's sitting next to me.'

All the other sailors thought Dad was wonderful, the life and soul of the party. I was trying, as usual, to attract his attention.

The boat anchored by the beach and the younger kids all squealed about having to be carried through the waist-deep water. Dad came over to us and picked up one of my mates.

'Let me give you a carry to the beach, son, save you getting wet.'

Then he threw him overboard. Everyone cheered as Johnny came up coughing and spluttering, thinking it was the best joke ever. On the beach he organised all the kids into five-a-side teams and drew goalposts in the sand. The women went to set up the picnic and watched from under sunshades, laughing at Eddie who pretended to trip up while refereeing. He loved making the women and the kids laugh.

To watch him like this aroused mixed emotions: pride that my dad was this funny, jokey guy whom everybody loved, but frustration that he wasn't like this with me. He never played with me at home; he was always 'busy'. I couldn't help but notice that being 'busy' included sitting on his arse with his feet up reading the paper. Not that he was lazy, simply that playing with me didn't seem to be among his range of activities.

I ran up to the top of the sand cliff above the beach. The Mills kids followed me up and arrived breathless beside me, looking down on the adults who were now cracking open the beer and handing out the cigarettes. Everyone smoked, Mum, Dad, the lot. Eddie was in the throes of some story, his hands going manically to demonstrate some point.

I shouted down to him. 'Oi! Watch me! I'm going to jump off.'

The Mills kids looked at me agog. Even Dad stopped talking and looked up. He nudged the others and they looked up too. My heart started running away but now I had to do it. Then he picked up a camera and twiddled with the focus.

'Come on, son! Jump! Don't forget to bend your knees.'

A few paces backwards then full throttle forwards and I was in the air.

Life was on hold, everything frozen until the ground met me with a gentle thud, sand filling every orifice. I expected my father to pick me up and congratulate me but instead he was off running down the beach. So was everyone else. My entire audience were sprinting frantically down the beach towards the rocks.

'Hey, what about me? Wait for me.'

I ran after them before slowing down to a stop when I saw what they were running to. Something was flailing around in the water, surrounded by red. It was a body. Dad and two other men ran into the sea and pulled it out. It was red and floppy. One of the women was crying and screaming and it took three other women to hold her back.

They dragged the man's body onto the shore, leaving a red trail in the sand as blood poured from the chest.

'Oh God. It's Tommy Simms,' a woman said.

Eddie swam out to the boat and radioed to the naval base for help. All the kids went to sit on the rugs.

'Is he dead?'

'Dunno.'

'He's dead.'

'He looks dead.'

We listened to the women talking, trying to understand what was going on.

'He was trying to pull himself up on the rocks and he shot himself through the chest.'

Some of the sailors went snorkelling off the rocks with harpoon guns that they didn't let us kids touch because they were dangerous. Tommy had pulled himself out of the water and accidentally pressed the trigger, shooting himself through his chest. This first glimpse of death had a great effect on me. I viewed my impending eye operation with gargantuan levels of doom.

About ten years later, Mum showed me some photos of that day. Among them I found one of me, a spectacular midair shot. As so often, a higher power intervened and got in the way of our attempt to share a genuine boys' own moment.

*

I was used to wearing glasses with one lens covered in plaster to get the 'lazy' eye to work, but the doctors had told my mother that an operation would tighten the tendons behind the eye and stop it going north-west. I needed reassurance that going under the knife was totally necessary. The doctor shone a light into my eye and then sat back.

'Do you want the good news or the bad news?'

I shrugged carelessly. What did it matter? I was going to die anyway.

'If you don't have this operation, you will continue only to use your good eye and this will put it under so much strain that it will weaken to the point where you'd be virtually blind.'

'Oh.' I stared pitifully at the floor.

'The good news is that if this operation is a success, you'll be able to see out of your bad eye and you won't need to wear spectacles.'

The world brightened. 'No specs? Really?'

With everything perfectly crystallised in my mind, the operating theatre beckoned. I lay on my back, staring at the ceiling. Various nurses came into view. One of them asked me to count to ten.

'One ...'

I came round in a white ward with tall windows. People walked by, ignoring me. My head appeared to be stuck to the pillow, fixed with dried blood from my eye. The doctor came and sat on the bed.

'Let me help you.'

He peeled my face off the pillow and a giddy sensation came over me.

'My eye's going to come out.'

The doctor lifted the dressing and peered at it, frowning, before letting go and looking at me gravely. I feared the worst.

'Don't look so dramatic. It's fine.'

'What about the operation?'

He went on matter-of-factly. 'If you must know, I took your eye out and put it on your cheek and tightened all the little bits of string called the tendons and then stuck it back in.'

'Will I be able to see out of it?'

He shook his head. 'It won't get any better than it is now. The good news is that it won't get any worse.'

So there it was. For the rest of my life it would be blurred vision – like wearing a pair of greasy spectacles you could never clean. I didn't need glasses, though, which meant no one else would know that I was sight impaired.*

During my recuperation, Mum and Dad made friends with a Maltese man called Mr Busitill. One day he appeared in my room with some toys. Eddie introduced him.

'Son, Mr Busitill has agreed to be your godfather.'

He ruffled my hair and smiled. 'We gonna have loads of fun. Tell me, you want to go to the church?'

'Oh yes, he'd love to go to church with you, wouldn't you, son?'

Despite never himself going within fifty feet of a church, Dad was most insistent that Susan and I went, and very magnanimously gave us the choice over what branch of Christianity we followed. Whoopee.

'It's down to you whether you want to be a Protestant or a Catholic. I want you to think about it and make your own minds up.'

It wasn't a hard decision. One look at the pasty-faced Protestant chaplain delivering a dull 'repent now' sermon to an empty, creosoted Nissan hut and we were running for the rosary. The Roman Catholic church Mr Busitill's family went to was a fully formed God centre with incense, singing and expensive-looking Christmas decorations.

On Sundays the naval base was empty and lonely, whereas down the hill at the Catholic church it was high drama with imagery, rituals and question-and-answer singing. For me it was about being part of a community. After the service I'd stay with the Maltese kids and play football, loving the 'crowd' mentality. The good thing about a crowd was that I could stick out if I chose or melt into it and become invisible. Either way it was better than being at home on my own.

---

* I actually qualify for a white stick. If I walked round with a white stick now people would think I was taking the piss. But if I swung round on the tube and knocked someone under a train, I would have the excuse of being blind (which is more than you'd have).

THE SIXTIES

THE SIXTIES

Chapter 4

THE MALTESE KIDS were skilful footballers and taught me tricks with the ball. We played on the school netball courts with a tennis ball, which helped my ball control.

'See, son, that's the best way to learn. We'll have you in the England team in no time.'

Dad would referee the school team in tournaments that took place on Saturdays. My first pair of boots were leather past the ankle, and instead of studs they had three leather bars across the bottom, which if they made contact with an opposition shin would pare off the skin like grating cheese.

'Go on, son. Get in there,' Dad would rant as he sprinted up and down the pitch blowing his whistle and giving me instructions.

Talking of ball control, my own were starting to make their long journey towards my ankles. Apart from Miss Street, I was having prepubescent stirrings about Rhona Smith. We were in the same house at school, the Blues. The girls had to wear a blue sash round their skirts. Rhona's blue sash looked lovely. She had long blonde hair that went all the way down to her blue sash. Funny the things you remember.

Along with hair product and voluntarily washing my armpits, early forays into what was for me very early puberty included this particular young lady. She was even more gorgeous than Miss Street, plus she had youth on her side. Me. She'd walk by my desk and leave a trail of destruction in her wake as my emotions went crashing to the floor. Her house was about an hour from mine but this was a small price to pay to stare at her front door.

That one could be so attached to a front door was a revelation to me, as was the discovery that this adoration of an inanimate object was commonly called love. And there was something else. Not for me the awkward blushes and hand-holding of prepubescent love; I wanted to devour Rhona whole.

One day, on the circuitous route home, instead of passing and staring I took action and knocked on the much celebrated front door. Rhona Smith's mum looked up and down at me.

'Yes?'

'Is Rhona in?'

'Rhona! There's a little lad here who wants to see you.'

Little? Lad? Surely she mislaid the words 'strapping beast'? She left me cringing on the step. Did mothers have to do that? The sight of me bright red and awkward was what greeted Rhona. She stood and waited, apparently disinclined to put me at ease.

'Will you be my girlfriend?'

'No.'

'Why not?'

'I don't want to.'

'Why not?'

'Dunno.'

'OK then. Don't tell anyone.'

'OK. I won't.'

Her not telling anyone was suddenly the only thing that mattered. Rhona Smith and her beauty were no emotion at all compared to being the target of playground ridicule.

There is a story that when the stoat escaped from its cage, it still wasn't happy and had to escape from the room. When it was out of the room, it wasn't happy until it was out of the door and in the garden. Then it still wasn't happy until it escaped into the field. Even then it wasn't happy, and tried to get out of the field … you get the picture. Welcome to Keith 'The Stoat' Allen. (Except that I don't have furry bollocks – except at Glastonbury. See below.)

When Dad was out on exercises with the sub, it was a chance to piss off on my own to seek out danger and thrills. The bombsites became my playground and I enlisted all the local kids to play with me.

'Right. This is the secret society HQ. We're going on a top-secret recon mission to what was number twenty-three and is now a pile of rubble.'

Inside number twenty-three, a weird feeling came over me as I imagined people sitting there eating tea when the bombs struck. What if someone had died there? It was oppressively hot and flies buzzed round piles of human shit. My recon mission lost all its allure and I ran all the way home to have a bath (things must have been bad). On arrival the security guard commonly known as Mum blocked my way.

'Where've you been?'

'Nowhere.'

'Well, nowhere must be bloomin' intrestin', Keith. You spend most of your time there.'

This was the beginning of Mum's 'Wait till your father gets home' routine, which was to last well into my teens. I always ignored her, unable to resist the call of the wild and my innate desire to roam. I always found ways of escaping, often walking for miles and miles out in to the countryside, stopping to rest and cool off by swimming in isolated bays.

A romantic image, I grant you: a young lad stripping off and exploring his innocence through the wonder of the natural world, but not when you dive into the middle of a swarm of jellyfish.

The first one stung my cheek and made me thrash around, only to be stung repeatedly in a sea of pink globules. I ducked under to escape but it was worse there. Hundreds of tendrils swirled and forced me up through the jelly field, my head swollen and pounding. Thereafter I had a pathological fear of the fuckers but it didn't put me off roaming.

Our next-door neighbours were a Maltese family called the Navarotts. Their son Henry was the same age as me and occasionally we used to play toy soldiers. I thought toy soldiers were for little kids but sometimes I was desperate enough to play with him.

'Mum, can I go and play with Henry Navarott?'

Mum was clutching a hanky and listening to the radio perched on a chair, one buttock off as if she didn't dare sit on the whole thing, as if perching was better than whole sitting, which qualified as being a lazy cow and not getting on with the housework.

'You don't like Henry Navarott.'

'So? I still want to play with him.'

The wonderful thing about being a kid is that you can apply reverse logic to a situation and flummox an adult. This time anyway she wasn't in a mood to argue. Something *very* strange was happening in the wider world. My mother, Mrs Fraser and Mrs Mills would spend all day huddled round the radio. All I knew was that the word 'Cuba' kept coming up, in close association with the word 'war', which was not generally one of my favourites.

Henry's house was an oasis, and even though I had my suspicions that his neat hair and moustache aged seven were slightly odd, it was better than being at my place. We set up our armies and faced off.

'I'll be the Nazis.'

All he ever wanted to do was be the Germans. It was Nazi this and Nazi that. I didn't know much but I knew that serious interest in a dictatorship at seven was unhealthy.

'Don't you ever talk about anything else?'

Henry smiled at me, a warm, caring smile.

'If you want, I'll show you something …'

As we walked through the hot dusty yard, the noise of the radio carried over from our kitchen. My mother let out a wail, the kind you never hear – the kind that is reserved for death. Henry pulled me downstairs into the cellar. At least we could hide down there. For once Henry's Airfix kits were a welcome distraction from the stress of living in the forces.

'I've heard it's going to be World War Three.' Henry rammed a pilot into a cockpit.

'What is?'

'Cuba.'

We didn't know if Cuba was a place or a man or a bomb. It was just Cuba and it was scary.

'We could just stay down here if you want,' Henry chirped.

'OK.'

Then he smiled, not the warm, caring smile any more, but a strange, faraway, yearning smile. I stared at the haircut, a neat sweep of blond hair across his forehead, blue eyes and girlish complexion. He leant over and put his hand on my cock.

I don't remember much about the journey back to my house but I do know it could have beaten various land-speed records. In the kitchen everyone was crying. It seemed appropriate to join in. All of a sudden I didn't hate the Cuban Missile Crisis nearly as much I hated Henry Navarott.

My father was due home the next day after sea exercises on the sub, but he never arrived. All Mum did was cry.

'Where's Dad?'

'Mind your own business, Keith.'

'I'm minding it. Where's he gone?'

'Don't push me, Keith.'

Mrs Mills turned up for a cup of tea and the two positioned themselves round the kitchen table. What they didn't know was that I was under it. Despite now being eight and considering myself a grown-up, I'd lost none of my infant desire to drive submarines up women's skirts.

'Bob said they weren't even allowed off the sub. Said they came back from exercises in the Med, stored for war and sailed right back out again.'

'They could have let them come home for the night. To see their wives.'

'They couldn't. It's a security risk. What if it had slipped out?'

'What slipped out?'

'Where they're going.'

'Where are they going?'

'Cuba, I suppose.'

'Don't say that, Nora.'

'Well, it's true.'

Dad's sub had been scrambled and put on alert in the Atlantic. We all waited for news, which we knew we wouldn't get unless it was the bad kind. Perversely we wanted it anyway; anything was better than nothing.

Life became extremely serious and there was even less talk in our house than usual so I put a lot of additional energy into buggering off on my own. On one such jaunt to the Maltese outback, the sky turned abnormally dark and grey matter started to fall.

It could only mean one thing. Cuba. The end of the world. I ran all the way home, convinced that when I got there my family would be dead. But as usual Mum was washing the pots.

'It's here.'

Mum dropped the pan in the sink. 'What is?' She thought I meant Dad's sub.

'The Nucular War.'

Susan pulled the spastic face. 'It's a volcano, you doo-da ...'

Etna had erupted in Italy, covering the Med in a layer of fine grey matter. Mum was angry with me because she'd got her hopes up that Dad's sub was back.

Then one day, with no warning, he walked through the door. It was this that told us the crisis had passed. He'd been away for three months without any contact.

Aged about ten I started to observe the local builders to pick up tips on manhood. They worked in the heat of the morning, bare-chested with fags hanging out of their mouths, cursing professionally in Maltese and whistling through their teeth at the passing girls. They would stop for lunch at two when the heat got unbearable and take out a huge lump of bread and a tomato. First they would rub olive oil into the bread and then the tomato. What resulted was a kind of delicious raw pizza.

'Mum? Can I have bread and tomato for my lunch tomorrow?'

'No.'

'Why not?'

'Because it's not proper food.'

'What am I having?'

'Tinned corned beef and tinned peas. Proper food.'

I could see that I wasn't going to get anywhere with her so it was off to the bakers to buy my own lunch. Then, with a wobbly doorstop of bread and with some unattractive-looking tomatoes peering out of the side, I sat with the builders, thinking this was true maturity. Then a bit of tomato fell between my legs. It was a signal for the whole thing to fall apart. Before I could even contemplate becoming a builder there was clearly still a lot to learn in the business of sandwich construction.

I did also know that the Maltese builders had an unhealthy interest in getting their cocks out – I noticed that in every bombsite I played on, there would always be one hiding furtively behind a pile of bricks with cock in hand. They enjoyed hugging each other as well, I noticed. Perhaps it had to do with the war, and them still being upset.

There was one with a very big cock who used to flash at Susan and me on our way to play with Dr Busitill and his kids, out of whom Nadia was the one who finally explained to me the rules of Doctors and Nurses.

My new maturity continued with my first solo trip to the cinema. The local flea pit was showing *Sergeants 3*, starring Sammy Davis Jr, Dean Martin and Frank Sinatra. Sitting on the back row, I observed the adult codes of behaviour that accompanied such a sophisticated pastime as 'cinema'. These consisted of eating pine nuts and spitting them on your neighbour, burping loudly and putting your feet up on the seat in front.

The film started with our heroic trio of Las Vegas cabaret singers being pursued by Indians. As the film came to a climax, all my sophistication went out of the window. There was severe danger of dissolving into tears and crying for my mum. Sammy, Dean and Frank were hemmed in by Indians and they were all going to die. No one in the cinema seemed to care. The youths in front were chatting away and the courting couple were more interested in swallowing each other whole. It was awful, terrible, tears ran down my face and there was no one to make me feel better. Convinced that people knew I was crying like a girl, I made for the exit. Next time it would have to be a proper action flick, not a weepy movie like *Sergeants 3*.

The world outside my puberty concerned itself with moving on in great inventive leaps. My father loved new gadgets. One day he brought home a reel-to-reel tape recorder.

'There you go, kids, that's the latest in new technology, that is.'

He gathered us all into the front room with the intention of creating a ground-breaking piece of family history: *The Allens in Conversation*. The idea was to send the tapes home to all the grandparents in England so they could hear us talking. Why we didn't just phone them was a mystery to me.

Dad pushed a microphone in my direction.

'Go on, son, say hello to your grandmother.' I stared at the mike.

'Er, hello, Nan. It's Keith here.'

Much tutting and rolling of the eyes from Eddie. 'Well, go on, son, say something else.'

'It's very hot here.' Pause. 'And we're having a lovely time.'

More eye rolling. 'That was Keith, here's Susan.'

Susan got her bid at fame. Could she do any better?

'Hello, Nan. It's very hot here.'

It went on like this and while maybe it was in some way pioneering, *The Allens in Conversation* wasn't about to turn heads at the BFPO radio station where our staple Sunday night listening was *The Goon Show*.

Then Dad made us all sing, leading with a low voice.

'Come come ... dah lah lah dah at the Old Bull and Bush.'

He carried on while us kids trailed off, unable to remember any more words and feeling more than a little idiotic.

Of course, Grandma and Grandpa Allen also had a reel-to-reel and sent us a reply. I can't remember the exact message but I'll hazard a guess it went something like this: 'Hello, Eddie. Hello, Mary. (pause) Hello, Keith. Hello, Susan. (pause) Hello, Kevin ... (clearing throat) ... Here's your Grandma Allen (sounds of protest). Just say something, woman! Hello, Eddie ... it's your mother ... Uncle John sends his best.'

One thing I learnt from this was that my father's choice of songs wasn't going to stand me in good stead in the modern world. Particularly one he introduced me to in the car one Sunday afternoon on the way to the beach:

'Oh Old Mother Riley she got drunk, fell in the fire and burned her bonnet ... then she had no hair upon it ...'

Eh? I didn't understand it. We bombed along in a green Consul convertible, Mum, Ethnie and Nan screaming, the frantic sea bubbling eight hundred foot below the sheer cliffs. A whisker of land between road and death. Eddie continued to sing.

'She got drunk and burned her bonnet.'

Who cared? We were all going to die. Dad was showing off, doing seventy on a clifftop road. Nan and Ethnie had come to stay with us, which meant me and Susan were relegated to the front room so they could have our room (all the kids shared). But that was OK because Dad had plenty of campbeds. A famous Allen motto was: 'Son, you can never have too many campbeds.' Other families have signet rings engraved with stirring messages like 'Find Strength in Valour'. Ours, had we had one, would have read: 'You can never have too many campbeds.'

'Oh! Old Mother ...' he went on.

Dad was steering and singing manically, Nan and Ethnie had gone white, I closed my eyes and saw heaven, and Mum just kept a stiff upper lip.

'Will you stop it, Eddie,' Mum finally said, not referring to his reckless driving but to his constant singing of this song. I couldn't understand why she should be so bothered by it.

'She got drunk, fell in the fire and burned her ...'

Chapter 5

AMONG THE FIRST signs of puberty is being interested in popular music. When my father came in one day in 1963 and announced we were going back to Gosport, it was Elvis Presley's 'Wooden Heart' that became the theme tune to our leaving. Everything became that song: packing up the house, saying goodbye to all my Maltese friends, leaving a life of picnics and beaches and sun. It would be the sun that I would always miss. The kind of heat that killed most people was my life force; Mum used to say there was more than a touch of the tar brush buried somewhere in me.

As we touched down at Brize Norton it was cold and raining. The radio in the car that took us away was playing a song called 'Love Me Do' by a band called The Beatles.

We didn't have a house to go to. We were on a waiting list back at the old estate in Gosport so we went to stay with Nan in Llanelli. The main change was that now she had a television. You had to put a shilling in the back to make it work, though, and consequently it had the annoying habit of turning itself off in the middle of *The Flowerpot Men*.

Susan and I were enrolled in the local schools for two terms and attempts were made at normality. Compared to the local kids we were exotic, what with having lived in Malta and all. Everyone wanted to be my friend. I started sneaking out late and staying up when everyone else was in bed. One night about eleven I got back and decided to watch TV. It burst into life with a grainy and serious-looking man telling me that the President of the United States had been assassinated.

Because of the Cuban Missile Crisis, everyone knew who Kennedy was – the man who had taken the world to the verge of obliteration before pulling it back from the brink to be lauded as a hero.

My thoughts turned to my father. I could hear the sound of him snoring upstairs, along with the barn-like noises coming from the bed that contained the lumbering forms of Auntie Ethnie, my mother and Susan. Should I wake them? I weighed up the kudos of being able to tell everyone that Kennedy was dead versus the pain of the clip that would inevitably follow when they learnt I'd been out. No, best leave it. Besides, Kennedy would still be dead in the morning, so I removed my socks and folded myself under the stinking duvet next to Uncle Gwyn.

Soon things began to go wrong between Dad and Nan. Used to being the man of the house, he was put out at having to live under Nan's rules. One Sunday he took us out for lunch, ignoring the fact that Nan had cooked a roast dinner. When we got back there was a row. My father marched out to the car and began loading it with suitcases, Mum running after him.

'Calm down, Eddie.'

'Get the kids. We're going home.'

In the car again I pondered the word 'home'. Not at all sure where home was, I knew that now wasn't the best time to ask. Home turned out to be one room in a motel in Fareham, the town next door to the naval base in Gosport. We were back in familiar territory – I was going back to the same school as before Malta – but for the foreseeable future this one room was all we had for three kids and two adults (one of them with an extremely short fuse).

After we left for school, Mum would put the mattresses in the communal hall so there'd be some space until the following bedtime. For a man of my father's levels of pride this was a lot to bear, but it was preferable to living with his mother-in-law. At least here he was in control.

For once it wasn't me who was the focus of my parent's ire. In Malta Susan had been a model pupil, straight As all the way. But the combination of returning to England, starting at a mixed senior school and a revolution in popular culture did for her.

Susan arrived back at the motel breathlessly clutching a record to her breast.

'What's that?'

'"Baby Love", that's what.'

Turned out 'Baby Love' was by someone called Diana Ross. The only place to listen to 'Baby Love' was in the hallway outside the room where there was a spare socket, and there we sat, moving our heads in time to the music like two nodding dogs. Susan added a little sway and, although an interesting move, I didn't think it appropriate for a boy to sway. Nodding, on the other hand, appeared to be fairly cool.

'Sawn-off …? Why? What does it mean?'

When we returned to England I started at Holbrook Primary. I didn't know many of the boys there from my pre-Malta days as most of my mates' parents had been posted elsewhere. I set about making new friends and football once again afforded me access to the kids that mattered. The school team was run by Mr Tomlinson, who could have stepped straight out of an Enid Blyton book – if she had ever written *The Firm But Fair Unmarried Favourite Uncle Who Drank Too Much*.

As I walked home from football practice, something was bothering me. Swimming round in my head was my new nickname. I'd been looking forward to this event in my life. Dad was always talking about his submarining mates and their adventurous tales of derring-do, and they all had nicknames. It was 'And Chubby White did this' and 'Stompy Jones did that', or 'We had a two-ring commander called Nuts O'Brien' and 'I'll never forget that Chief Petty Officer called Two Tots Simpson' … It was endless. Nobody in the navy seemed to have a proper name. Even my dad had a nickname: Dapper Derbs. He was also known as Derby Allen – apparently 'Derby' was reserved for all men in the navy called Allen. Why, I have no idea. And Dapper?

Dad fastened his belt, lifting each foot slightly to adjust the trouser slack.

'It's because I'm always smartly turned out, son. I'm known for it. Always have been. Always dapper.'

A nickname about being clean and smart? Good grief.

I trudged through Bridgemary Estate considering my recently acquired nickname. I'd been at football practice and me, Mickey 'Cheese' Rolls, 'Popeye' Hewitt, 'Desperate' Dan Langdon (you get the picture) and 'Spangles' Newington (always had a packet of Spangles on him) were called over by Two-Patch Tomlinson (leather patches on his sleeves).

He'd decided it was a good idea to enter two teams into the Gosport and Fareham Under-Elevens six-a-side competition on the grounds that we were so good we'd probably meet in the final.

'The teams will be Holbrook A and Holbrook B. Sawn-off? You're to captain Holbrook B.'

We all looked round to see who would captain the B team.

'You, Allen. You are the captain.'

I pointed at myself questioningly, unable to take it in. It then became clear that Sawn-off, the blunt and stubby (but deadly) shotgun was my chosen monicker. Hmmmm. Add to that the insult of playing in the B team and then getting beaten up for the first time in my life, and it wasn't a happy return.

Jimmy Farrin from the neighbouring school, Bridgemary Primary, lorded it over us, taunting the kids who didn't dare retaliate. Jimmy wore a bright red jumper, a big angry fat red jumper. That's all he was. It didn't take him long to focus his attention on me, the new face.

'Oi, Shorty. Is your dad a dwarf?'

'Get lost, Fatty.'

Jimmy jumped on me and took me apart in front of all the other kids. I was cocooned on the floor as the kicks and punches rained down. I hid my face because I was crying. It was the worst thing that had ever happened to me. And it hurt like hell. Now I was humiliated and knew what it was like to be scared.

More than fear, I discovered the definition of 'cowardice'. From then on I went out of my way to avoid Jimmy. If I knew he was playing in a certain area I'd take evasive action. I was a coward and this preyed on my mind. Not a nice feeling, and one of the earliest 'feelings' I can clearly remember having, good or bad.

*

'Oh Christ, what have you done now?' said Dad in a voice about an octave higher than usual.

We'd been allocated a new house back on the naval estate: number 2, Stocker Place. And I was in the bath. I looked at the bathwater, rapidly changing colour from clear to deep red. He seemed to be suggesting I'd done it deliberately, and I guess technically he was right. The blood was pouring from my nose. The fact that he'd gone to clip me round the ear as I was getting out of the bath, causing me to slip and smash my nose into the taps, seemed to pass him by.

'For fuck's sake, son, can't you do anything right?' His voice was getting higher. 'Look at it, look what you've done.'

He was exasperated, but I detected a note of fear in his voice too.

'Always bloody trouble with you, isn't there?'

I couldn't help but think this was a *bit* unfair.

'Hold your head back … hold it back, for Christ's sake.'

He passed me a flannel, said, 'Put this under your nose,' and ran out of the bathroom to get me some clean clothes. I sensed that this was serious. Dad was only gone a minute but when he got back the flannel was already soaked in blood, which was dripping onto the bathroom floor.

By the time we got to the hospital the small bathroom towel we'd taken with us was soaking too. This was the first time I'd ever seen Eddie afraid, and in a peculiar way it made me feel good. Although there was a lot of blood there was no pain and not very much discomfort. He hadn't meant to beat me, it was just a clip round the ear, but this display of fear for my safety was novel, and nice. It meant he cared about me. Two hours later we got home and he let me stay up and watch TV. I didn't even have to clean up the blood.

'Susan!' Dad shouted down. 'Have you not bothered to clean up this blood?'

'What blood?'

She'd only just got in, she was late, she was in trouble …

'Just get up here and clean this up before your mother gets in.'

Mum was working at the Black Cat Café in Gosport. Susan started to clean up the blood. Eddie watched, fuming.

'What time do you call this?'

'Eight o'clock.'

'Eight o'clock, yeah. And what time were you supposed to get in?'

'Seven o'clock,' she mumbled.

'Yes, seven o'clock, right. Clean up then get to bed. I'll deal with you later.'

The register of Dad's voice had lost its fear and was back to normal.

'But Dad? I was only at Helen's doing homework.'

One of my nose plugs popped out and onto my cheese sandwich. Susan and homework had long since parted company. She was nearly a teenager. It was 1964. For most teenagers being alive in what would become known as the 'Swinging Sixties' should have been an unforgettable collage of musical and cultural influences that would shape both the individual and the latter part of the twentieth century. For Susan, it was.

'Homework? Homework? You think I was born yesterday? Clean up that blood, get to your room – and when I come back up I'll get the truth out of you …'

I took the plug out of my sandwich and popped it back up my nose.

The next morning breakfast was eaten in silence. Mum was upset with Dad for being too harsh in getting Susan to tell him the truth. Sue was upset for obvious reasons. She had a sore arse and wouldn't be hanging out with biker boys and smoking for at least a fortnight. Dad was upset because he couldn't understand what he'd done to deserve any of this. At least that's what he kept saying. And Kevin was getting upset because he was five years old and kept being told to be quiet and 'nobody's in the mood'. I wasn't that upset. But I had noticed that my nose was starting to swell.

Along with cocaine abuse, mobile phones, anal sex and croissants, anger management was unheard of in the Allen household. In fact, in 1964 anger management was an unknown concept anywhere this side of the Atlantic.

The philosophy of the late sixties to 'let it all hang out' had not yet been developed by the country's (soon to be empowered) youth, and it certainly hadn't permeated the branch of the navy known as the secret service. In fact, as philosophies go it would have fallen on deaf ears for those five hundred feet below the ocean's waves. No, a more apt philosophy, literally and metaphorically, was 'to keep a lid on it'.

My dad knew that the engines he pumped clean, repaired, watched over and kept running were what enabled this deadly machine to function and its occupants to stay alive. A submarine is basically a large gun with people inside it that spends most of its working life hidden from view. It will only operate efficiently if there is a virtually symbiotic relationship between man and machine. It was the perfect environment not to allow feelings to get in the way. Too much depended on it.

Nowadays, on every one of Her Majesty's nuclear submarines there is a ship's welfare officer who will deal with such events as the theft of gay magazines from Number 1 Forward Torpedo crew's mess rooms, the organisation of the Keep Racism out of Submarining forum when the boat is next in Plymouth and the loss of Chief Petty Officer Jones's set of chrome metal bum spanners (naval slang for dildos) somewhere between Gibraltar and Portsmouth. In the Royal Navy of the sixties, however, everything of an emotional nature was left back on shore. In the diesel-electric machines, air was at a premium – and there certainly wasn't enough of it to share with a 'welfare officer'.

'What have I done to deserve this?' Dad shook his head again, looking round the breakfast table at his gathered family.

He wanted to know why. Why? Well, two reasons.

1) His job. If you live life with 'a lid on it', trouble was what you got. Had he known that he could talk about things and communicate with his family – instead of treating us like a submarine crew – he may have realised that although he'd done nothing to 'deserve' trouble, it was bound to follow.

2) The second reason was about to walk in the room.

Eddie jumped up and answered the door.

Grandpa Allen loomed. 'For Christ's sake, your bloody mother, stupid mare. Get out here and help her push the car in.'

For some reason Grandpa Allen was incapable of reversing his car.

Perhaps he thought it was some kind of blasphemy against God or devil worship. When he arrived that day, he made Grandma Allen get out and push it backwards into a parking spot. Dad made us all go out and help her. Soon we were straining and pushing the car up to the kerb.

If Grandpa Allen didn't 'dig you out', that was his version of being nice. He didn't do compliments. He came from a long line of hard men and was a strict disciplinarian. He had never let my father get away with anything, and my father, with due consideration for family and tradition, conscientiously tried to do the same for me. In the war Grandpa had gone off to fight and Dad had been evacuated to the countryside. On Grandpa Allen's return it was clear he'd been badly affected by the war. My father grew up in this emotionally austere, constrained environment.

When we went in and sat back at the breakfast table, I sneezed. A few moments later, Nan looked at me, screamed and fainted. Dad and Susan backed away from me in horror. Mum started crying. My eye was swelling up and my eyeball was popping out grotesquely. Dad grabbed a coat and rushed me back to the hospital.

What had happened the night before when Dad had clipped me one was that a tube had been displaced between my eye and my nose. After I sneezed, I displaced it further. The inhaling and exhaling that had previously been done through my nostrils was now being partly done through my eye, thus forcing my eyeball out. It was gruesome to behold.

Of course I was thrilled with this new addition to my arsenal of physical vulgarity and did it all the time at school to thrill the lads and make the girls scream. Unfortunately, as the hospital said it would, after a few weeks it corrected itself and I returned to normal.

My father got busy convincing me that I was going to fail the eleven-plus, his attempt at punishing me for my increasingly errant ways.

'You see, son, they're clever, not like you,' he said for the umpteenth time.

Of course, he didn't *mean* it. He hoped his kids would have the chances he never had. He won a scholarship at the age of fourteen, but his mother wouldn't let him take it up. She sent him out to work instead because the family needed the money. Denied the chance to 'better himself', he transferred his aspirations onto his children. He dreamed of the cap and gown for us, and of basking in the reflected glory. These were notions with which he infected my mother. They both thought it was all going right with Susan, but since she spent most of her time at school desperately trying to find a pair of rails to go off, their hopes were transferred to me.

At around this time my parents' social aspirations found an outlet in the purchase of their first home. It was a detached house on an estate that featured communal landscaped areas, all of which had signs up saying 'Keep off the Grass'. My hatred of suburbia started here, as did my loathing for Cuprinol.

The top half of every identikit house was covered in wood, which everyone else painted in matt paint of one colour or another. Dad, for some reason, decided to keep the wood cladding 'natural'. I stared up at the house and asked myself why Dad wanted bare wood. Soon enough I realised. So Dad could send me up the ladder every weekend with a tin of Cuprinol. My hatred of suburbia comes from work, the idea of maintenance, of having to 'beat the Joneses' and, more than anything, from the smell of fucking Cuprinol.

In fact, I never saw much of my parents, such was their devotion to improvement of various kinds. Weekends were religiously observed. But not in the way that you would observe religion: that is, quiet time of reflection with a cup of cocoa and *Songs of Praise* on the TV. No – their weekends were spent religiously cutting grass, clipping edges, fixing gates.

All over the estate, men in slacks tended to front lawns and begonias while ladies wore frilly blouses and expensive-looking cardies and washed windows in rubber gloves rather than their bare hands. The estate was so new that it was surrounded by acres of mud and rubble, isolating us from the town and shops and all community.

The petty bourgeois code of conduct among the occupants of the new estate was pervasive. It was as if moving house gave my parents licence to be rude about the families we'd left behind on the naval estate.

'Don't you go back to play on that estate, it's full of layabouts. Not our kind of people.'

'Mrs So and So hasn't got this; Mr So and So can't afford that.'

'Look at the state of their frontage.'

The new house was a temple to this mentality. It was full of new things. A new television set. A new pouffe for Dad to put his feet on. The front room was so new it was out of bounds. One day he called me in. He was sitting, feet up on the pouffe, opening a bottle of wine. Wine was his new tipple, it was very sophisticated, 'very upper class'. He took a sip and waved his hand across the room.

'See, son, this is what you work for. All this.'

These words were intended to motivate me. His line may have back-fired.

On the day of the eleven-plus results I waited for my name to be read out in the list of 'failed'.

'Allen, Keith, pass.'

'You what?'

'You've passed the eleven-plus, Keith. Now stop graffiti-ing your desk or I'll have you before the headmaster.'

I ran all the way home, following the tractor marks through the wheat field, not even bothering that it was scratching my legs. Mum and Dad were in the kitchen. All I wanted was to see the delight on his face.

'I passed.'

Mum gave me a hug and Dad patted me on the back. So I wasn't stupid after all. I may even be *clever*. He went out and Mum winked at me. There was a present coming. What would it be? A Beatles record? A football strip? Money?

'Here you go. Well done, son. We're proud of you.'

Dad handed me a tennis racket in a press. What on earth was the man thinking? A tennis racket? I'd never played tennis in my whole life. My father pointed out its shiny press, no doubt imagining me bounding about at the All England Club in starched whites displaying heroic manners. The tennis racket went under the bed, where it would remain.

Some time later a letter arrived. We all bent over it, apart from Dad who was sitting rod straight, a pen in his hand, as if he was about to sign the armistice that world peace depended on. I waited with baited breath as his pen lingered between two boxes. One said 'Grammar', the other 'Comprehensive'. That word was a mystery to me, but my father had been talking about it for months with great excitement.

'See, son, this is progress towards a socialist state. The first comprehensive school in Hampshire is opening right here in Gosport.'

I'd passed the eleven-plus so it was natural to go to the grammar school where all my mates (the entire Holbrook footie team) were going. Dad slowly lowered his pen and put a mark in the 'Comprehensive' box. My world promptly collapsed.

'It's progress, son, that's what it is, and being a socialist I support it fully,' he said, folding the letter into the envelope.

So I was off to be a socialist when all my mates were going to Gosport Grammar. Brilliant. Thanks, Dad. There I was battling with the principles of socialism while my father sipped wine, subscribed to *Reader's Digest* and strained to move another rung up his new stepladder of social betterment.

Even worse I was carted off to the local school outfitter with my father and measured up for the new yellow and black uniform of Brune Park Comprehensive. Why they bothered taking my measurements I don't know as Eddie insisted I get trousers and blazer at least three sizes too big.

'No point in getting something that fits you *now*, son, is there? You need something with a bit of give.'

I looked at myself in the mirror. There was no sign of me, just a boxy blazer and three metres of trouser.

'You'll grow into it in a couple of terms.'

Even if I'd put in a growth spurt to rival Jack's beanstalk I'd still be hidden under the mountain of fabric in two decades.

There were no two ways about it. As I walked through the school gates with my regulation short back and sides and oversize uniform, I looked like the biggest twat in town. One cursory glance at my contemporaries confirmed this. It was 1965 and the kids were all in Chelsea boots and drainpipes, already adopting the new 'go fuck yourself' expression promoted by The Beatles and the new pop culture. The lads had long hair and wore earrings while the girls clicked round in stilettos chewing gum.

We sat an entrance exam so that we could be streamed according to our intelligence. In other words, thickies together and swots together. Looking round at the thick-headed youths, I thought I'd sailed through, but was mortified to find I'd been put in the set below the top.

All I could think was that I could have been playing football with all my mates down the road at the grammar school. Instead I was at the wrong school with the wrong haircut and the wrong uniform. There and then I decided to get my own back on my father by perfecting my study of the ancient art of rebellion.

Chapter 6

'TEA, KEITH?' TONY'S mum looked at me resignedly. 'Again?'

'Please,' I murmured, slinking in to sit round the table. It was the fifth night in a row I'd gone to Tony's house for tea. Tony's mum put an extra chop on the grill. The air was thick with grease and smoke.

The house smelt of food, the house smelt like a home. I knew that Mum would have left tea for me at home, as usual, but our kitchen had an extractor fan and smelt of dead space.

An ashtray was overflowing on the table. Tony's dad came in and shouted at his mum, who shouted back.

'Keith having his tea again?' Mr Lardi ruffled my hair. 'Haven't you got your own family?'

'No. I'm an orphan.'

Everyone laughed. As usual I'd used humour to cover up my awkwardness. But I really wished I was.

How to build a good den:

1) Have five shillings in your pocket – with which to buy a porn mag and some rolling tobacco.
2) Have parents who are rarely there or always busy.
3) Read all the Enid Blyton novels – dens will seem much more exciting if you do.

The problem with being moved up the social ladder against one's will is that one attempts to climb back down again. As did I, with monotonous regularity. The kids my age on the new estate were not the kind of kids I wanted to play with. I was three miles from my old mates on the old estate, so I used to have to cycle back there to call for them. Remember these were not only pre-mobile-phone days, but many people didn't even have a landline. I'd cycle up to Ollie Staples' house. Knock knock.

'Is Ollie in?'

'No.'

'Know where he is?'

'No.'

'OK then,' and I'd have to cycle back home again.

My solution was to run away. The woods between my house and school seemed like a good location to move to. I stole some beans and bread and found a clearing in which to build the mother of all dens. I'd built dens as a lad in Wales, and my skills were well honed. I dug down into the earth and hollowed out a living area. Then I put carpet down and corrugated iron on top, followed by sods of grass on top of that. The entire thing was subterranean, invisible from above. With the fire burning and the bread toasting I reckoned I could last out there for six months. Then it started to rain, and I needed a poo. However bad my father's temper, it was better than a leaking roof and sitting in your own crap. Six hours later I was snuggled up under my Beatles duvet. There were drier, more comfortable dens that I would consider after a good night's sleep.

On another aimless cycle ride to Nowheresville I found my new den. There were mountains of bricks on the half-built estate, waiting to become houses. If I removed the bricks from inside the centre of the stack, I would have my own little 'house'. So I did, and I started to spend many hours on my own there. Then the builders arrived to see their brick mountains had increased from my burrowing out. It was lucky that they caught me before the entire stack caved in on my head.

Fictitious situation: The Allen family on *Mastermind*.

Magnus Magnusson: 'Welcome to *Mastermind*. First up we have Keith Allen, aged twelve.'

I take the chair. 'Hello, Magnus – my specialised subject is: smoking and how to get away with it.'

The main gang at school was run by a lad called Billy Fox. To be in the gang it was necessary for me either to grow or to smoke. Since there was not much I could do about the first one (except, in hindsight, not to smoke), I chose the second.

Everyone in our house smoked. Dad, Mum, Susan, me. I even think little Kevin had the odd puff. My first cigarette was a Player's No. 6 I stole from Uncle Gwyn. The cigarette was so strong it nearly took my arse out. Standard order for all navy personnel was two hundred Capstan blue-liners – so called because they had a blue line all the way up to signify they were for the services and could not be sold on.

I would steal two or three singles at a time from Dad's packet so he wouldn't notice, and each day dinner money was duly spent on tobacco and rolling papers instead of corned-beef baps. But the *coolest* thing was to have a cigarette case, so I nicked one from Dad. Then I spent an entire week of detentions rolling cigarettes to go in it.

On the walk home I opened and shut the case several hundred times, perfecting my chat-up lines. I didn't notice the white Ford Prefect shadowing me until it was too late. The window came down and I was greeted by the increasingly familiar look of utter disappointment on my father's face.

'Get in, son.'

I got the belt and was sent to my room for the foreseeable future. He hid the fags but it didn't stop me.

Keith Allen on *Mastermind*:
'My next specialised subject, Magnus, will be: inventing excuses in order to get away with smoking.'

Eddie stood in the doorway and examined my school blazer – the white lining of the sleeves was stained yellow-brown with nicotine.

'What's this, son?'

'Erm. That's a dog, Dad.'

Whatever Dad intended to come out of his mouth didn't make it. Instead his head slowly tilted to one side and he turned an ear towards me. He offered an astonished, 'Come again.'

'It was a dog, Dad.'

'A dog.'

'You see, er, at school, I used my blazer as a goalpost, and, er, a dog sat on it.'

As if this was enough explanation for him.

'Yeah and then what?'

'Well, er, the dog must have had a dirty arse.'

'A dirty what?'

'Sorry, Dad, a dirty bottom.'

Dad shoved the offending armpit under my nose.

'Smell it! Does that smell like dog shit to you, son?'

I sniffed. Paused. Had another little sniff.

'Er, no, Dad.'

'No, son. That's because it's nicotine, isn't it?'

No answer.

'Isn't it?' (Louder.)

'Yes, Dad.'

'Right, home from school and straight to bed – for a week.'

What he'd correctly worked out is that on the smokers' wall at school, to avoid detection by teachers watching from classroom windows, we would take shady puffs and then blow the smoke down the arms of our blazers, leaving a dirty brown stain on the inside. Dad didn't buy my dog-crap excuse, but it came from the top drawer of good ones. Years later, doing stand-up comedy, someone asked me how I managed to think so quick on my feet. Smoking is my answer.

My devil-may-care attitude spread its wandering tentacles in the direction of Dad's car.

'I'm going down the pub, son. Don't bleeding touch anything in that garage.'

'No, Dad. Course not.'

He bowled down the road, arms slightly out to the side – a small but perfectly formed alpha male. I snatched the car keys and decided to go for a drive. I'd been observing the process carefully enough and was pretty sure I could do it. I got the car started, drove it out of the garage, roared up the street and came to a shuddering halt in front of number 76. OK, put it into reverse and turn it round. The rear wheel touched the kerb and bounced the steering wheel away from me. A dull crunch followed as the car made contact with a lamp-post.

It was bad – a big dent in the wing. A dent that was bad enough but would be nothing compared to the dent in me if Dad found it. Survival mode kicked in. On adrenalin I managed to drive the car back into the garage, then locked the door and went to work with old newspapers, forming a papier-mâché filler for the hole. Time ticked by.

'Bugger bastards fuck shit.'

Swearing helped me focus as I applied several coats of model paint over the drying paper. It didn't look bad at all. A neat colour match too. Problem solved.

The following morning, shouting came up from the foot of the stairs.

'Keith! Get out of your pit and wash that bleeding car.'

Dad had taken the car out of the garage and parked it on the street without noticing a thing. I got the buckets, connected the hose and turned on the water, all the while thinking in a rather junior way about fate and what a cunt it was. I managed to wet the entire car apart from the dented bit. Dad was watching from the garage and getting increasingly frustrated by my idiosyncratic washing style.

'Not like that.' He grabbed the hose off me. 'Like *this*. You start from the roof and work down.'

As the water trickled down the wing it washed away the paint and moistened the paper, bits of which started to fall away.

'What the bloody hell …' Dad's jaw tightened and his tongue came forward over his lower teeth.

I backed against the hedge. 'Please … It wasn't me …'

At that moment our neighbour Taff Davis stuck his head over the fence. He started to laugh.

'Bloody good piece of repair, eh, Eddie?'

His laughter threw Dad into confusion. He knew I deserved to be punished but he couldn't do it in front of Taff. More to the point, if he didn't laugh, Taff might think he couldn't take a joke. We all waited for the decision. He smiled tightly at Taff and cocked his head at me as if to say 'get inside'. As I went Taff shot me a conspiratorial look and a wink.

The car fiasco was followed by a lengthy period of not talking. Eventually the silence was broken. Dad stuck his head round my bedroom door, sleeves rolled up, holding a hammer.

'Come on, do something useful for a change.'

He beckoned for me to follow, clearly on a DIY mission. He shouted instructions at me, getting me to roll back the carpet in the upstairs corridor while he banged away at a floorboard. He was so preoccupied he hadn't noticed that all I was wearing was a pair of Y-fronts.

He'd installed a revolutionary central heating system in the new house and went on and on about how we were the first on the entire estate to have it. The theory was that two wall-mounted heaters downstairs would heat the upstairs of the house through holes drilled into the ceiling. Dad wanted me to help him fit metal louvres to the holes.

It just so happened that Nan and Auntie Ethnie had come from Wales to stay. Nan was in the kitchen cooking up a storm of Welsh cakes, and Auntie Ethnie had been detailed to mow the lawn.

I had to hold the louvres in place in the holes in the floorboards while Dad secured them with nails. We were both on all fours, the smell of baking coming up from below. When he stopped to wipe his forehead, I took this as the signal for a break. I got up and stepped backwards, and went straight through the hole in the floor, sending the new metal louvre crashing into the room below.

Dad remained on all fours, frozen, his heating system in tatters.

'Dad! It was an accident.'

I struggled to free my foot as I counted down and watched his tongue come forward. The moment it hit the inside of his lower lip it would be too late. Still on his hands and knees, every inch of his skin was pulled tight with rage. My foot came free just before he lunged at me.

'Nan, Ethnie! Help!' I ran downstairs and through the kitchen, past Nan as she withdrew the latest batch of Welsh cakes from the cooker. I shot out of the door, surprising Ethnie as she laboured over the lawnmower, and made for the street.

A woman came out of number 21.

'What are you doing outside in your underpants?'

'I'm looking for my brother.'

The answer seemed to satisfy her. I wandered around for a bit then crept back.

'Pssssssst! Nan! Post me some clothes through, will you?' Nan's eyes met mine through the letterbox. 'I'm flipping freezing.'

She waddled off to find Ethnie, who by now was billeted to keeping Dad in the kitchen. A pair of jeans and a jumper emerged through the letterbox.

'Of all the stupid things to do. I don't know why you two can't just get along.'

'Shoes, Nan! I haven't got any shoes.'

My father's shadow filled the corridor behind Nan.

'Who you talking to? Is that Keith?'

In her haste Nan had brought me a pair of Kevin's jeans and a jumper. I was forced to wander the estate barefoot, looking like I'd fallen asleep in a tumble dryer. I didn't dare go back home until Mum was there to protect me from the worst of the fallout.

And then there were girls. Up to now I'd been defined by boys. I'd never had female mates, and apart from Rhona Smith my forays into the realm of women were nil.

That said, I was fast turning into a walking hormone, albeit a very small one. The girls congregated at the back of the classroom and boys would hang around them, mouths open, feeding off scraps of exotic conversation like:

'Mine's a C cup, she's a B cup and hers are Ds.'

This was about as clear an explanation to a group of twelve-year-old lads as Newton's law of physics. I was never invited to extracurricular assignations with the chicks, having not been able to shake off the first impression of 'little twat in the ill-fitting uniform'.

The easiest route to experience this thing called 'fucking', it seemed to me, was to get in with the lads who had 'done it', hoping they would introduce me to girls who were 'up for it'. I started hanging out with

Tony Lardi and Gary Davis. Tony was my best mate, the leader. Gary was a swot but he was OK because he lived next to Tony and knew how to mend motorbikes. Tony's balls had dropped and he had a very deep voice. He wore flared hipster trousers and had long hair that he greased back. His dad, a big man, was also a greaser and drove a Zephyr and wore cable-knit jumpers (very in with the greaser crowd was cable knit). What I especially liked about him was that he swore all the time. My old man only swore when he was angry. Mr Lardi would use swear words descriptively when he talked to Tony. 'Fuck me, son, I'm tired.' I took heed then and stuck to this principle throughout my life (as you well know).

Me, Tony and Gary used to bunk off school. It quickly became obvious that there was another reason to let Gary hang out with us. His mum. One day he took us back to his house. It was a run-down semi on the local council estate with an overgrown garden and bits of motorbike everywhere. Gary's mum was divorced. This was incredible in itself because no one was in those days. It was *very* exotic. She was also very vivacious and a bit naughty. The whole set-up fascinated me and opened up possibilities that my family could never offer me … (perhaps even that the family unit *per se* could never offer happiness).

Gary's mum wafted into the kitchen with a fag on the go and a look that said she didn't know what housework was.

'Want a cup of tea, loveys?' she cooed.

'Ta …' we all murmured, staring at her tits.

She was wearing red lipstick and full make-up in the middle of the afternoon and she was the sexiest woman I'd ever seen. She started to make tea, and as she leant into the fridge her breasts and her fag dangled invitingly.

'Sorry, there's no milk.'

By the state of the fridge it looked like there had never been any milk. Every week after that we'd be round at Gary's and while they all fiddled with the big end of Gary's motorbike I took to fiddling with my big end while exploring the contents of his mum's knicker drawer. She had negligees in every colour and I held them over my face and relieved myself all over the bed.

Gary called up the stairs to me and interrupted my negligee-sniffing.

'Keith! We're off to fuck Rose – you coming?'

This was the news I'd been waiting months for and I threw myself down the stairs and caught up with the lads as they marched excitedly down the street, pooling their shillings.

Half-a-Crown Rose was in the second year and was what you might call a free spirit. Essentially she was the school bike. She only became known as Half-a-Crown Rose on the way across the fields to the assignation point because that's what our pooled resources came to (after three ciggies, a packet of Spangles and a can of pop at the corner shop).

The assignation point was a dry dock where the navy kept jump boats for repair. Contextually it was an appropriate venue for my first sexual experience: a fish out of water surrounded by boats out of water. The whole pace stank of diesel and you could still smell the war in the rusted hulls. I wondered why Rose had chosen this spot. More to the point, would she turn up at all?

Tony Lardi had spoken to her that morning at school and offered her money in return for sex. It seemed like a perfectly reasonable arrangement to me, not having yet been introduced to the word 'prostitute'.

'Bet she doesn't turn up.'

'Bet she does.'

'I'm first for a jump.'

'Fuck off, Lardi, I'm first.'

'OK, you, then me.'

'What about me?' I chimed in.

'You're last.'

'Why am I last?'

'Because you've never done it before.'

'Fuck off I have.'

Rose arrived chewing and casually picked her knickers out of her arse. The excitement that I'd been feeling turned to panic. I had no fucking idea what 'fucking' was.

'Who's first then?' She was deadpan.

We all followed her on to the deck of one of the jump boats and broke into the cockpit. Tony went in first and as we listened to the grunts and moans I made a mental note to do the same.

Finally it was my turn. Rose was lying on the floor with her skirt up. I could see that her knickers were half on and didn't know what to do about it. Without stopping to think about how I should achieve my aim, I lay on top and lunged at her mouth, humping like mad. After a minute she broke away.

'Aren't you going to put it in?'

'Yeah,' I replied defensively. I was annoyed that she seemed to sense my lack of know-how. Point was – how to put it in?

I rummaged around inside her knickers and located an entrance. A leg entrance.

'What are you doing now?'

'Shut up.' I was dangerously close to shooting my load anywhere. I continued my search and thrust a finger somewhere warm. This must be it. Meanwhile Rose was getting restless, tutting and moving.

'Hurry up, will ye.'

It was more a hit and hope, but all I seemed to be doing was getting serge-grey panties in the way of me and my future. Then finally … it felt like I was in, warm and sort of – At that precise moment, Lardi opened the door.

'Get off, Allen. Someone's coming.'

No sooner was I 'fucking' than I was fucked. Rose sprang up and out with the energy of someone glad to get away. I followed doing up my trousers and wondering what all the fuss was about. Even at that tender age I couldn't help thinking that Gary's mum would have been a better teacher.

Schoolboy scrambling was our favourite pastime. And no, it isn't making eggs in the cub scouts. Motocross was a massive sport when I was kid, and me, Tony and Gary all loved bikes.

Gary had a Billy Bantam, the Rolls-Royce of all scrambling bikes, and the three of us together bought an old banger to take scrambling at an old army training ground nearby. It was so heavy it was like pushing a removal van up Snowdon. At the track it immediately blew up and caught fire.

Dad enquired about my hobby when I returned with singed wellies.

'Tony's bike just blew up,' I said, reasonably honestly. Well, he'd caught me on the hop and I was still a bit shocked over the bike.

I was even more shocked by his response.

'I'll help you build a new one if you want.'

Dad had obviously decided this was a good way to show he cared. It worked. He was brilliant with his hands and knew everything about engines. Together we made a James 175 motorbike. Even Tony and Gary were invited into the garage to see. Dad's suspicions of my mates were suspended and he talked engines to us for hours. Then we took the new James out for a spin. I'd never been so proud.

On the way home Tony and Gary both said, 'God, your old man's fantastic.'

I didn't understand. Who could they possibly be talking about?

Chapter 7

'GET IN, HURSTY son.'

Dad was slightly squatting, looking as if he was about to pop out more than a couple of buttons.

'What a save! See that, son? What a pass. What a pass! Is that it? We've done it. We're there!'

The final whistle went. England were through to the World Cup finals, and to face who? The *Germans*, of course. It was almost too beautiful to bear. Dad attempted a dance that was a cross between the haka and some early ska and for once he didn't mind us laughing at him. He barked instructions at my mother.

'Mary, get the beer in for next Saturday, and some fancies … you know the sort … and something for the kids. We'll make it a day to remember.'

Ever since Eddie and Grandpa first took me to a Fulham game, football had been the one thing that had never failed to unite our family. After finding out that Eddie nearly played for Fulham, I decided (like every other boy worth his salt would) that I wanted to be a footballer.

In Malta I'd once watched Dad playing for his submarine team so I knew he was a decent player. Once he turned up to play without his shorts and had to play in his boxers. I remember him tearing down the right wing, me and Mum and all the navy wives hollering support, and then his cock fell out of his boxers and they all turned away in horror. I remember being very embarrassed.

In 1966, aged twelve, all my hopes and dreams of being a footballer loomed large. Unfortunately the throb of youth was getting to me and my behaviour was deteriorating commensurately. On the Saturday of the World Cup final I arranged to meet the gang in town to while away the hours till kick-off.

Portsmouth town centre was a mixture of bombsites, docks and new concrete developments. We bowled along in a big group, smoking, swearing and cussing each other.

'Bet Hurst gets the winner.'

'Bet your mum shags the postie.'

'Bet your dad's the milkman.'

We stopped outside a sports shop, loafing by the window and shouting obscenities at girls passing by. Me and Lardi stared at the display commemorating the England team with a replica red England shirt as the centrepiece. The shopkeeper's face appeared from behind it and gestured to us to clear off. Lardi stuck two fingers up.

'Dare you to go in and nick something.'

'Fuck off. Why me?'

'Go on, Allen. It's your turn. I nicked that football last week.'

All the other lads looked at me as if the outcome was predetermined.

'All right, go on then,' I sighed wearily. 'You lot distract him.'

The shopkeeper looked up when the door bell jingled and scratched his crusting beard.

'If you touch anything you're out.'

'I'm only *looking*.'

I scanned the display racks. Rugby balls were too cumbersome, and though proud of my developing manhood I wasn't fool enough to think I could get away with a cricket bat down my pants.

Outside I could hear Lardi picking a fight with Ollie Staples. The owner tutted and left the cash register to check out the commotion. I saw Lardi throw a punch that looked painful. (The distinction between staged fighting and real aggression was barely observed.)

'Oi! You lads, clear off or I'll get the police.'

All I could focus on was a pile of tennis balls. It was a low-grade steal and one I was surely going to regret, if only for its pathetic size. I ran for the door to catch up with the lads but a hand grabbed me by the scruff of my neck. The shopkeeper stared down at my bulging pants. It was a fair cop. The police arrived and looked at me as if an attempt had been made on the crown jewels.

'Do you understand the consequence of your actions?'

I was trying not to laugh. It was a fucking tennis ball. Lardi and the lads were now back and staring through the window, pulling imaginary cocks out of their heads to demonstrate what they thought of me.

'Where do you live, son?'

All of a sudden a bigger, more devastating consequence popped into my head. Dad.

'Um. I don't know.'

'Well, I'm sure you'll remember at five to three when the game's about to kick off … unless you want to watch it down the nick, that is.'

The game. I'd forgotten about the game. I gave them the address, and they put me in the back of the squad car. We drove to the edge of my estate.

'Er. You can drop me off here if you like.'

They looked at me as if to suggest that I had indeed been born yesterday. As we pulled up outside our house, several neighbouring curtains fluttered. I squeezed my eyes shut, praying for some kind of divine intervention, or even sudden death.

Dad spoke to the policemen in the front room quietly, he thanked them as they left and shut the door softly. My eyes watered up as he turned to look at me. Perhaps the tears and the humility would move him to forgive me?

'Get to your room. I don't want to see your face again today.'

'But what about the match?'

'You should have thought of that, son.'

I was twelve; I didn't think.

'I swear I'll never nick again, I swear.'

'You've brought it on yourself.'

He went into the front room and closed the door behind him. I went up to my room and closed my door. The window was ajar and the noise of a hundred televisions flooded in. I pressed my ear to the carpet and noticed bits of fluff and hair while straining to hear Kenneth Wolstenholme's voice. Every so often my father would boom, 'Go on, son. Get it in,' followed by, "Ow the bleeding hell did he miss *that*?'

The air was still, the street quiet. Everyone was together, then a massive overwhelming noise.

'Yeeeeeeeees!'

I could tell my dad was jumping up and down. I put my nose under the door and sniffed like a dog after the Sunday roast.

'No! You prawn! Noooooo.'

One-all. I could tell by the silence that it was tight. Very tight.

The afternoon wore on. I lay on the carpet and stared at the ceiling, wanting England to win more than I wanted to turn the clock back to erase the Great Tennis Ball Robbery. Suddenly there was a thunderous noise on the stairs. The door burst open and nearly shot off its hinges.

'Yeeeeeeeeeeeeeeeees!'

Dad was on his knees, fists clenched, head back as if waiting to be mobbed by ten strapping men. I joined him on the floor, mimicking his pose.

'Yeeeeeeeeeeeeeeeees!'

We jumped around the room and the ceiling shook, everything forgotten in the euphoria of the moment.

'He's only gone and put it in the net, son.'

'Was it Hursty?'

'Course it was, he's a bloody genius.'

We both made for the door eager to get back to the television as if our presence would be enough to make England hang on through the final ten minutes. Halfway down the stairs he stopped, remembered and turned.

'Where do you think you're going?'

I shuffled back up the stairs to my prison. I didn't 'think' it was all over, I knew it was.

It was clear to my parents that I was hanging with the wrong crowd (not that Brune Park Comp gave much in the way of the 'right crowd'), and out of the blue my father told me I was to take a naval scholarship.

Another motivation lay behind the naval scholarship. Dad's new sub,

HMS *Onslaught*, was being posted to Singapore. He told me about this only when it was announced that I'd passed the exam and on the strength of it been accepted at Brentwood public school in Essex.

'It's a boarding school. Your mother and I think it's for the best.'

My parents must still have been holding onto their cap-and-gown fantasy. Either that or they decided they couldn't handle both me and my sister in Singapore. (Even with my limited knowledge of sexual misdemeanours I knew that Susan was fast becoming 'experienced'.) While my parents were building their dream existence, their children were busy dismantling it.

I immediately put the thought that my family were soon to fuck off to the other side of the world without me to the back of my mind. Instead I was quite looking forward to the new school. It had been such a major upheaval when I went to comprehensive the September before that nothing would ever again be a jolt quite like that. Besides, I was sick of cycling back and forward to the old estate to see my mates. Plus, as you know, I'd read all the Enid Blyton books and knew boarding school meant dorms and other kids and, I suppose, I was desperate for company.

The idea of a tuck shop also loomed large. The whole thing sounded like a great adventure. I had no idea about the class difference, which was apparent after the first few days. Dad had made me a tuckbox out of bits of old wood, but I soon realised all the other boys had posh, shop-bought ones and I cursed my father's failure to appreciate that I needed to be the same as everyone else. At school, no one wants to be different.*

As I stood on the gravel at Brentwood School, waving goodbye to my parents, I realised that I was becoming something of an expert in 'fish out of waterness'. Another new school, another set of strangers and yet another oversized school uniform.

It didn't take long for me to make my mark on the school in my own inimitable fashion. For those lucky readers who don't know, boarding school is divided into 'houses'. Mine was originally called School House.

---

* Twenty-five years later I gave this box to my son Alfie when Alison decided he was to go off to boarding school – showing the same lack of appreciation for his delicate teenage tendencies as Dad did for mine. Oh dear.

In the assembly room boys had been scratching their names into the oak panelling for more than one hundred and fifty years, boys like 'Johnny Pascoe 1899' and 'Teddy Mallingham 1910'. But not for me the crowded graffiti of the north wall; it was the clear unblemished wood of the south wall that was to be privileged enough to bear my name. I scratched away, tongue protruding, until 'Keith Allen 1966' was etched into the panel.

It wasn't until I was in the headmaster's office that I understood the phrase 'safety in numbers', and that there was a time to stand out from the crowd, and another one to hide like a girl within it.

'Right, Allen. As you are a new boy, I shall be lenient.'

I was bent double with my hands on my knees. The headmaster moved about, humming a tune. He selected a weapon, a leather-soled slipper, and tested it with a thwack on the back of his hand.

'And remember … I don't like this as much as you don't.'

As my arse got battered, I knew that his idea of lenient and mine would never meet.

Football was called soccer, rugby was called football and fagging was definitely not smoking. It was all Dutch to me. Fortunately my 'soccer' ability redeemed me, but, as was so often to be the case in the coming years, it also afforded me more opportunity to fuck up.

It worked like this – I would do something good, get put on a pedestal, get carried away, do something idiotic and get taken off the pedestal again. My early life might have been easier if someone had taught me the value of *consolidation*. I never had much chance to enjoy success because as usual I was on to the next thing. Had I been good at nothing, my life would have been one long continuum of trouble without the need to raise the hopes and expectations of my father. But it must have been frustrating for him to see glimpses of what could have been.

I was able to keep the ball for a long time, and it was fucking hard to dispossess me. In Tenby a few years later I was the star of the beach football kickabout matches, and regularly kept the ball away from all the other players for whole tracts of the game. (The rules of kickabout football, if you don't know, are that anyone tackles anyone and the game kind of goes on like that.) Even at the age of thirty, at Glastonbury Festival, I kept the ball for thirteen minutes – none of the New Model Army could get it.

Playing 'soccer' at Brentwood School I was the star, but no sooner was I running the line for the school team than an overeager tackle left me with a handful of broken metacarpals and I was forced to watch from the sidelines as my house team went two-nil down in the semi-finals of the inter-house cup.

I harried our teacher. 'Sir, you've got to put me on.'

'Aren't you off games?'

'Erm … no, I'm, erm, OK now,' I lied.

'All right, get stripped off.'

The ball fell to my feet immediately and rounding all four defenders I slotted it into the corner of the net. We were back in it and the midfield was mine. My header dropped nicely for Simmons to make it two-all and with five minutes to go the game was there for the taking. All my energy was gone but the word 'hero' loomed large as I collected the ball deep in our own half and laid it off to the right wing. I skimmed the prefects Tippet, a big bully, and Walters, who was the best player on the other team. My heart thumped along with my feet all the way up the pitch in what seemed to take forever. I raised my eyebrows and spread my arms wide, appealing for the ball that Simmons had manfully held up for me. As it came I stretched to get a toe forward. It connected and beat the goalkeeper. The whistle blew and I was lifted by ten people and chaired back down the chase to the house.

After showers the coach gathered us in the dressing room.

'There's been a complaint. From the opposing team. Apparently Allen shouldn't have been playing as he's technically off games.'

I hid behind the coat pegs, pretending to be dressing.

'As a result –' I looked up. Everyone was looking at me bemused but it was the coach's expression that said it all '– I'm afraid you've been disqualified from the competition.'

Everyone turned round to me and the insults flew.

'Allen, you penis.'

'Allen, you dick.'

'Allen, you cock.'

You get the picture. In the space of half an hour I'd gone from hero to villain and for the rest of term Coventry was where I resided.

Luckily the prefects, Tippet and Walters, took a shine to me because of my natural athleticism. At least I think it was my natural athleticism. Or more likely it was my boyish good looks and the fact that I washed their shirts with my nailbrush once a week. Perversely I took great pride in this and turned out to be good at it. They offered me fags but fagging wasn't my scene, certainly not what they had in mind. Only two things interested me: masturbation and music.

Exposure to illicitness was limited and therefore my flowering into a disaffected youth remained in incubation. I started going round with Charlie Higson (not *that* CH!), who was three years above me and considered to be the Antichrist. It was rumoured that Higson smoked something called 'pot'. We stole out of school to go shopping in Brentwood.

'Like music, Allen?'

Higson threw me a look and I followed him into a record shop, fingering the tuck money in my pocket and knowing that if I wanted to be cool and buy 'House Of The Rising Sun' by The Animals I'd have to do without a Mars Bar. The Animals won.

On the way back to school, Higson lit a joint and smoked some of this 'pot' stuff.

He inhaled it and kept it in there for about five minutes. Well, that was the end of any conversation. Not that it had been in great supply in the first place.

Charlie was an enigma. Sometimes he'd completely ignore me so I was forced to make another friend, Douglas Adams, whom I liked simply because he was filthy rich. As we waited for our parents to pick us up at the end of term we made jokes about poor people and how uncool they were. At that moment Mr Adams turned into the gates and drove up in a huge shiny new Bristol.

'What car's your dad got, Keith?'

'Oh, er, same as yours.'

'What colour?'

'Silver.'

Our conversation was interrupted by a rattling engine labouring up the school drive. Douglas Adams frowned.

'Who on earth is *that*?'

I shrugged as if I didn't know and turned away as my father pulled up in a newly acquired second-hand Standard 8. He got out, pulled up his trousers officiously and rocked backwards, legs apart, before spotting me and putting a hand up in recognition.

'Hello, son! Over here.'

He waved manically and then strode purposefully towards me. I died.

'You going to introduce me to your new friend?'

Chapter 8

ANOTHER TELLING SIGN that the cut of my gib was not right at Brentwood was that I had been unique among the kids of my age in Gosport and Wales in having been on a plane. At Brentwood I quickly discovered that all the boys were jetting off willy-nilly round the world. Ian Mickey's dad lived in Malaysia and Walters' in Australia. All the lads who smoked used to lie on their backs on the sports field and plane-spot, and they were much more knowledgeable than me. But I soon got to know the planes, particularly after the odd day out with Grandma and Grandpa Allen, who used to pick me up and take me to Heathrow Airport. (Their idea of a good time.)

By the beginning of 1967 my parents were in Singapore. At least being picked up from school in the battered Ford wasn't going to happen again. On my first solo trip out to see them, aged thirteen, I stayed the night with Ian Mickey at his aunt's house near Heathrow. Ian was going with me to Singapore, then on to Malaysia to see his father.

Perhaps it was just me or maybe all little boys have awkward sexual moments. Anyway, mine seemed to come thick and fast. As I lay in bed excitedly imparting my great knowledge of the features of the Boeing jumbo jet, Ian fell asleep with his hand on my cock. Perhaps he thinks it's his, I thought. I moved his hand, but back it came. This was not part of the holiday plan and I shot out of the double bed, got dressed and waited downstairs for five hours before it was time to go to the airport.

I spent the entire journey smoking at the back of the plane, thinking

I must look at least eighteen. And the entire journey being told to put my fag out and return to my seat by the air hostess.

Singapore was a visual feast but it flitted by the window of the car too fast. In the forces residential areas there was an eerie air of British familiarity. The Frasers were there, as was the Mills family. Most of the time we went swimming in the pool at the naval base. We were bussed in and out of the complex, missing all the interesting bits, all the places where the natives lived, which I was sure were my kinds of place.

I went exploring the first chance I got and decided that I fancied a haircut and a new shirt. I picked my way through alien streets, nearly being run over by old men on bikes in bare feet and being accosted by people frying bits of fish, their weird chatter so unfamiliar it wasn't worth bothering with. The luxury of an incomprehensible language is that you don't even try to speak it.

I developed a keen awareness of how to make myself understood most of the time. It involved taking a large wad of seemingly useless notes out of my pocket and pretending to count them.

'Shirt. *Shirt*.'

I tugged at my breast pocket and flicked my money at a tailor, who nodded and smiled. He took my measurements and made me two shirts with my initials on the pocket. They came to less than fifty pence. What impressed me was how little everything cost and therefore how much money I could spend.

The barber shop was my favourite place, despite the fact that I was totally whiskerless. I did, however, have a few pubes round my cock. I counted them. One, two, three. I used to check they were still there – all three. Yes. I was convinced I had more than the other lads in my class. There were four of us now, me and my three pubes, taking on the world.

The tiny barber offered up his fag packet and we'd sit all day communicating in the universal language of smoking. Dad now seemed to turn a blind eye to my habit, preferring to think of me as the model son and distinguished sportsman.

As ever, Dad encouraged my football, knowing that it was the thing most likely to put me on the right path in life. He put me forward for the

HMS *Onslaught* football team, and Kevin came along to watch the match against an army eleven. Because of the rivalry between the forces there was a lot riding on it. Kevin cheered me on, seeing me as his impossibly cool older brother (if only he knew …).

'Come on, Keith, score a goal.' Kev and his mates jumped up and down.

I took on a naval rating with the ball and nutmegged him before turning on the speed and leaving four or five twenty-year-olds for dead and finished by wrongfooting the goalie and burying the ball in the left corner. What a goal, what a feeling. That was the only goal of the game and decided the match in our favour. Things were looking up between me and Dad. If I could make it as a footballer, I would never have to worry about being a disappointment to him again.

Susan, on the other hand, was most definitely on the way down. She and the Fraser girls, who were all fifteen, were going to dances on the other battleships and dating sailors.

One humid night, I lay soaking on top of the bed sheets listening to the mother of all arguments going on downstairs. Susan, who hadn't come home the night before, had now, at last, turned up.

'Where've you been?'

'At the Frasers'.'

'Don't lie to me, girl.'

'Why don't you ask 'em then?'

'I know what you've been doing.'

'Why don't you just piss off and leave me alone.'

Susan ran upstairs and locked herself in the bathroom. A minute later there was the thud thud thud of Eddie Allen and a powerful thump on the wooden door. I wasn't about to put myself in line for a medal for gallantry at that moment so I stuck my fingers in my ears and pretended nothing was happening.

Mum managed to calm him and finally we were all able to get some sleep. The next morning there was no Susan. She'd packed and gone to stay with the Fraser family, who were promptly disowned as family friends for siding with my sister.

I never felt bad for my sister. But kids are selfish. I just thanked God it was her, not me. We, all three kids, knew Dad had a temper. We didn't need to defend each other and make it worse.

Summer at Brentwood meant another trip to Singapore. I was almost fourteen by now and mortally self-conscious, but I had a trump card. It was June 1967 and The Beatles' *Sergeant Pepper's Lonely Hearts* album had just hit the shops. England was truly the hippest place to be in the world. I boarded the plane clutching my copy of the album, safe in the knowledge that none of the other kids out in Singapore would have a copy.

As soon as I arrived, an orderly queue formed round our record player to listen to it. My sister was back at home and a truce had been called by Mum. Susan's mates twisted their skirts and pointed their toes, giggled and tossed their hair as they pored over the album cover, which was the coolest thing anyone had ever seen.

'I love John. I don't know what to do. If I met him I'd die.'

'I love Paul. Look at that hair.'

'I'm going to faint.'

Their skirts were made of floaty stuff which rode up towards their thighs as they moved. Janice slipped her shoe off and rubbed her legs with her toes.

'You coming to the summer ball?'

'I suppose.'

'Good. You're cool. Bring the record with you.'

She stared at me as she balanced on one leg, feeling for her shoe without looking down. Eventually she found the hole and slipped it on. It was so erotic it was all I could do not to get the most enormous hard-on.

The summer ball promised much and I washed my genital area ambitiously. Dad came into my room carrying a suit. He stuck the hanger on the back of the door and ran his hand down the suit.

'There you go, son, my best old suit. I had it taken in for you. You'll look tip-top in that.'

Oh dear oh fucking dear. I strode onto HMS *Terror* in a double-breasted suit with collars that could have flown me home and turn-ups that could have housed several baby kangaroos.

Janice was already dancing, her flowery print dress nipped in at the waist in the fashion of the time. She was holding her nose with one hand and pretending to pull a chain with the other. This was accompanied by a shimmy downwards, bending the knees. Another girl tried to copy her but looked more like she'd had a massive crap and was trying to pull the chain to get rid of it and holding her nose to overcome the stench.

I bummed a cigarette and tried to smoke my way out of fashion hell. All the kids were in shirts and T-shirts while I stood sweating unattractively in a woollen suit and tie. Janice looked over and smiled. It was the sort of smile that brings you back from the brink of suicide. It said one thing to me: sex. Since Half-a-Crown Rose, I was still waiting for my first proper shag.

'Hi, Keith! You know, after you've given it to Jane Murphy can I have it?'

What was she talking about? Who was I giving it to and when? My groin stirred.

'Yeah, course … er, what exactly am I giving you?'

'*Sergeant Pepper's*. Can I have it next?'

'Oh that. Course. Sorry. You want to … er … dance?'

She nodded, and turned sharply to hit the dancefloor. My contribution to the 'Submersible' dance was something akin to a stranded penguin unable to get a foothold on slippery ice. What was great and extremely unexpected was that Janice seemed to think I was cool.

'Do you want to go outside?'

'All right then.'

Janice's heavenly skin touched mine as she took my hand in the middle of the dancefloor. With my free hand I took one last pull on my cigarette, American style, hand cupped round like the soldiers did, and mullered it with my shoe.

A sudden sharp pain almost sent my legs from under me. Janice stepped away in shock. Someone had hold of me and was dragging me off the dancefloor.

'You think it's clever to smoke, do you?'

Eddie marched me outside and threw me against a wall.

'Get home. And take off that suit. You're not fit to wear it.'

He went back inside and I walked home contemplating how to murder him and get away with it. He couldn't wait and humiliate me at home. Oh no. It had to be in full view of all the older lads. 'Little Allen in his wanker suit being sent to bed for smoking.' Ha ha.

Nothing much mattered apart from smoking and girls. I spent Christmas in Wales, nicking and doctoring a pair of Auntie Ethnie's fur-lined boots in an attempt to create some fashionable gear for myself. For Easter 1968, however, I was stuck at boarding school with time on my hands. Something was going to give and it wasn't going to be me. I wandered into the chapel and sat down, hands in pockets, breathing in the smell of old Bibles. My gaze fell on the organ and its complicated structure of pipes. A plan formed in my stupefied mind. It was simple enough, but I didn't have a clue how easy it would be to move the pipes. I tried one and with a delicate lift slid it out of its hollow.

On the first day of the summer term we all filed into the chapel for the service. The choir checked their sheet music and the boys fidgeted in the pews, whispering and nudging each other.

'All rise for the first hymn.'

The first hymn was 'Jerusalem'. The organist struck up. What followed was less Jerusalem and more Beelzebub. It sounded as if the organ was being played backwards in some kind of devil worship.

The organist stopped playing at the very moment that Douglas Adams leant over to Ian Mickey and said at some volume: 'It's Keith Allen! He's switched the pipes.'

The entire school looked at me with a mixture of admiration and pity. It was a genius stroke, but one that also sealed my fate.

I was taken straight to the headmaster. From the way he resignedly scribbled notes it was clear that something serious was going to happen.

They sent for my dad, who was nearing the end of his draft in Singapore. He came back early and appeared at school wearing his naval uniform, looking grave. We walked round the running track together, no noise but the crunch of rubber on cinder, our steps in time. This was the same track on which for two years running I'd earned my athletic colours, beating school records for the 800 metres.

'They're going to expel you.'

'Me? What for?'

'What for? For leading the other boys astray, that's what for.' He wiped a tear from his eye. 'What have I done to deserve this, son? Eh? Your mother and me gave you everything. What did we do wrong?'

We crunched on wordlessly. I looked down at my shoes, my main thoughts along the lines of: Thank fuck I don't have to run round this track again.*

I was shipped back to Brune Park Comp and walked in to the familiar sight of a bunch of blank faces. Here we go … Still, I'd done it before and I'd do it again.

Except this time there was one massive difference. I joined my new class and found a desk at the back. A girl looked round at me and smiled. I smiled back. The teacher saw us.

'Esther Williams, get on with your work.'

'Fuck off, miss,' Esther shot back.

I couldn't believe what I'd heard.

'*You can't tell a teacher to fuck off,*' I rushed, under my breath.

She looked at me as if I was an alien. There was no getting away from it. After two years at boarding school, I had become posh. Esther turned and whispered to her mates, who stared at me and giggled.

'Oh you *can't* tell a teacher to fack orf, *can't* you?' said Esther, mimicking my accent.

My face coloured up. There was only one thing for sure. Posh was *not* staying.

I immersed myself in football, trying to regain some cred. With some success. Me, Stevie Mills and Mike Newington all played for Gosport and Fareham in the local boys league. The Southampton scout came to watch us play and noticed me. He loitered about after the final whistle, chatting to the sports teacher. They called me over.

'Allen? This is Ken from Southampton FC. You caught his eye.'

'Well played, son.' Ken wasn't giving much away.

'Thanks.' I continued limbering down.

'I'd like you to come for a trial.'

---

* I found out later that this was what my headmaster had said to my father: 'He'll either win the Victoria Cross or go to prison.'

First H-bomb goes off above
Malden Island 1957

Dad 1953

Avenger being 'ditched' at the end of
Operation Grapple.

Mum and dad on their wedding day

Dad, Nan and Grampa Allen,
me and Kevin at the pool

A very vivacious mum, 1950

Showing off, Malta 1962

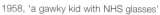
1958, 'a gawky kid with NHS glasses'

Kevin holding the family
tortoise, Malta 1962

Sue about to hit me

Nan and Grandpa John, Mum and Kevin outside Nan's house

Open day on Dad's sub – Kevin watches as mum goes down the hatch

The best football team I
ever played in

With llamas on a day out
from Borstal, aged 18

Me (far left) playing Oedipus at the Welsh College of Music and Drama.
Peter Garvey whose knee I unwittingly ruined is in the middle

AUNTY ETHANCE + UNCLE CYRYL 1973

Dad having left the Navy, dancing with Mum

Nanny John with Uncle Gwyn

At the ICA, 1976, in front of one of Ken and Bob's Posters

My flatmate

'Great. When?'

'We'll be in touch.'

I sprinted off to get changed – a trial for Southampton FC? That would impress the girls, and Dad. What could possibly go wrong?

'Hello,' said the rating from HMS *Handmedown* chirpily.

'Yes, sir, what can I do for you?'

'Drawers.'

'Drawers, sir.'

'That's right, son. Run out of drawers.'

'Size, sir.'

Much laughing and winking with the senior sales assistant.

'Extra large.'

Off I run to cabinet number 3 and rummage round for a pair of extra-large men's briefs. I run back and hand them to him. He stops laughing.

'Only kidding, son. Medium will do.'

I go back and swap the extra large for a pair of medium. Why didn't the stupid git ask for medium in the first place?

To set the scene, earlier that morning Allen junior (me) stood in the shadow of a brewery in a shady part of town called Queens Street, looking at his shiny shoes for an inordinately long time.

Greenburg and Son Gentlemen's Outfitters looked harmless enough from the outside, but I had a feeling that once I'd crossed the threshold things would deteriorate.

Oh well, I thought, I might be measuring up a rear admiral for a suit or something equally exciting. A couple of hours earlier I had reluctantly pulled on one of Dad's double-breasted retailored suits with enough give in the arse to float the navy in. I felt like I was being evacuated from Poland as I boarded the Gosport Star Ferry bound for Greenburg and Son Gentlemen's Outfitters.

Dad had decided that a stint as a shop assistant would be good for me. And where better to smarten me up a bit than a clothes shop? But any dreams I had of such glamorous tasks as measuring up a rear admiral were swiftly dispatched by David Greenburg, the son of the Greenburg and Son partnership.

'Right, Allen. Junior salesmen start in Pants and Socks.'

Right. I ambled over to the display cabinets and folded some men's briefs. Fan-fucking-tastic. I was to fetch and carry smalls for the naval ratings. Worse still, the shop was permanently in the shade and the stench of old hops from the brewery hung in the air. By five fifteen I was thoroughly depressed.

Eddie Allen mantra – depressed? Work your way out of it.

Keith Allen mantra – depressed? Steal something.

What I was about to learn was that stealing sets off a chain of events that changes the course of your life. For example, if you get away with the steal, you benefit materially. If you get caught, you get sacked, or there are other consequences, such as beatings. All of which at least mean things are not the same as they were before, the same as when you were depressed.

I was bored shitless. Casting a junior sales assistant's eye on the display cabinets, I noticed a series of lighters. The jackdaw in me was attracted to the shiny metal. Imagine the joy when I discovered the cabinets weren't locked.

When questions were asked by Son of Greenburg it seemed ridiculous to me to own up and give the lighter back and therefore be sacked for theft and criminal charges. Why not insist it was one of the few sockless ratings who'd had it away?

I was immediately dismissed and waddled back to the ferry in my demob suit (nothing in Greenburg's having caught my eye). I waited for the ferry for about an hour, scared of telling Dad, putting off the dreaded moment. As I finally walked the gangplank down to the ferry, my attention was caught by what looked like Portsmouth's Am Dram Urchin Club. A crowd of strapping young Pomponians were playing about happily in the mudflats under the pier. It looked like South Hampshire's Paedophile Festival had just got under way. In fact what I was witnessing was the quaint Pomponian tradition of mudlarking.

I noted people throwing coins into the mud (most of them were over forty and had massive erections) for the youths to chase. This mudlarking seemed marginally preferable to facing Dad, so it was a relief to throw off the shackles of the suit and jump in.

Oooh. The blow landed on my left temple.

Aaah. The second connected with my chin.

The mudlarks were not charitable chirpy chappies after all. This was high-stakes begging. And I had muscled in on their patch. Still, weighing up the choice between getting a beating from Dad for nothing and getting a few clouts from the gyppos in the mud in return for money – well, no contest.

(Looking back, I guess most of the people who threw us coins were northerners, holiday-makers going on the ferry to the Isle of Wight. I reckon it reminded them of home, scrabbling around in the shit for a few pennies. It must have been nice to see their southern cousins doing it for once.)

Back at home Dad said, 'Turn out your pockets, son.'

There on the kitchen table spilled a hundredweight of small change. He looked at me suspiciously.

'Er, tips, Dad.'

'Tips.'

'Yes, Dad. From the customers.'

He couldn't complain since my mudlarking takings came to a small fortune. Later, brushing past me in the hallway, Mum commented on how lovely and soft my skin was.

And so it went on, me showering and changing in the local public baths before going home.

This established a theme in my life. My parents thought I was doing one thing when actually I was doing something completely different, but I'd always come home with a bag full of money.

'Hello? Speaking … Yes, that's right. He's my son.'

Eddie looked towards the kitchen where I was eating my tea. I quivered in my socks as he stared at me, nodding seriously as he listened to the person on the phone. I wondered what I'd done now. Was it the police? Someone's mum ratting on me? Greenburg's the Gentlemen's Outfitters informing him that his son had been fired?

'Right you are. I'll tell him.'

Eddie put the phone down softly and stood looking at me from the hall. Mum turned away from the sink, wiped her hands and stood in front of me, as if to protect me from whatever was to come.

'That was Southampton Football Club.' He looked serious. 'They only want to offer you a trial, son.'

Eddie did a little jig. Mum hugged me and I breathed a sigh of relief. I was saved. For now. I was having a trial for a division one football club. At last Dad could be proud of me.

But in the true tradition of that elusive theme called 'rites of passage', I was too involved in the drama of my young life to enjoy a period of peace. Oh no. I had to fuck up. The next fuck-up was to be the most spectacular one so far.

So it was that a couple of weeks before the trial I turned up for a local tournament wearing the colours of Fareham and Gosport; Mike Newington and Stevie Mills had also been offered trials and the three of us were talking excitedly in the changing rooms.

The coach wandered in.

'Allen – you're on the bench today.'

Stevie and Mike looked at each other. I was fucking pissed off. I was not very good at being rejected – and that's how I saw it. Along with all the other subs I took my place on the bench. In keeping with the Keith Allen school of illogic, what I did next was a kind of 'well, fuck you then, if I'm only good enough to be a sub, I'll go and nick something'.

While the other subs were warming up down the line, I warmed up in the other direction – that of the opposing team's changing room. This was a new thing, stealing people's possessions. But it was just happening faster than I could stop myself. I checked a few trouser pockets and found a wallet. I stuffed it into my tracksuit bottoms and ran out to rejoin the other subs. Back on the bench I considered whether I should put it back. Hmm. But if I did then I wouldn't be able to spend the twenty quid that was in it … decisions, decisions. At full time the decision, as ever with my life, was taken out of my hands.

As we approached the changing rooms, our coach stood talking with the opposition coach.

'Right, lads. Empty your pockets. One of their lads has had a wallet nicked.'

Everyone turned out their pockets, except me, who only turned out one.

'Empty your pockets, son.' The coach looked very sorry for me, sorrier than I felt, having not, as he obviously had, thought about the consequences.

Had I had any idea about this thing called 'the future' and 'consequences' and how it related to me, I wouldn't have done such a stupid thing with a trial for Southampton coming up. The reason I suppose is this: no matter how bad was the thing I had done, I never in a million years thought Dad would punish me by stopping me going for the trial.

The police were called to the football field and I was taken to the police station where I was given a court date. Dad collected me and took me home. He didn't speak; as ever, this was more unnerving than the rage. No words, no emotions. Dad went into the front room and shut the door, while I was sent to my room. Eventually he came up.

'Son, you're a waste of space. You can fend for yourself now. You're going to live with your nan in Wales. I'm taking you out of school, you're going next week.'

'But what about my football trial?'

'Your what?'

'My trial at Southampton. If I go next week, I'll miss it.'

He cocked his head. It was no good – I knew I'd blown it.

'You should have thought about that, son.'

Dad drove me to Wales himself the next week, so that was the end of any chance I had of a football career. My mates Stevie Mills and Mike Newington both went to the trial and were taken on as apprentices, so since I was at least as good as them, I probably would have been as well. Stevie Mills* (who by the way was the greediest footballer I ever played with – he'd never give you a pass in the box) went on to play for England Under-21s. Mike played for Southampton before retiring with a leg injury and playing semi-pro for Waterlooville.

Me? I was shipped off to Llanelli to get a job. Aged fifteen and a half, I was going to be a man.

* Stevie Mills later died of leukaemia.

Chapter 9

EASTER 1969. I'd left school and was going to live with my nan in Llanelli. The Severn Bridge had been completed so no more road journeys via Gloucester. Dad drove, and not much in the way of talking was going on. I totted up the pros of the situation.

1) I had finished school. (Great.)
2) I would be starting work. (Brilliant.)
3) I would be a man. (I had watched men. I knew what to do. Start smoking more.)
4) I would learn to drink. (I'd already perfected the art of not doing very much and telling jokes so no problem there.) And of course: sex.

As I stared out of the car windows to see Cardiff disappear into the Welsh hills behind me, I decided to cross the 'sex' bridge when I came to it, and got to thinking more about what I might do when I became a working man. It wasn't as if I'd gone through the school's careers advisory process. One minute I was a schoolboy with no thoughts about my future, the next, because my parents had come to the end of their tether, I was about to start work.

Options: Hairdressing? No. Farmer? Fuck that, too much like hard work – although I had loved going to Uncle Les's farm so I didn't dismiss it completely. By the time we pulled up outside Nanny John's I'd decided that bus conducting, catering, manual labour, carpentry, armed services, motorway construction and road sweeping were definitely not for me. No – the long trundle from Gosport to Llanelli had afforded me all the time necessary to consider my future. As I unloaded the car outside Nan's, I had decided what I wanted to be.

The wayward issue of Eddie and Mary Allen had decided to become – A Cub Reporter. As far as I remember, this is the first time I was to employ the kind of condensed thinking process that was to inform the rest of my life. I said above I ran through all kinds of employment possibilities, as though I'd carefully weighed them up. In fact, I just shot through a mental checklist at high speed. It works like this. In my care is a set of predetermined responses, which go: *fuck that – fuck this – bollocks to that – you must be joking – yeah right – as if.* These are subconsciously applied to anything I ask of myself or anything that is asked of me.

In other words, I react instinctively. As you get older, trusting your instincts is harder; it requires more faith. The trained mind runs on rigid, pre-set lines. When you are following your gut reaction, however, all your senses are aware. You will make the wrong decisions, some catastrophic (stealing wallets, trashing nightclubs), but if you are, in essence, a good person (which I think I am), and don't wilfully wish to harm anyone, then overall your decisions will turn out to be the right ones. Anyway, that's what the rest of the world is there for, to help make decisions for you. Just like the way you don't consciously choose your friends, but are drawn to certain people.

So when 'cub reporter' entered my mind and none of the usual responses had popped up, I thought, yeah, why not? I loved English at school, it was my best subject, and wasn't Superman really a cub reporter? I think it was the word 'cub' that swung it. Cub meant 'cheeky, cuddly, don't really do anything except play about with other cubs and get fed'. Yes, that was the kind of job I wanted.

Somewhere between Swansea and Llanelli I had also flirted with the idea of being an airline pilot. None of the *bollocks to that, fuck it* or *you must be joking* responses had appeared when I thought of it, so it seemed to qualify as a possibility. Also, I was definitely the one fifteen-year-old in Llanelli in 1969 who had been on a plane, and not only that, had been asked from the age of eight to tell all the Welsh lads what it was like. So there was a kudos attached to it, and I knew something about planes. Not technically, but I knew them all by name.

Hiding behind the bushes and smoking at Brentwood's playing fields I'd watched BAC 1-11s, VC10s, Boeing 707s and Comet 2s and 4s leaving from Heathrow and shooting off to all points of the globe. I yearned to be on them, getting as far away from the hell-place as possible. It's amazing how the brain records and retains information of an apparently useless nature if there is some kind of emotional landscape it can be anchored to. Being able to remember all the Division One results (Premier League now, of course), having heard them only once, is a good example of this. It means you can be one of the lads (pathetic but true). My knowledge of military aircraft was rooted in the events in Malta that took place around Henry Navarott's hand, my cock and Airfix kits.

But the thought didn't last long. Not even I could see how I was going to be an airline pilot having just left school with not one qualification. Surely you had to know something of maths and physics? Still, not to worry – English was my favourite subject, therefore I would be a journalist.

As we crossed Loughor Bridge on the last three miles of our interminable car journey to my manhood, Mum pointed at a sprawling industrial complex that bore the legend INA Needle Bearings. This was where they churned out the vast majority of the ball bearings required by British industry in the late sixties, and my Uncle Gwyn had joined the workforce three years earlier. He had now, Mum informed us, saved enough for a car. In the Allen household this meant: 'Why don't you try there for a job?'

And my response: 'Wow! What car is it?' really meant: *You must be joking – fuck that.*

'A Triumph Toledo – good car,' said Dad.

For 'good car' read 'sensible'.

Hmmmm. I'll be a cub reporter with a very large, very fast motorbike, then.

I wondered if Triumph Toledos came without windows. I was sure that Uncle Gywn's exploding arse wasn't restricted to bedtime.

Fuck it. I'd just realised that for the first two years of my working life, while my parents were in Singapore, I was going to have to share a bed with Gwyn. As we carried my bags into the house, the words 'merchant' and 'navy' appeared in my mind.

Fast forward a couple of weeks to my first job: at the Etherington printworks.

'Fuck fuck and fuck again.' I stuck the base of the index finger of my right hand into my mouth and sucked furiously. There are certain things in a man's life that are inevitable. Getting your cock stuck in your fly is one, and paper cuts another. Nothing prepares you for the pain but you are supposed to learn and ensure that these are one-off experiences.*

It was only lunchtime on my first day and I'd managed to re-cut the papercut where the thumb meets the index finger three times already. The three cunts who worked there thought this was one of the funniest things they'd ever seen. *The* funniest thing they'd ever seen, however, was what happened when I returned with their lunchtime order. They shovelled whatever permutation of faggots, peas, fish, rissoles, pie and chips they wanted onto their plates and I sat in the corner by my machine and set about Nan's packed lunch. Nan's packed lunch was part of the deal for my 'keep', as negotiated two weeks earlier by chief petty officer E.C. Allen RN on my behalf.

Even with my limited understanding of chemistry and physics, I knew that if the brain was starved of oxygen for any length of time there were likely to be catastrophic results. I'd read of men falling off high mountains, pilots losing consciousness at altitude, etc, so my father's thinking process must have been permanently damaged after having spent up to two months at a time over a period of fifteen years two hundred yards underwater in a tin breathing in fetid air with other smelly sailors.

---

* Twenty-five years later I was trying to soothe my son Alfie with this pearl of wisdom. Unfortunately I had denied him part of the learning process by catching his cock in his zip for him. I was dressing him in his first tailor-made suit (a black velvet number). With his sisters Sarah and Lily he was to be presented to Princess Diana that evening at a royal gala showing of the film *Hear My Song*, which his mother, Alison, my first wife, had produced. As he lay on the floor screaming in agony, an agony about to increase tenfold as the only way to free his little trapped foreskin was to pull the zip back down again, I remembered my first day as an apprentice lithographic printer all those years before.

Obviously his ability to apply logic had taken a battering. At the dole office interview (with my dad), I had struggled to see the sense there was in starting my working life as an apprentice lithographic printer (a fucking *what*?) when what I really wanted to be was a cub reporter on the *Llanelli Evening Post*.

'You need qualifications for that, son, and you haven't got any.'

'Well, of course I fucking haven't. You've just taken me out of school before I could take any exams.' I *thought* this but of course I didn't *say* it.

I think Dad registered my disappointment and attempted to cheer me up with these immortal words: 'Listen, son, the world will always need paper and something printed on it.'

Computing and IT were a microdot on a very distant horizon back in 1969. I'd gone for the interview (with my dad) at Etherington's and they'd immediately recognised that I was the right person for the job. (I'm always reminded of this scene when I watch *Oliver Twist*.) I didn't hear a word of what they were saying because:

A) I was still sulking from not being allowed to be a cub reporter, and

B) I was looking at my future workmates (the Three Cunts).

If I had listened, though, I'm sure that this is *not* what I would have heard:

'Every lunchtime he'll have to run to the fish and chip shop and he will have to run back because the boys don't want their orders cold. It might sound harsh but he'll come to enjoy the daily jog. It will interrupt the mind-numbingly dull and boring tasks that are the lot of the apprentice lithographic printer. These will include scraping, cleaning and filling the machines' inktrays, collecting and collating the piles of printed paper and, having removed the misprints, taking the soiled paper to the guillotine to be cut, then wrapping the paper for dispatch. Oh, and tea-making. Lots of it.'

As me and Dad drove back to Nan's I remembered the scene a few years earlier when Dad's hand had wavered between the 'grammar' and 'comprehensive' boxes. Did he really think this lithographic printing was for my own good? I don't think so. I had to be gainfully employed before the family went off to Singapore again for Dad's second posting there, and I was too young for the mines or the steelworks.

Eddie switched gears and changed lanes in that super-efficient way of his. Checking his mirror, he repeated: 'The world will always need paper, son.'

I guess I was supposed to somehow make this meaningful, but the three pounds fifteen shillings a week (£3.75) take-home pay suggested otherwise.

'Oi! English? Want a chip?' asked the long-haired foreman cunt. It was my first day, so why would I suspect anything?

'Er, yeah, thanks.' As I leant over to take a chip, he began to pour vinegar enthusiastically over them and my paper-cut hand. It hurt like hell. I leapt round the print room howling. As their laughter and my pain eased, I slyly looked to see if there was someone I could take it out on. There was nobody. I was fifteen and three-quarters, five foot tall, and the apprentice. My life had come to this – I was the company gimp. *Fuck this, bollocks to that* and *you must be fucking joking* quickly formed a disorderly queue in my mind.

Now fast forward and I'm sitting in the holding cell at Paddington Green Police Station, waiting to be taken to Stamford House Remand Home in Shepherd's Bush. The judge, in discussing that my parents were in Singapore and that I'd run away from home, decided that I was 'in need of care and protection'. How had this come to pass?

Well, it was a combination of things really. There was my extraordinary footballing skill, my ridiculously low wages and of course the desire to hang out with the older boys. The coolest of these were Ritchie Phillips, Steamer and Lucky. They all worked in the Rolling Steel Mill next door to Etherington's. At lunchtimes there would be a pretty large football game organised at the Stacking Yard.

Ritchie, Steamer and Lucky were famous in Llanelli (quite a boast). Of course, famous *then* didn't mean falling out of Chinawhite nightclub with a couple of tarts or wanking a pig on reality television. It meant surviving a car crash which scythed your head into two parts, then repeating the feat with astonishing frequency. The crash that made these three famous happened after Ritchie was being chased by police through

Swansea in a stolen car. Rounding a corner at seventy, they hit a lamp-post and cut the car in half. Of the five in the car, three got out with cuts – including Ritchie and Steamer. Lucky underwent brain surgery, and the other one, sitting in the middle in the back, was killed outright.

They became the faces to be seen with. Ritchie's nickname was Scruff. He was called Scruff because he had a scruffy beard, but apart from that he was very smart. He wore Ben Sherman shirts and well-faded Levis with turn-ups. He walked like a geezer and was born to be an entrepreneur. (He's now a millionaire scrap merchant.) Lucky was so named because of the crash, after which he had more metal plating in his head than there was in the steelworks. He also acquired a nervous twitch as a result. Steamer looked like Pancho Villa. He had a ridiculous moustache and compared to Ritchie and Lucky always dressed like the poor relation. Nevertheless, these three weren't smalltown-minded. They were often bombing off to London in a stolen car to buy drugs.

I quickly realised that this existence (working at the printers for £3.75 a week) was *not* going to be my life. Impressed by my footballing skills, Ritchie took me under his wing, and to the Waterloo Pub. I was underage but it just so happened that Norman, the landlord, was queer (the old-school type who didn't like other queers) and took a shine to me because of my youthful good looks – and the fact that I was in with these young, glamorous car thieves.

Norman let me in the card school at the Waterloo, and I started to win. The problem with this was you needed a stake, and money to play with. On my wage this was impossible …

In 1969 Llangenydd on Gower was one of the best surfing resorts in Europe and the place was awash with VW camper vans. The beach head was a twenty-minute hike from the sea at low tide. The surfers sheltered from the cutting wind in the dunes, leaving their clothes in a pile before heading down to the waves for more torture.

The petty theft started one cold day when a couple of surfers came and undressed, leaving their clothes in heaps in the dunes near to where me and some mates, Kenny, Alan, Dylwyn and Jack were sitting smoking. Kenny was the hardest kid in Llanelli, with a long blond feather-cut. Once he had a drink inside him he'd fight anyone, but he was actually very funny and kind.* Alan Jones had hair like Paul Weller, flared turn-ups and, best of all, a scooter. Dylwyn Williams with his pallor looked like he was to the prison born. Jack Jones was a skinhead; he had the latest Lee Cooper denim jacket and white flared Lee Cooper jeans. Anyway it was fucking cold and we huddled together sharing our last fag as the surfers stripped, waxed their boards and ran towards the sea. We watched them go and shivered.

'Lunatics.'

'Idiots.'

'Wankers.'

The wind was picking up. Nan's roast and home-made cake loomed large in my mind. We sat there smoking in the wind, watching the waves in the distance.

'I'm fucking starving,' moaned Jack, 'and freezing.'

I chucked the cig and went over to the pile of clothes the surfers had left under a stone.

'No, Keith ... we can't do that.'

'Why not?'

I fished around in the jeans and found a wallet.

'It's not right.'

'Not right? Serves them right for being soft fucking hippies.'

After carefully considering the evidence in front of them, the lads decided they were indeed soft fucking hippies and joined me in pillaging their wares. We did that pile and moved down the beach and did another five.

Meanwhile, I carried on at the printers, getting more mindnumbingly bored by the hour, until a lucky event occurred. A van with big letters on the side turned up at the printer's – the letters said 'GENO WASHINGTON'. Out of the van stepped Mike Pearson. He was twenty-one and to me this was a grand old age. He had long brown wavy hair, a moustache and a beard. He was the spitting image of George Harrison. He had been a printer but was now a roadie and had come back to say hello to the lads. Everyone went down to the

* Kenny died in prison, aged twenty, from a heart attack.

Waterloo that night and met up with him and Cracky, who was head roadie for Geno Washington. The two of them were off on tour.

Cracky was about twenty-eight and didn't have an arse to speak of. When he wore flared trousers – trousers, never jeans, because he had no hips – where there should have been arse there was just air. Together with his permed hair, gold chain, loose-fitting T-shirts with flared arms, aftershave called Screamer (or something like that), wheezing cough, Capstan full-strength fags and man bag, Cracky was just about the most loathsome stereotype for a rock roadie you could ever hope to meet. That said, he was very good at his job.

'Get 'em in, Keith,' roared Cracky. He looked like someone had stuck a scrunched chamois leather on his head and called it a face.

'I'm, er, a bit short.'

'We know that,' he guffawed.

Mike laughed and dealt the cards.

'You in, Keith? Two-bob stake.'

'Yeah, why not …'

I'd run out of money and already owed from the card game the day before.

'Yeah, man, we've got the gig, three weeks on the road, booze, drugs and women.'

'Can I come?'

Everyone went quiet and looked at me, as if it was a very bad joke or a very good idea. Cracky ran his tongue round his lips and took a long pull on his cigar, like Clint Eastwood deciding to give a guy a chance.

'Why not?' He exhaled, casting his eye over my fast-developing fifteen-year-old frame. A slow smile spread over his face. 'We ship out in the morning.'

I snuck out of Nan's before anyone was awake with a couple of pairs of underpants in a holdall. Cracky and Mike were waiting for me outside the Waterloo, clearly nursing hangovers but already on their second roll-up and racked by the kind of cough that carried away consumptives. They looked as if they'd just been dug up.

'Hurughhh.' Cracky cleared his throat of a ball of phlegm about the size of Wales. 'Didn't think you'd make it.' The phlegm hit the tarmac.

'Nothing to stay for.' I slung my holdall in the back of the van and squashed in between them, the tender meat in the rough-as-arseholes roadie sandwich. Off for an education in sex, drugs and rock 'n' roll.

I wasn't disappointed, except the sex and drugs seemed to have been left off the 'junior roadie Monopoly' board game. Those bits had clearly fallen down the back of the sofa . One thing I didn't need for my board game were instructions; the only rule was that there were no rules. But there *was* a hierarchy and I was at the arse end of it. Literally.

The first night was a short hop to Cardiff and we offloaded the kit and Mike and Cracky started setting up drums and amps and guitars. All I wanted to do was get on the drums and start bashing.

'Can I help?'

'You're not touching the kit. Go and find some good-looking girls and tell 'em to come backstage after the gig.'

Out front there was a group of seventeen-year-olds, busy flicking their hair and nattering.

'Oi! You lot. Want to come backstage and meet George Harrison?'

The others had told me that this was the chat-up line to use, that passing off Mike Pearson as George was a surefire way to get the girls into the dressing room.

'You're with the band?' The girls looked at me doubtfully.

The hairs on my neck stood up with pride. 'Yeah, I'm with the band.'

'Isn't it past your bedtime?'

They all laughed.

'There's a party after.'

'Yeah? What are you having? Ice cream and jelly?'

Unconcerned by their extreme lack of foresight, I shrugged and left them in the wind, bare legs mottling like pickled tripe. Girls could wait. I wanted to hear the music. Backstage the band was warming up, which entailed loads of booze and smoking and banter.

Geno Washington was the best band I'd ever seen. That it was also the only band I'd ever seen made the experience even more seminal. The band were made up of four brass parts, bass guitar, drums and an organ.

About midnight on the first night we loaded up and went to eat. I'd never been to a restaurant without my parents. I was still waiting for someone to tell me to stop slurping my Coke and get up from under the table when the waitress arrived to take the order.

'What you havin'?'

I looked at Mike and Cracky, my surrogate parents. 'What am I allowed?'

They cracked up laughing and passed me a red-cushioned plastic menu.

'I'll have a prawn cocktail and a large steak,' I said.

Everyone stopped talking.

'A prawn fucking cocktail?'

'What's wrong with that?'

'If he wants a prawn cocktail, let him have one.'

I looked from one to the other in a bid to establish why having a prawn cocktail was wrong.

'It's a bit bloody poncy, ain't it?'

'I have them all the time,' said Cracky.

I'd never had one and didn't know what to expect. Mum used to talk about them. Whenever she and Dad went out it was: 'Oooh, I had a lovely prawn cocktail. Very nice. Very posh.'

It looked like an ice-cream sundae: six or seven prawns on a bed of lettuce with a round of brown bread and a slice of orange. I tucked the napkin into my shirt and raised my eyebrows in concentration while squeezing the orange onto the prawns with a flourish. Ten musicians and roadies watched me tuck in before turning away and muttering.

I didn't care. On the road with Geno Washington aged fifteen and a half? Prawn cocktails and steak? No parents in sight? I was the most sophisticated geezer in the world.

The mock Tudor inn had rooms and everyone wandered off to crash out. Cracky motioned to me and set off down the corridor hacking like an old lady. He kicked the door open and picked up my holdall.

'Is that my room?'

'Your room? You don't get a room.'

'Well, where am I sleeping?'

'You're with me.'

He went inside without a word. The doorway was suddenly the gate to hell. It wasn't just the fact that Cracky lived his life with all the professionalism of a park-bench tramp. He was also a screaming gay.

'You can share the bed.'

If my eyes didn't deceive me, the bed was a single with a duvet cover that could have held its own in a bucket of puke.

'The floor will do.'

Lying on a carpet that had probably seen the underside of more truckers' boots than I cared to think about, I was welcomed to the other side of 'life on the road'.

'You awake, Keith?'

Cracky's seduction technique was to breath smoke in my ear. At this point I hoped for an early death. He leant over and prodded me with I know not what. I went into spasm and thrashed around as if in the midst of a sudden bout of epilepsy. The suddenness of my movements sent Cracky leaping back into his own bed. I'd kept him off for now but my heart sank as it dawned on me that every night I'd have to work hard to avoid Cracky's not-so-romantic overtures.

We toured towns in southern England and my main job remained inviting girls backstage for the band, the road crew, the bus driver – in fact, for everyone apart from me. I would prowl the bars for the pretty ones, and if there weren't any, the drunk ones. The London dates were the climax of the Gino tour. We drove through Marylebone in the battered Gino truck agape at the drop-dead-gorgeous women in the latest Mary Quant minidresses, and youths with razor-sharp haircuts and velvet trousers. This was more like it. We parked the van outside Oxford and Cambridge Mansions, which housed a roadie bolthole. The five-floor walk-up gave way to an open door and loud rock music. Three or four hairy men were rolling joints and staring at the television.

'Hey, Cracky, hurry up, man. We're about to fucking set foot on the moon.'

Neil's small step was greeted with mayhem and an excuse for the mother of all piss-ups. Unfortunately the alcohol brought Cracky's queerness to the surface again.

'You're sharing with me tonight, Keith.'

'The sofa will do fine, ta.'

'Mike's on the sofa.'

'The floor then.'

Everyone looked away from Neil and Buzz to stare at me in amazement. I looked at the floor, which was an eiderdown of bacteria with several craters of its own made of mounds of mould which may once have been beans on toast.

'I've slept on worse.'

This was a lie, a superhuman one. It would take all my courage to use several types of fungi for a pillow. One giant leap for all mankind it may have been, but I vowed to make it an even more impossible mission for Cracky to get his hands on my arse.

(Still, he did take me to La Chasse Club in Wardour Street where Keith Moon and the other rock aficionados used to drink in 1969, along with Chas Chandler who tried to turn a bunch of hippies – The Who – into a bunch of Mods by shaving their hair.)

After hanging round the flat for a couple of days I got some more work on another tour: Jimmy James, going up north to Stoke and Nantwich. I'd never ever been Up North before and it was grim, but didn't shock me, after industrial Wales. The head roadie for Jimmy James and Alan Price lived in the flat and asked me if I'd do an Alan Price gig in Brighton, where I met Ian Leak, the head tour manager for John Hiseman's Colosseum. It was all so fucking exciting compared to changing the ink in print machines in Llanelli.

After a while, though, the other roadies in the flat started wondering what a kid was doing hanging round the place. A couple must have felt uncomfortable, because Cracky suggested I go back to Llanelli. The thought of going back to the printers was horrible, but I needn't have worried – they had no intention of giving me my job back.

I returned to Nan's but the welcome was muted. I'd thrown in my job, I'd left home without telling anybody and now I was told I'd better get another job to pay for my board and lodgings. What little money I'd saved from roadie-ing ran out after a fortnight. Sitting in the sand dunes of Llangenydd waiting for the surfers to kindly leave their valuables unattended, I turned to Dylwyn and Alan and said, 'Shall we fuck off from this shithole?'

We piled on to the bus with only the clothes we stood up in. I knew Nan would be beside herself but my reasoning was simple. You can't run away if you tell people you're going to do it. We got a lift with a lorry and then a few cars and in between we walked. The next day we were heading down the A303 in the rain. A car pulled up.

'Where you going?'

'London.'

'Pompey no good?'

It was back to Portsmouth. What a small world. My old stomping ground did not appear to be very forgiving and with our resources dwindling we bedded down for the night under Southsea pier.

'Keith.'

'Yeah.'

'There's a rock sticking into my arse.'

'Who fucking made me dad?'

I removed the offending rock from Alan's jacksie and pondered our joint future. Luckily, the next day I found a mate from school in Gosport. Kim Lawrence, who I'd mudlarked with, was now working as a bingo caller on the pier.

We quickly worked out a scam. Alan and I sat in the front row waiting for Kim to call the numbers.

'Two fat ladies …' Kim winked with all the panache of a man with a bluebottle in his eye.

'House!'

Alan waved his card manically and Kim pointed at him.

'We have a winner, ladies and gentlemen! Come and claim your prize.'

Alan went up front to get his fifth prize of the morning. We sold the prizes on to parents trying to pacify screaming kids and managed to make enough to live on. It took as long as a week for us to get busted. Alan was relieved.

'Fuck it. I've had enough anyway, let's go home.'

'No way.' I chucked a cig end defiantly in his direction. 'Let's go to London.' I rolled up my stuff and shoved it in a plastic bag.

'Er, can't we go back to Llanelli?' Alan whimpered.

Dylwyn punched him, firmly with me on this. 'What for? You scared?'

'No.'

'Well, come on then.'

We jumped the train and arrived at London Victoria tired and hungry. I pretended to know where the fuck we were going and tapped my finger on the tube map, tracing a route.

'Right, yeah, yeah … I know this … Yep, Piccadilly Circus, that's where we're heading.'

But Piccadilly Circus was shit. Everything cost a fortune and we were nearly out of cash. We dived back on the tube intending to kip down at a train station for the night but we got lost and ended up in Wapping.

'Well, I must say that London is rubbish.'

'Shut it, Alan.'

All of a sudden a side door of a pub opened and a column of piss sprayed us. A large skinhead was on the end of it, knob in one hand, can of lager in the other. I jumped back to avoid the piss.

'Watch it!'

'Watch what, you fackin' caant.'

We cowered, walking backwards rapidly, when his contorted expression turned into a smile.

'Skinheads.'

We remembered our crew cuts and now thanked God for them.

'You a London firm?'

'No, we're a Welsh firm,' Alan chipped in.

'A fucking what? You fucking Welsh?'

I could see 'Welsh' register nul points on the threatening scale. He calmed down and once again contortion turned to smile. The next thing we knew we were pogoing up and down with him and his gang. They did crazy stuff like set each other on fire and beat each other over the head with trays. They were by far the coolest people we'd ever seen. As we bade goodbye to our new brothers that night, they gave us a pint glass full of coins.

'We 'ad a whip round to get you caaants 'ome to Wales, yeah.'

The coins added up to about three quid. We slept among the

deckchairs of Hyde Park then the next morning set out looking for a square meal. Hyde Park and Marble Arch were very impressive but a cream bun would have sufficed. We stood like pathetic orphans outside Lyons Corner House.

'I want to go home.'

'We can't go home. You know how much trouble we'll be in.'

Dylwyn and Alan had started arguing and I was getting sick of them.

'Wait here. I'll go and steal something.'

I found my way through the guts of the Corner House and was just about to dip my hand into a jacket in the staffroom when I was intercepted by a large fat black waitress. (Black people were a relatively new one on me.) Amazingly, she took pity on me. While Dylwyn and Alan froze outside, I was fed and watered by kind-hearted Phyllis.

'You took your time,' said Dylwyn.

'Me and Dylwyn are sick of London. We're off home.'

'Fine. See you then,' I said.

This parting of the ways was inevitable and they strode off to the train station without a backward glance. We wanted different things. I was the adventurer who'd been to Singapore and Malta. They were the home-town lads with narrow margins and narrow minds.

My mind turned to basic survival techniques. Money, food and a place to stay. It was a warm day and the doors to the offices of the rag trade that littered the area behind New Oxford Street were all open. I wandered into one and followed a corridor that opened into a courtyard with a fire escape. With a cheery whistle I mounted the stairs and slipped through an open window. The office was deserted but there were bags lying around spewing wallets aplenty. I took one and climbed back out of the window. A voice stopped me.

'Oi! Come back here! Thief!'

There was a fat bald office worker staring at me, clutching a newly purchased beef pasty, which he dropped and ran after me. I had a head start down the fire escape and didn't rate his chances of catching me, except that my escape route was now locked.

'Stop the little fucker. Police!'

Back up the fire escape. There were now several pairs of feet clanking down the metal stairs as I opened another window on the ground floor and jumped through to the connecting building. After about twenty minutes everything was quiet. I pushed the door open and straight into the clinch of two policemen waiting patiently on the other side.

'Think you're clever, eh, son?'

'You're not clever, son. You're nicked.'

Fat Bald Office Worker clapped his hands in delight as if he'd just made the acquaintance of a giant apple pie.

I was taken to Marylebone nick.

'Right, Allen. Where's home?'

'Dunno.'

'Where are you from?'

'Not sure.'

'We'll find out. How old are you?'

'Eighteen.'

'Pull the other one.'

'Where are your parents?'

'Singapore.'

'Course they are.'

I was charged and sent to Stamford House, a halfway 'holding' house for delinquents. I was still under sixteen, and obviously meant to be under 'care and protection'. I was there for six weeks, during which time I had no idea whether any attempts were made to contact my parents or my family in Wales. The judge stuck me in a children's home in Paddington. The stench of unwashed adolescents in the dormitory made me want to throw up. A couple of disaffected youths came over and sized me up.

'Who are you?'

'Mind your own business.'

'What you doing here?'

'I'm not staying.'

'Where you going to go then, shithead?'

'Somewhere where I can't smell your fucking rotting feet.'

They kicked my head in, which was good because it meant I could run away again. Except I didn't have anywhere to go apart from Oxford and Cambridge Mansions. Still, even the stench of Cracky's aftershave was preferable to the foot odour of twelve junior recidivists. Three days later the police turned up and I was arrested for absconding from the home. It was the end of my summer of love. Cracky argued fruitlessly with the arresting officer.

'He's in my care and protection.'

'Well, sir, I think you should look at yourself.'

And Cracky wasn't a pretty sight. Unshaven and followed by his own personal swarm of flies, he didn't exactly enhance his claims to be my legal guardian.

(I don't know how they found me there – I think I must have told the police I had a part-time job as a roadie and given that address.)

This time the police contacted my parents and Mum flew home from Singapore. She and Ethnie came to London for the court hearing. Mum persuaded the judge to let her take me back into her care, so I was to go back to Nan's with Mum and Kevin and Susan. Nan didn't much want me back at hers – I was the first in the family to get into trouble with the police and she didn't want the accompanying shame. So after a while we moved to a new-build estate in Gorseinon – so new-build that it wasn't yet built. Ours was the only house in a sea of mud. It didn't even have a cooker.

'Get in.'

Muffled laughter from seven teenagers as I was pushed into the boot. Lid closed.

'It's fucking dark, you twats.'

More laughter. Car moves off. I knock my head on something. Curled double. Car veers round corner. More laughter from the front.

'Aaaaaaaaaah.' I hit my fucking head.

Screams from the girls in the front.

Another corner, this time the other fucking way. Hit my head again. Brakes. Swerve. Screams from the lads.

Airborne. I feel it. We're turning over. Screams. I brace myself. Against what? Fuck knows.

We land. Silence.

I was alive. I checked, everything moved OK, but I was cursing my stupidity for accepting a lift with Ritchie Phillips. They'd put me in the boot because there were five of them in the back and two in the front. I couldn't hear anything from the car so I felt round for a way out. I knew we'd turned over and feared I was trapped. I could hear moaning and whimpering. My hand felt something hard and wet underneath. It was the road. The boot was open a crack; Ritchie hadn't shut it properly. I crawled out and saw that all the others were trapped inside the car.

'Get the door open, Allen, for fuck's sake, the engine.'

Petrol was leaking out of the car and the engine was still running. I pulled at the doors and they writhed to free themselves, terrified of the car catching fire. All the girls were crying and the boys shocked to silence. We ran away from the wreck of the car to hide from the police who would surely follow. Once a safe distance away, the lads recovered some bravado. Ritchie took out what I recognised as a lump of hash and started building a spliff.

'Thank fuck I was in the boot. Otherwise we might all be dead by now.'

Ritchie nodded and inhaled, passing the spliff to me. 'Dope. Have a pull. It's fucking mental. 'Specially after a car crash.'

Although I'd seen Charlie Higson smoke it at Brentwood, I'd only ever pretended. It was a few minutes before my legs became heavy and my mind soaked like wet cottonwool. Then everything was hilarious.

The trouble was that this dope-smoking session was the trigger to me spending the next three months locked away in my tiny boxroom doing nothing except indulging in teenage paranoia. Suddenly everyone in Llanelli 'was talking about me'. They were all out to get me. Even a trip to the corner shop was an exercise in Orwellian surveillance.

Mum was rarely in, as usual. She'd got a job waitressing at the Copper Grill in Swansea and was out until eleven most nights, so during this time of teenage angst, all the lads and their girlfriends came round to shag in our house. Stephen Warlows even went so far as to fuck in my brother Kevin's bed, while Kevin looked on from the corner of the room. Of course I swore him to secrecy (or was that 'terrorised'?) and got extremely good at removing all traces of teenage occupancy before Mum got back.

My depression and paranoia extended to my criminal activities. Around Christmas time I took up again with Ritchie and began siphoning petrol out of cars to fuel his ice-cream van, the legitimate 'front' for selling on stolen goods round the local estates. I must have hit one particular road more than once because the residents grassed me to the police, and one evening when I went along to do my first car I noticed a police car pull out. I legged it but got caught and bundled into the back.

'Where d'you live, son?'

'Mrs John, Lewis Crescent, Llanelli.' Fuck, why did I say that? I didn't live with Nan any more but they could trace me this way.

The car moved off. I knew I had to escape. They slowed down to corner so I kicked the door open and ran into the night. Such was my paranoia at this time, I imagined they would have a full-scale police search out for me. I found a building site and hid under a tarpaulin for two hours. Thank fuck for my duffel coat. But not thank fuck for my hair. My crew cut had grown out and I was sure my longish hair made me easily identifiable. You must bear in mind that *Mission: Impossible* had just hit the screens and 'fugitive from justice' summed up my mental state. I walked furtively down an alley and came to a depot full of trucks. I crawled under one and turned on its diesel tap, filling my cupped hands with diesel and greasing down my hair so as to be unrecognisable to any passing police. (Uh-huh.)

It was in this state that I turned up at the back door of the Waterloo and asked Norman the landlord to hide me. He stood and stared at me.

'What the bloody hell 'ave you done to your hair?'

I had diesel streaking my face, and I stank, but thankfully Norman had a big heart. He bundled me onto the back seat of his car, concealed me with a blanket and drove me home. I trod silently on the back doorstep, but Mum pulled the door open before I had a chance.

'The police have been round,' she said. 'Have you been stealing petrol again?'

It seemed like every time I tried to avoid crime, opportunities stared me in the face. Well, if people leave petrol in their petrol tanks they're asking for it, aren't they?

The same happened one night when I was hitching home. Everybody hitched in Llanelli. It was the way you got around. One bus connected my estate with the other estates, and apart from that you hitched. One night I got dropped near Loughor Bridge and noticed a cottage with no lights on. Closer inspection revealed a louvre window at the back of the property, so I removed it and slipped in. Though I did feel terrible about being there, especially about taking someone's Christmas presents, there was also something alluring about being in someone else's house illegally. I made off with a carton of cigs, a watch and a bottle of the best brandy. Like I say, I did feel awful afterwards (though this probably had something to do with smoking four hundred cigarettes and half a bottle of brandy).

I justified it because there was nothing to look forward to about Christmas: me, Mum, Kevin and Susan in a still unfinished house with no furniture.

In a bid to lighten Mum's mood I cooked Christmas breakfast on an oil heater. Even then I enjoyed cooking 'commando'. My den in Gosport a few years before had regularly seen fry-ups of stolen eggs, meat, beans, bread and cheese. So on this Christmas morn, eggs sizzled and bacon crackled while we all huddled round for warmth. I broached the subject of my old man.

'When's he coming back then?'

'Soon.'

'When soon?'

'Soon enough.'

'You won't tell, will you? About everything?'

Silence. After observing her perfectly cooked egg, she replied, 'He might look a bit more kindly on you, Keith, if you got a job.'

After breakfast, we all piled on to Nan's for Christmas lunch. But something was missing. After much persuasion from Uncle Gwyn, Nan had replaced her stone hearth with a brand-new Canon gas fire. Thus the family hearth, the bedrock of the Welsh working classes, had disappeared from her home. I remember feeling depressed about this, though that could have been the continuing after-effects of my dope-smoking.

Selfishly, I couldn't see that this might have been of *benefit* to Nan. For the life of me I couldn't understand why Nan didn't *want* to be on her knees at 6am black-leading the grate and building fires to heat the water to bathe the men before they went downstairs to eat their freshly baked Welsh cakes …

THE SEVENTIES

Chapter 10

TAKING MUM'S ADVICE I got a job at the Co-op supermarket, where among other things I quickly learned how to open the safe. One night me and Dylwyn climbed over two roofs and broke in through a skylight. Still rather paranoid and still watching *Mission: Impossible*, we were convinced there were lasers guarding the door to the office, so instead we crawled to the checkouts – in full view of the front windows – to steal all the cigarettes. We left them round the back under the bins for Ritchie to pick up in his ice-cream van the next day.

I invested the proceeds of this contraband in my first suit. The form was to go to the local tailors and choose the fabric. Mine was bright green. The jacket came down to my knees and the trousers had 30-inch flares.

If your town wasn't big enough to accommodate a Top Rank, you had to make do with the local ballroom. Llanelli's was called the Glen. Like all such places, it had its own resident eight-piece band, which had to play the entire Top Ten every week. There can be nothing so ridiculous as the sight of eight old toupé-wearing Welshmen attempting to play Hendrix on the saxophone.

Saturday nights in towns all over Wales were the same. We would get our suits on and head out. At some point in the evening there'd be a 'sing off' between rival groups of lads, usually our own renditions of the latest hits. However, unlike the Welsh lads, my voice had more in common with a grunting toad. My repertoire extended only as far as a sickly version of 'Dreeeeam, dream dream dream, dreeeeam'.

*

Dad was finally home from the navy and had got a job at the West Glamorgan water board. Reinstalling myself on the sofa, the job at the Co-op now history, I put my hand down the back looking for some coins. Surely there was enough to buy a pint? The door went. It was Mum returning from another eight hours' hard graft down the café.

'What the bloody hell do you think you're doing?'

'Er, looking for a job.'

'Well, you won't find it down the back of that sofa.'

She threw me the paper and I scanned the vacancies section. The only thing going was for an apprentice lathe-turner. I sighed and hauled myself upright. Another try at being a model son. It all went wrong when I discovered that being an apprentice lathe-turner had less to do with lathes and more to do with making tea. Not only that, the senior operators decided it would be a funny joke to send me blind.

I was dispatched to take tea to the spark welders who were mid-weld at the time. Fortunately for them they were wearing visors. Unfortunately for me I wasn't. I dropped the tea and lurched about like a lunatic, blinded by the white light. I was forced to take the rest of the day off and consequently told not to bother returning.

The honest trade of the working man was never going to be for me, but there wasn't any point in telling my parents this. Instead we carried on as normal, me leaving for work every day, hiding round the corner, waiting for them to leave then going back inside. There was one problem: cash. Thinking around the problem I came up with a solution: window cleaning. Dad had ladders in the garage that could be used each day while he was at work. In addition, the fact that Mum and Dad hadn't been there long, and that their work ethic didn't leave much time for socialising, meant they didn't know anyone on the estate. So I could work to my heart's content without fear of being busted.

My window-cleaning business went from strength to strength and I was earning four times what I would have done as a lathe-turner. The irony, of course, was that I couldn't share any of this with my father, who might have been quite proud of my enterprise.

But it all went tits up when I was cleaning the upstairs window of a house and spotted a fantastic Bush radio. Up to now I hadn't nicked anything but this was too good an opportunity to pass up. The occupants were out somewhere so I climbed in the bedroom and scooped up the radio. At that moment a little girl, aged about eleven, walked in and screamed. She was wrapped in a towel. Thinking suddenly about rape charges and all sorts, I legged it out the window, down the ladder and all the way home, only to remember I'd left some rather incriminating evidence – Dad's ladders.

That evening the police came.

'We need to establish your movements this afternoon. Were you at 2 Davis Place cleaning windows?'

'No. I was at work.'

'Is it true that you have a window-cleaning round?'

Mum butted in. 'Don't be so ridiculous. You don't have a window-cleaning round, do you, son?'

'No. I'm a lathe-turner.'

'Yes, he's a lathe-turner, not a window-cleaner.'

'In that case, sir, we need you to come down the station tomorrow and take part in an identity parade to rule you out of our enquiries.'

Doesn't take a rocket scientist to work out that I never turned up. Instead I was on the A48 hitching to Portsmouth, intending to make enough money to buy a one-way ticket to France. There's a hill on the A48, and three trees below it. As I passed this landmark it dawned on me that I was now on the run and would never see that hill again.

Somewhere round Bristol I got a lift that took me in the opposite direction to where I wanted to go. On this occasion, happily, it was to Bath, which was hosting the annual Bath Jazz and Blues Festival. I saw Led Zeppelin, Pink Floyd, Johnny Winters and Country Joe McDonald, whose song 'The Fish Cheer & I-Feel-Like-I'm-Fixin'-To-Die Rag' – which I'd never heard before – has stayed with me to this day. Mainly because it was going round my head for two days while I hid under a plastic sheet after ignoring the immortal words: 'Don't touch the brown acid.'

I left Bath, arrived in Portsmouth in the dead of night and headed for Billy Manning's fun fair in Gosport. I needed funds. The amusement arcades offered opportunity, and I was soon chatting to an Irish gypsy who owned three hoopla stalls.

'Just passing tru, are ye?'

'Yeah. I'm off to France.'

Seamus explained to me the mechanics of running a business, while his Down's Syndrome son busied himself with headbutting my shins.

'Don't mind him. He's a sweet kid. Brains of a feckin' tea bag but we tink the world of him.'

Seamus laughed; his wife laughed. They lived in a caravan behind the stall and invited me for tea.

'Got anywhor te stay, have ye?'

They made me a bed and told me how they'd started with nothing but now had a little empire. For the next two days I worked the stall with Seamus.

'See this, Keith –' He gestured proudly at the stall '– I'm not qualified in anyting at all but I made this stall wid me own hands, and I've got me own bisniss. You could have it all, son.'

He was right, I could do anything I set my mind to. Then came the downer: I was on the run, with no hope of staying out of jail this time.

He entrusted me with one of his shooting galleries to run on my own, and I found another geezer working on the fair who had a flat and kipped on his sofa for a few weeks. I was doing really well, particularly when the US naval fleet came in. The sailors had so much money to spend that I was making a fortune. The shooting gallery worked by paying for pellets so I bought a job lot of pellets from the gun shop and skimmed money off the stall that way.

The fun fair was also good for something else. Sex. Girls always want sex at fun fairs, and my stall was away from the main drag in a corner all on its own. Girls would come up and flirt, I'd give them a go for free and then say:

'D'you want to come round the back? I've got something to show you.'

Sometimes the girls would giggle and tell me not to be so cheeky, but more often a few jokes and a promise of a night on a sofa was good enough for a quick in and out. A cold damp fumble, a few stabs and a quick climax with not much thought for Norma Sue from Selsea. Hmmmmm.

All in all being on the run wasn't so bad, except that the temptation of having so much money running through my hands from the stall proved too much. One night, as I was counting the day's takings (about eighty quid), the Allen guide to decision-making kicked in again. Should I steal the lot and run? Well, let's see:

1) I could stay and shag women on the fun fair for ever (only moderately attractive as the deal included going to work).
2) I could stay and shag women on the fun fair for a few weeks until I was spotted by the police (or MI5) and hauled off to jail.
3) I could go home and stand trial for nicking the Bush radio. (Yeah, right.)

So quickly the *fuck that*, *fuck this* and *yeah right* turned into 'Fuck this, fuck that, yeah right, I'm off.' Seamus – the man who had been so good to me – was shoved unceremoniously to the back door of my mind and booted out of it.

I took the money and went back to the flat I was staying in. The geezer had a portable reel-to-reel tape recorder I lusted after. Well, fuck it, might as well take that too. This time, though, my conscience got the better of me. I took it but I left him the money to buy a new one. I set off before dawn to catch the first ferry to Le Havre.

Stealing from Seamus had to be my worst ever shame. Nothing could redeem me now. I stood at the stern of the boat and watched England disappear. With a tear in my eye I took out the reel-to-reel and pressed 'Record'.

'Mum, Dad, Nan, Susan and Kevin, this is Keith. I just wanted you to know that I'm sorry for what I've done, and any trouble I've caused you. I'm going to France and you won't ever see me again ...'

The only thing missing was the sawing of the violin.

Chapter II

FRENCH CIGARETTE SMOKE first entered the Allen lungs at just past one in the morning on the dockside at Le Havre, France, sometime in late summer 1969. Having cleared customs and passport control, I'd stepped into France eager to make my way ... well ... I didn't know ... I hadn't really thought about it. Anywhere I suppose. I plumped for Paris as it was one of the only two places I'd heard about. The other was Dunkirk and I wasn't ready to give up just yet.

'Hey my friend, you are eenglish?'

The friendly French voice was just what the tired young English fugitive needed to hear.

'Yes.'

'Where are you 'eaded?'

'Er, Paris'

'Are you 'itchhiking or do you wish for ze train station?'

I told him I was hitchhiking so he very kindly offered to give me a lift to the main Paris road on the outskirts of Le Havre. He also offered me a cigarette. I sat in the front of his car

'A what! A deux cheveux!' I choked as I took a drag on the lump of the horseshit he'd given me. The engine wheezed into life which was more than could be said for me. We coughed and spluttered away from the port. Me trying to come to terms with the fact that I'd lost my arse and lungs forever whilst his girlfriend who was sat in the back explained that this tin with four small deckchairs in it was the french equivalent of the Volkswagen.

They dropped me off somewhere on the outskirts of town. I settled on the side of the road and took stock of my situation. I would go to Paris, find the road leading south and slowly make my way down to the Mediterranean, where I would get a job, probably as a fisherman, meet a woman, start a family and then when the dust had settled back in Blighty – probably in about ten years – contact my family and take it from there.

After about an hour of fruitless thumb waving – there was very little traffic – my lungs had settled down enough for an English fag. I fumbled about in the pockets of my ex-army rucksack.

'I'm sure I put them here'. I went from pocket to pocket.

'That's weird … I know I had them when ….HANG ON!'

I furiously went through the pockets again. In desperation I opened the rucksack and poured everything out onto the road. I searched through what few clothes I had, went through the empty pockets again, nothing.

'YOU CUNTS! YOU PAIR OF FRENCH CUNTS!' I screamed.

'Sit in ze front, zere is no room in ze back, is ok leave your bag zere.' I remembered him saying.

I'd been in France for two hours and already I had no passport and no money. They'd stolen them. Too young to understand the implications of John Lennon's instant karma, I furiously stuffed my meagre possessions back into the rucksack. I hadn't exactly packed for an extended run: a pair of jeans, some socks, one pair of sandals, three t-shirts and a portable reel-to-reel tape recorder. And no sleeping bag. It wasn't cold but it wasn't warm either. I walked but was tired and hungry and after a while I did start to get a bit cold. I came to a petrol station that had some flag poles in front of it with large blue and yellow fleur-de-lys flags on top. It was closed so I shinned up a pole and tore one down. It served as a good blanket. Wrapped in my flag on the side of the road somewhere outside Le Havre was not how I'd envisaged my glamorous life as a fugitive from justice.

It must have been about four in the morning when the car pulled up. He wound the window down and said something in french.

'Je ne suis pas français. Er, Paris?'

'You are english?'

'Yes.'

'Come!'

I sit down next to a large French black man in a tracksuit. He tells me that he is going to Paris but via Rouen where he has to stop for a couple of hours. He says I can either wait for him in Rouen in the car or he can drop me off on the main Paris road. I say that I'll wait.

After twenty minutes in which he explains to me that he is shagging this married woman in Rouen whose husband worked nights, he pulls over for a piss. He asks me if I can drive.

'Er, yeah, of course.' I lied.

He passes me the keys to his beautiful triumph MGB GT Mark 2 (amazing what you remember) and settles into the passenger seat. He explained that he'd been driving for over six hours and was knackered. Pre-auto routes most roads were built by the Romans. Straight as a die that go on forever - perfect conditions for learning to drive. After a couple of false starts and stalls, explained away by it being left hand drive and a tricky gear box, I soon get the hang of it, a piece of piss really. Throughout my childhood sat in the back of Dad's cars I'd copy whatever Dad was doing for whole journeys: foot on the clutch, put it into gear, hum along with the engine knowing when it reached a certain pitch it was time to press down on the clutch and change gear again. I'd been preparing for this moment all my life. By the time we'd reached the outskirts of Rouen at about 5.30 a.m., I had one elbow on the open window, was steering one handed, and was convinced that I could speak French.

Rouen wasn't awake as we parked up outside a block of flats on a sprawling council estate. Two hours later when a grinning Antoine returned with the car keys it definitely was. It's one thing bowling along the open French countryside at 4 o'clock in the morning in a dead straight line with no other traffic, but it's quite another having things to negotiate - like cars, traffic lights, t-junctions and rush hour. Antoine sensed that maybe I was having trouble driving on the right and thankfully took over. By the time we'd reached Paris, I'd explained to him that

I'd had my stuff stolen. He was so affronted that his countryman had done this to a visitor that he insisted on driving me to the National Sports Institute. He was the coach of the French karate team. He gave me a full French cooked breakfast and drove me out to the road that went south, dropping me off and putting twenty francs in my hand. Happy days.

I was standing on stage in front of about 20,000 people whilst a compere held up my arm and read out what was written on it.

'I AM AN ENGLISH STUDENT WHO HAS HAD HIS PASSPORT AND MONEY STOLEN. I MUST RETURN TO ENGLAND TO HELP DEMONSTRATE AGAINST AMERICA'S OCCUPATION OF VIETNAM.'

Huge cheers. The compere took off his hat, gave it to me and pushed me into the crowd. The seething mass of student communist sympathisers waiting for John Hiseman's Colosseum to hit the stage were soon filling my hat with their loose change.

Two days earlier having been dropped off by a lorry driver in Aix en Provence, I'd been wandering around with not very much money and even fewer prospects when I'd come across a poster for a local music festival. No-one could have been more ecstatic to see the names John Hiseman's Colosseum than me. John Hiseman's Colosseum meant Mike Pearson, Mike from Gino days. I'd met Mike backstage and he'd steered me through catering and introduced me to a posh groupie who would write my message on my arm, in French.

I'd only been a fugitive for four days, and yes, it was exciting but that night as Mike drove away from the festival leaving me with a hatful of change, I did feel a little bit lonely.

Suddenly a huge cheer went up from the crowd. The mayor of Aix was on stage and had said something that had obviously gone down well.

Apparently to avoid any trouble - this was 1969, one year after the student riots that had swept across France - he had offered to provide 20 coaches to take the 1,000 hard core communists across France to another festival near to Juan les Pins. The deal stood if they left that night. There was another huge cheer.

Sat on the roof of one of the buses with six of my newfound communist mates driving across France by moonlight, the warm mistral air blowing against my soft juvenile skin, I didn't think life could get more romantic. I was right. I woke at day break, the bus had stopped on the outskirts of Juan les Pins. Most of the people were still asleep or were waking. The communist who'd slept next to me was already up, and had gone, so had my hat full of money.

Skint again, I wandered round the little town, looking for anything really. All I had was the now fading writing on my arm, so I showed it to passing Frenchmen, who snorted at me until one old geezer read it, walked off, then stopped and came back. He gave me a fifty-franc note and walked off again. It was a beautiful moment. My breakfast of croissant and coffee tasted incredible, sunning myself in a little French square. Quite astonishing for a little criminal from Llanelli. After my feast I searched round for alternative transport to get me the rest of the way to the festival in Beot.

En route I befriended a Frenchman called Bertrand. He was in his twenties, with a penchant for American students doing the 'backpack' tour of France. He had a beard and – yes, my favourite accessory – a moped. He stopped and asked me if I needed a lift and on I climbed.

'Mmmmm. Mmmmmm.' Bertrand humped away with the pretty American student. I was busy fingering the other one (she wouldn't let me do it to her). I was still very short and not nearly as manly as Bertrand so finger penetration was all I got.

'Mmmmm. Mmmmm.' Bertrand was having a great fucking time.

We were sleeping on the side of the road on the way to Beot, except there wasn't any sleeping going on. In the morning Bertrand seemed more interested in petting than moving, so I decided to take the moped and drive ahead to have breakfast in Juan-les-Pins with our luggage. I waited for a few hours but he never showed. I remembered that he'd told me where he lived, a village nearby called San Raphael, so I left his luggage at the railway station and bombed off there. It was a small village and someone pointed me in the direction of his sister and I told her to tell him that I was driving his moped to the festival in

Beot. So I wasn't stealing it – it was a bona fide borrow. (The kind of borrowing I'm very good at – you ask to use it after you've finished borrowing it.)

On my way out of the village I was stopped by the police – who obviously weren't au fait with my definition of 'borrowing'.

'Zis is your bike?'

'Er, yeah.'

'Zis is Bertrand's bike.'

'Er no. I'm borrowing it. Borrow? You know the word.'

They didn't know the word. They read my arm and called the consulate to come and interview me. Of course, I still thought there would be a huge Interpol search for me and expected the flying squad to turn up and take me home. Nothing. Instead I was left to rot in a provincial French police-station holding cell for thirty-six hours (like American cop-show jails it had chicken-wire walls so you could be watched at all times, and nothing else but a tiny bench). Here I remained while the consulate tried to find out who I was, without success. By this time I was happy to give up being on the run. In French jails then, you had to pay for your own food. So I sent a policeman out to buy me a sandwich. He came back with a ham baguette coated with curdled margarine. I puked all over the cell and the pigs made me clean it up myself.

Yes, I was definitely ready to go home. I was deported for stealing a moped and was met by police when I arrived in Dover. A couple of phone calls revealed I was wanted on 'failure to turn up to an identity parade'. They gave me money for the train to Swansea, where Dad would pick me up.

'Son.'

'Hi, Dad.'

Open car door. Get in. Watch Dad change gears. Watch the road ahead.

'Sorry, Dad.'

Dad indicates. He hasn't looked at me once.

'Your mother's been worried sick.'

'Yeah. Sorry, Dad. I won't do it again.'

An imperceptible shake of the head. A tut. An air of extreme disappointment.

I admit to stealing the Bush radio.

Bus stop outside the house at Gorseinon. Mum and Dad and me. Mum can't come to court because she's got to work. Nothing interrupts Mum's work at the restaurant. I am to answer charges of theft and absconding. We get on the bus and Dad says to the driver: 'Two returns and a single please.'

'A single? Dad.'

'No point in wasting money on a return for *you*, is there?'

Mum cries. Mum carries on on the bus to her work and me and Dad get off at Penclawdd Magistrates' Court. The judge clears his throat. 'Ah hem. Mr Allen. I would give your son a hefty fine, if you think that would do him some good.'

I look at Dad. Dad won't look at me.

'I'm not paying it.'

I look at Dad again. What does he mean, he won't pay it?

'In that case, I have no option but to give your son a custodial sentence.'

My legs go. The judge writes something down. I look at Dad; he turns white.

'Keith Allen, I sentence you to three months in juvenile detention.'

Penclawdd was such a tiny courthouse I had to wait for the prison van in the secretary's office. Dad comes in and I can see that he is genuinely shocked and upset about me going away. I suppose it is a crumb of comfort that he cares.

The journey to Cardiff nick was OK. The coppers taking me were local boys and told me not to worry. It was actually quite exciting being put in a cell with other men, because I knew I wouldn't be staying there. The next day I was off to Usk. Then one of the other men told me about Usk. It was hard.

The next morning I was collected in a van with two of the prison officers from Usk Detention Centre. All my fears were confirmed. They chatted to me on the way, seeing I was shitting myself and all that.

'It's tough in there, son. Just keep your head down and you'll get through it OK.'

One of them gave me a cigarette as we wound up through the Monmouthshire countryside. The weather was grey and drizzly. All I wanted to do was cry like a kid and run home. I leant forward to get a light, my hands trembling.

'Make the most of it, son. It's the last one you'll be having for three months.'

Chapter 12

'WHAT ARE YOU looking at, you ugly little fucker! Move!'

I'd made the mistake of slowing up a little. You had to run everywhere. Out of the cell to the toilet, from the shower to the refectory, from the refectory back to the cell.

'Don't fucking walk, Allen, you little toerag – run.'

Everywhere you went, you went fast. I was put in the induction wing and told that if I behaved, I'd be moved off it. It was the first night. The cell stunk. The door banged shut and was locked. Fuck me, I was scared. After lights out I could hear crying, not just one lad, a few. It was that bad.

There was a pipe that ran through all the cells, the central heating system. I'm not trying to make out that this was some kind of romantic *Papillon* moment, but I was woken by someone tapping on the pipe – the noise carried along, the tapping getting more urgent. Someone was trying to communicate with me.

At 3am, door unlocks, lights on.

'Get up, you little wanker. Who's been tapping on the pipes?'

A screw drags me out of bed, big ruddy-faced cunt. I stand in my pants shivering in the corridor with the other boys while the screw strips down my bed and searches my room for fuck-knows-what. Then he moves to the next room, and the next.

'When I find which one of you little fuckers was tapping on the fucking pipes, you are for the fucking high jump, you understand?'

'Yes, sir,' we all murmur.

Next day I repeated this story to a lad called Tony Sullivan. His shoulders were stooped as if he carried a heavy weight on them. Only eighteen, he already had two kids and was on a two-year stretch. A two-year stretch in this hell-hole was unimaginable. I barely knew how I was going to survive three months. Tony was quiet, in that ticking-bomb kind of way. You knew that if he lost it, it wouldn't be pretty.

'It was the screws,' said Tony.

'What?'

'Banging on the pipes. It's their little game, man. Think it's funny to fuck up the new lads. See who they can break.'

It was clear to me that Usk was going to be fucking miserable. The hours passed like days. There was no end in sight. Three months was a massive ask. Luckily my growth spurt had finally arrived and I had reached the heady height of five foot five and a half.

After a week on induction wing they gave me the regulation light-blue shirts and blue cotton trousers and put me in a cell with Tony Sullivan.

Mornings began with a cold shower and then a swift run to the gym where we'd have to play murder ball. This was the arena where bullying and petty squabbles were worked out between the lads. The screws looked on, leaning against the sides of the gym, arms folded, while the weak got beaten up and the bullies prospered.

The aim of murder ball was to transport a medicine ball from one end of the gym to the other, a sort of working-class version of the Eton wall game (but with no Pimms afterwards). Anything went: an average game would see bloody noses, dislocated fingers and bruised ribs. There would be blood everywhere.

Mum and Dad came to visit me at Christmas and Mum cried. They didn't come again. I was so desperate for a cigarette I even considered asking Dad for one. I never did, though. Instead I smuggled a horsehair brush into my cell, pulled some fibres from it and rolled them up in newspaper. I borrowed a match from the bloke in the next-door cell – who was busy splitting a normal match into eight parts with a razor blade (yes, eight). I was trying to light my horsehair fag when Tony came into the cell trembling, his face drained of colour.

'Allen. You're going to have to break my hand.'

I pulled on the 'fag', laughed and choked. Tony only had three weeks to go before he got out: two weeks on work duty and the last week on cleaning. He'd just come off the work roster. There was a fat Australian screw who had it in for Tony and was forever provoking him, trying to make him snap.

'Did you just say you want me to break your hand?' I spluttered.

'If you don't, I'm going to kill him.'

I passed him the horsehair fag and he looked me in the eyes, right down to the core.

'I mean it, Keith.'

I believed him. Tony was nearly out but if he murdered a screw he'd spend the next twenty-five years behind bars. The only way he could get off work duty and therefore avoid the screw was to get an injury that meant he couldn't work.

'No fucking way.'

'I'm begging you.'

'Oh man.' I paced. 'Oh man ... *fuck*.'

We discussed how to do it and I pushed a towel in his mouth for something to bite into and muffle any screams.

'Jesus Christ, Tony.'

'Just do it,' he said through the rag in his mouth.

He put his hand between two sticking-out drawers and I raised a boot above my head and brought it down on top. Tony bit hard on the towel. We looked at the results. I'd managed to push two of his fingernails down into his fingers. I looked away and collapsed, holding my own fingers as if it was me in pain.

'Ow, man ... ow ow ... OW.'

'What are you crying for? It's still not broken. You'll have to do it harder.'

I stopped rolling around and looked at him. 'No way. No fucking *way*.'

Tony stuffed the towel back in his mouth and closed his eyes. Now I was worked up. I raised the boot high and junped up, bringing it crashing down. There was a sickening crack and Tony slumped to the floor in agony. His knuckles were smashed and he appeared to be going in and out of consciousness.

'Get up! We have to be quick.'

I pulled him to his feet. We smeared blood on the door hinges and yelled for the screws.

'Help! Quick! It's Tony, he's trapped his fingers.'

They came running and examined the door frame, then Tony's hand.

'What's going on?'

'It was an accident. I opened the door quick and he had his hand on the joint on the other side.'

One of the guards took Tony to the sick bay. The other sat on the bed and looked at me. We played a game of dead eye.

'He didn't trap his fingers in the door, did he, Allen?'

We stared some more and then he left. They let it go. I think they admired our ingenuity.

I walked out of the gates to freedom on a freezing February morning in 1971. I was going to stay out of trouble because there was no fucking way I was going back there. They gave me some money to catch a bus from Usk village square into Cardiff. I got to the train station, bought my ticket to Swansea and spent the rest on twenty fags. I waited until the train moved off to light up. It was a beautiful moment. The power of the nicotine made me giddy and high. I was free.

Arriving home at my parents' empty house I remembered how free I'd felt with Seamus's takings in my hand at the fun fair in Portsmouth. I remembered why I'd done it – there was nothing stopping me, nothing to stay for. Who cared about me? No one apparently. Mum and Dad were at work, Susan long gone, fuck knows where, and Kevin at school. I didn't even know him. Still, it had to be better than Usk.

'I'm going to get a job …'

Eddie stared at the road.

'I mean it, Dad. I'm going straight.'

I didn't want to get in trouble again. Everyone in Gorseinon now knew I was a thief and it muddied the family name. The only consolation was that no one ever told Nan. They didn't want to upset her, and nor did I.

'You better had if you want to live under my roof.'

Joining civvy street hadn't bothered Dad. As long as he could work all the hours God sent, he was content. Work for him was like a process of cleansing the ills of the world, and doing the right thing was his way of proving his manliness.

Nevertheless, there was effort on my part to be the son he wanted.

I started looking for an honest trade among the mining communities of the Welsh valleys, which was as far away from my dreams as it was possible to be. I enrolled at the miners' training college. Apart from impressing my father with my application, there was another reason to choose mining. I was a bone-idle little fucker and the Bryn Llywd Colliery was only a short walk from our house.

Dad was pleased that I seemed to be settling down. Little did he know that the only settling down I was doing was on the sofa. After he and Mum had left for work, me and a couple of the other apprentices would bunk off and play cards at my house. We stole rolls of plastic sheeting from a factory yard and covered the sofa so the coal dust wouldn't rub off on it. At the end of the day the house would be clean and Dad none the wiser.

My first day underground was an education in how not to live. In the changing room I was issued with standard overalls, helmet and lamp. Around me the hardened faces of the miners confirmed my worst fears. I was going to hell. We were loaded into the cage and sent down. No one said a word.

At the coal face it was stiflingly hot and cloying with black dust. Up top, summer was approaching, which made it even more insufferable down below. The apprentices – me included – shuffled over to join a crew of men using cutting gear to shave off the coal. After a mind-numbing and nerve-shattering few hours a foghorn sounded and it was a thing called 'lunchtime'. I didn't see how such a word was relevant in the bowels of the earth. Talking of bowels, I was taken by the urge to empty mine.

'Where's the toilet?' I enquired of a couple of men chewing their sandwiches, leaving black fingerprints on white Mother's Pride. They looked at each other and smiled.

'There aren't any toilets down here.'

'So how do I go?'

'Use your bloody lunch box, innit.'

My lunch box contained an apple and some cake. Dispensing of its contents I duly went off and crapped in it. Hearing the men hooting with derisive laughter, I realised I'd been had. It seemed the main point of being an apprentice was to be the butt of all practical jokes.

That was the first of only three times down for me. I couldn't take it. We were sweating below ground like subhumans. I knew the other miners had learnt to live without their dreams, but I couldn't live without mine.

I'd done my time at Usk, but I still wasn't entirely free. Being in gainful employment was part of the court conditions keeping me out of borstal. To meet the conditions and maintain the peace with Dad, I secured a job at the butcher's. I lasted all of five days. It turned out that the glamour of bagging up sheep's bollocks for old Mrs Williams to broil was even less attractive than shitting in your own lunch box.

My career in butchery lasted about as long as an ice cube in a sauna. At the end of the week I collected my pay packet and told them not to expect me on Monday. On the way to the pub to spend my wages, I ran into my mate Jack.

'Want to buy some drugs and get off our heads?'

We counted our money to see what we could buy. Between us our wages came to a healthy thirty quid.

'Let's get some acid,' said Jack.

'And get to London.' I fancied buying some clothes. 'Get some new clobber down Carnaby Street.'

We rushed off to call on the dope dealer.

'Can we have half an ounce of Durban Poison, please?' The Poison was the strongest dope in Llanelli. Jack grinned at the dealer and winked. 'And four tabs of acid.'

We got a lift as far as the Severn Bridge. It was late and the chances of another lift were diminishing into the darkness. We didn't want a night on a kerb. We wanted bright lights and big city. All of a sudden an old yellow Post Office van ambled down the slip road towards us and stopped. A mullet hairdo emerged and disco music was pumping out.

'Where you off to, lads?'

'London.'

'Me too … get in the back.'

Climbing in the back of the van, we discovered that the Mullet was a mobile DJ, the new thing in Wales at the time.

'Just done a gig in Cardiff. Make yourselves comfortable, lads.'

If comfortable is sitting with one buttock lodged against a turntable and the other being penetrated by the corner of a speaker, then we were in paradise. So it was that we were transported to London. Jack cupped his hands and shouted above the music.

'Shall we drop an acid?'

'Go on then.'

We took one and waited for the effects, not thinking that doing an acid in an enclosed space was chemical suicide. But by the time we had reached the top of Edgware Road in the early hours of the morning, *nothing* was happening in the most spectacular way. So we took the rest. This a common and foolish mistake, because then when it happens, it happens double and blows your fucking head off.

'This is where we part, amigos …'

Mullet dropped us outside the Wimpy and disappeared on a raft of dodgy jingles. Jack felt round in his pockets.

'No! The dope. It's gone.'

'You what?'

'I must have left it in the van.'

'You fucking idiot. No dope and dud acid. Remind me never to try and have a good time with you again.'

There was no alternative but to eat our way out of depression. In the Wimpy a big black woman stood behind the counter.

'What are you having, lads?'

Her face started to melt. It melted into a dark brown blancmange and her voice slowed like a warped record, deep like the devil. I turned to look at Jack, slowly because my neck was stuck in treacle. He was lying on the floor with his hands over his eyes.

'I'm scared,' I said.

'Let's get out of here.'

We ran out of the Wimpy and into the safety of the underground. Rarely had a worse decision been made. Once down there we couldn't find an exit. People stared at us as we criss-crossed London on various trains, clinging desperately to each other. Eventually we collapsed on the Piccadilly Line platform at King's Cross.

'Let's just stay here and go to sleep.'

'What about trying to find a way out?'

'There is no way out.'

Everyone smoked on the tube then and someone flicked a fag butt on my head as he passed, thinking I was a down and out. Hauling myself upright I looked at my reflection in the window of a passing tube and screamed. 'Shit! Jack, I've died and gone to Hell …'

We ran out of the tube covered head to toe in dirt and soot. Back in the fresh air again the acid started to wear off. I checked a clock. We'd been down there for eleven hours. Drained of all human emotion we sat on the steps of Eros and watched the world go by.

It being 1971, the whole place was full of hippies hanging out, trying to start some kind of revolution with a couple of bongos and what appeared to be second-rate sparklers, which I later learnt were incense sticks. A couple of coppers interrupted my mental critique.

'Got any identification, lads?'

I suppose we did look like a couple of chimney sweeps who'd escaped from a Dickensian street scene.

'What are you doing in London?'

'Er, shopping.'

'Oh yeah? What for?'

'Clothes.'

They couldn't complain on that score, and since we'd taken all the acid and lost our dope they couldn't arrest us for possession. They let us go and we wandered off in the direction of Carnaby Street. We found a cool boutique, chose some clothes and went to the changing room. It wasn't our fault that the most unfortunate era in fashion was upon us. We emerged from the booths and checked each other out.

'What do you think?'

'Cool. What do you think?'

We were in identical crushed velvet flares, except his were black and mine were brown. He had a blue T-shirt and I had a red one. The T-shirts had loon sleeves and a satin star in a contrasting colour on the chest. Next we stopped in at Ravel. A pair of women's sixteen-hole lace-up white canvas boots with a Cuban heel caught my eye. Jack looked at me doubtfully, questioning my state of mind.

'Are you still on acid? They're ladies' boots.'

'I know.'

'You can't wear them.'

'Course I can, they're fucking brilliant.'

Mincing down Piccadilly in my white boots I fitted in perfectly. Being on the motorway trying to hitch back to Wales proved a little more challenging. The passing cars hooted and shouted.

'Poofs.'

'Fuck them. They don't know what's cool.'

What was all the fuss about? I'd watched my favourite band Slade metamorphose from skinheads into crushed-velvet flares-wearing buffoons, so I thought I'd have a go myself.

To complement our outfits, our faces were still smeared with filth from the underground. It took nearly two days to get home as we walked along the motorway like a couple of dandies who'd lost their wigs.

We got my dad to drive to Swansea and pick us up. Uncle Roy was with him and doubled up in hysterics when he saw us.

'What the bloody hell have you two come as?'

Dad just shook his head, anger bubbling under once again. He thought I looked like a cunt. For once, he was right.

Summer had arrived and I decided to go and look for a job in Tenby, a place I'd often visited before and where I'd made the acquaintance of

Charlie Edwards, a middle-aged man who ran a rock stall and hired out rowing boats on the beach. He was dodgier than a chair with three legs, but he always offered work and a floor to kip on. I went with my mate Tony Rees, called Peg for short, fuck knows why. Like me, Tony dressed in the regulation Lee Cooper, but unlike me he had a fashionable feather-cut. Tony Rees liked me because I was English. The lads in Llanelli thought anything English must be from London and London was the height of cool. I took every opportunity to exploit this.

Charlie put us up in his flat and gave us work on the rock stall, which left him free to work his boats on the beach. I also sold crockery on another stall and worked on my patter, which seemed to make people laugh.

'Anyone want some lovely fancies? Lovely ornamental teapot. What could be nicer on a Friday? Or some beautiful rock. Go on, sir, take some for your missus – she'll forgive you for falling asleep last night … come on …'

We started drinking in the Lifeboat pub in the harbour, where we met a bloke called Ginger Crockford. Turned out his family was one of the main players in Tenby with a great seafaring history. We got talking. Everyone knew there were two boats in Tenby that took tourists out mackerel fishing. Both boats had established touts who worked on punters ambling round the harbour and enticed them onto the trips. Bing and Black Ham were old boys who'd been touting for years. Black Ham was a big hairy man who'd shot himself in the foot to avoid National Service and also had two fingers missing.

If Ginger was going in with his own boat, this could be my break. I signalled the barmaid to bring me and Ginger another pint.

'I can do that. I've got all the patter.'

'Go on then, Keith.'

Ginger set up next to Black Ham and Bing. My pitch to the passing tourists was aimed at flattering the ladies and making the men laugh, cheeky but not too risqué.

'Anyone for pollocks? I said pollocks, you naughty girl …'

It was half slapstick comedian, half Norman Wisdom. Soon Ginger's boat was booming and the competition was fuming. They didn't like the little upstart beating them at their own game. Two weeks into the season me and Ginger were cleaning up. My take-home pay was a hundred and fifty quid a week, more money than I'd ever known.

Bing came up to me one day on a break. I was smoking by the boat store in the harbour. He pushed me into the store and asked me what I was doing on his patch. He was strong and meaty. After assessing my chances in a fight and deciding the odds were not favourable, I felt round behind me and came across a sturdy piece of wooden pole.

'Why don't you just take your lippy comments and go back where you came from?' he said, swinging his meaty fist at me.

I brought the pole up and hit him across the face. He staggered and fell to the floor, blood pouring from his nose. Outside the boat store a crowd had gathered and peered in, watching me stand over Bing and point threateningly at him before walking out, trembling with fury. 'Tell that cunt never to come near me again.'

This statement was motivated by fear, not bravado. It wasn't long before the harbour master got wind of the fight. He called a meeting, to which only boat owners were allowed, but I barged in, anxious to protect my job. Bing and Ham stood up and waved their fists at me.

'Get him out of here! He's not a boat owner.'

'I am. I own half of Ginger's boat.'

Ginger looked round at me. 'Since when?'

'Since the beginning. We went halves, didn't we, Ginger?'

Ginger recovered and winked. 'Yeah, that's right. Keith's got half me boat.'

My job was safe, and that called for a celebration. The weather was bad and the boats weren't taking tourists out, so we spent the whole day in the pub. Tony Rees came to meet me, along with some other wasters who had joined our gang.

'Stackridge are playing at the Pavilion.'

'Great. Lessgo.'

Stackridge at the Pavilion may not have been Hendrix at the Apollo but it was as cool as it got in Tenby. We turned up at the Pavilion half cut, to be greeted by unwelcoming looks from the bouncers. We wandered innocently round the back of the Pavilion. There was a window open, so we jumped in and found ourselves in the band's dressing room. Watches and wallets glinting in the night.

'Fucking brilliant, an easy steal.'

'We'll get caught.'

'No, we won't.'

We filled our pockets and the rest of the gang made for the window.

'Where are you lot going? Don't you want to watch the gig?' I said.

'Don't push it, Keith, we'll get caught.'

'No, we won't.'

We did. The next day the police arrested me at Charlie Edwards' hovel. We'd been spotted leaving the dressing room by one of the security men who, being a local lad, knew who we were. After interviewing the rest of the gang, they rounded on me as the leader and dobbed me in.

I requested that my case be heard in the magistrates' court. They bailed me to return three weeks later. It was to be an interesting three weeks.

Essentially life was good and there was nothing to worry about except getting drunk. Then I fell in love with a girl called Lindsey Dale. She was gorgeous, tall with long dark hair. The attraction was instant but her father had other ideas.

'Me old man's grounded me. He thinks you're the wrong sort.'

'Do you think I'm the wrong sort?'

'Dunno. Yeah, maybe.'

'But you still want to kiss me?'

She picked wool bobbles off her cardigan. Ah well, bollocks to her. There was always the old 'date the mate' trick. So I started going out with Lindsey's best friend Heather Turnbull, who reported everything we did back to Lindsey. Safe to say that was the end of their friendship. Heather had long legs (important) and full lips (very important). She had a lot of freckles and ginger hair. Most important of all she wore a very short skirt. She wasn't Lindsey Dale, but she was good enough.

There was a festival in neighbouring Saundersfoot and we tipped along, me, Heather and Tony Rees. We stopped in the car park to get some fish and chips. The guy who ran the shop was an enormous German. He glared as we joked around and took the piss out of him. His assistant came over and we exchanged unpleasantries.

'Have you got a problem?'

'Your boss is a German.'

'Why don't you fuck off and eat somewhere else then?'

'Do you want to take this outside?'

'Come on then, you little shit.'

The assistant launched himself at me and we scuffled. Heather and Tony egged me on until they saw the German stealing up behind me looking for a place to bury a pair of scissors and deciding that my back would do nicely.

'Keith! Watch out.'

As the German lunged forward I lurched back on the end of a square left hook from the assistant and fell over. The scissors missed my back and buried themselves in my scalp. By now the kerfuffle was attracting attention and someone had called the police.

The scissors had only cut the skin but the results were dramatic. I was carted off to hospital where my head was shaved and stitched, leaving a huge, ugly wound.

'Great.' I admired myself in the mirror. 'I look like a proper criminal now. That's going to go down well in court.'

My case was being heard the next day and my appearance, as I'd correctly predicted, did me no favours. The judge screwed up his eyes and looked at my head wound sceptically.

'You will be sentenced to two years' borstal training.'

The prison van took me off to Cardiff Prison and from there to Wormwood Scrubs for an assessment. The Scrubs was a place of brittle light and yellowing lives. It stank of hopelessness. The men here were decaying, morally and physically.

The screw came into my cell to confirm my name. 'Prisoner 455661? Allen?'

'Yeah.'

'You've been assessed according to your test results.'

'Please don't tell me I've got to stay here.'

'You've been allocated open borstal.'

'I like the sound of the "open" bit.'

He looked at me cynically. 'And by the way … you've got a message. That German who tried to kill you just got nine years for GBH.'

That cheered me up no end, and, to boot, open borstal was in green and pleasant Dorset and was not too bad at all. It was clean and bright and the boys weren't hardened criminals, just on the wrong track. Everyone was given the choice of a course to pursue, from bricklaying and carpentry to academic qualifications. I was anxious to avoid any contact with work benches, clamps and chisels, but wasn't sure what else I'd be eligible for.

In an uncanny echo of my old boarding school, we were split into 'houses', and after an initial spell in dorms were even given our own rooms. At the top of the bedroom wall was a gap of around ten inches, which was shared air with the boys in their rooms on either side. I could hear my mate Guy Marsh moving round in the room next door.

'Oi, Guy, you know what?'

'What?'

'These cells are *exactly* the same dimensions as my room at boarding school.'

I lay on the bed and took out a letter from Heather. Her letters usually smelt nice, but for some reason this one smelt of cabbage and egg. She told me how much she missed me and the stuff that was going on in Tenby without me. All the time the smell was getting worse. The letter appeared to be leaking an eggy stench.

Hearing muffled laughter I looked skywards and saw Guy Marsh's bare arse poking through the gap at the top of the wall.

'Like that fart, did ye, Allen?'

'Oh yes, very fucking funny. That's another thing we used to do at boarding school, but we used to light them as well.'

'Wait a minute, I'll do another one then.'

Guy tried to squeeze one out and I jumped up, flicked on the lighter and burnt his arse. He cried out with pain and the offending butt disappeared.

'Allen! When you've stopped being so juvenile, can you come out here and meet Mr Dennis.'

The screw had caught me in the act, but rather than being punished I was trooped along to an interview with a man who would become a mentor to me inside.

Mr Dennis sat across from me and opened a file. 'OK, Keith, I'm the PIO [Physical Instruction Officer]. I can see from the tests you did in Wormwood that you're a clever lad so we're going to enter you for O levels. You know what subjects you want?'

English language, English literature, maths, geography, history and economics were my subjects.

My English teacher was Dolly Jordan. She was over fifty but to me she could have been a twenty-one-year-old glamour model because she had the most enormous pair of tits.

'Keith, I want you to imagine what it would have been like to be sandwiched between a warring couple like Beatrice and Benedict in *Much Ado* …'

Unfortunately I was already fully employed on the business of imagining my head sandwiched between another warring couple – Dolly's breasts.

My libido had no outlet apart from wanking over Heather's letters and therefore I redirected it to exercise. I went to the gym three times a week and got fit. Mr Dennis, who'd taken me under his wing, enrolled me for the outward-bound courses. He told me that I had leadership qualities and gave me extra responsibility to lead the rest of the lads, which made me realise there were other things that came easily to me, and none of them criminal. I'd seen criminals in the Scrubs and didn't recognise myself as one. Had borstal been hard-line, there was a chance that I wouldn't have turned it round. It was the sense of the system trying to save me that gave me the encouragement I needed to work on myself.

Being institutionalised didn't bother me in the slightest.* It gave me

---

* We weren't nearly as criminal as Michael Howard was when he put a stop to the open borstals and encouraged prisons to take a hard line with young offenders. When this happened, Mr Dennis, the one person responsible for getting me back on the straight and narrow, was made redundant.

structure and routine. It was like a ready-made social system in which, surrounded by rebels, there was no pressure to rebel. Also, Mr Dennis was a great physical education screw. He recognised my footballing talent, and along with Peter Clutterbuck, we ran the borstal team. I've never played with such a great player – Peter was like Roberto Carlos. The ball went exactly where he wanted it to go.

Dad came down once to support me in a big match but unfortunately I was sent off for calling the ref a cheating cunt. Yet, apart from my temper, I knew I could play. Uncle Roy always said I was the best footballer he ever saw. Just before I went to Tenby I'd been playing in the West Wales Cup Final at Vetchfields. It transpired that a Leeds United scout had watched and wanted to invite me for a trial. Of course I never knew this – because I hadn't told anyone I was buggering off to Tenby and no one could find me. And from Tenby I got sent straight to borstal.

(The same Uncle Roy, when I played for my local team in Wales, misdiagnosed a torn ligament for a 'strain'. We were playing on the side of a hill, at a thirty-degree angle, and I collapsed in agony. Uncle Roy came tearing on with a bucket and sponge and advised me to play through it, boy. I got up and played on for ten minutes, which is hard when there is nothing holding your upper and lower leg together. The knee still hurts from time to time …)

Tony Diskin was my best mate inside. He was at best languid, at worst bone idle. A tall lad who was going bald aged nineteen, he had long fingers and could draw really well. He'd taken a lot of acid and was what you might call a pothead. Unlike Usk Detention Centre, fags and joints were readily available here. *

Me and Tony used to piss about mimicking famous people while we scrubbed the floor of the canteen. I grabbed a mop and slipped into the voice of an American mobster.

* Years later Tony contacted me. He was an art teacher at Worthing College. Then, about ten years ago, I bumped into him on Holloway Road, where he had the grey dead look of a junkie.

'We will fight dem on the fuckin' beaches, we will fuckin' kill their mutherfucker asses in the mutherfucking fields.'

'Why don't you get on the stage?'

'Fuck off.'

'You're good at it.'

'Good at what?'

'Dunno. All that shit. Voices. Acting. Making people laugh.'

'Don't be stupid.'

'I'm serious. I reckon a life of poncing about in tights awaits you.'

In the summer of 1972, after eleven months, three weeks and four days, I was out. Not that I was counting. Well, you do, of course. I was desperate to be out, but mainly because I had a great job to go to. Because of my good work on the outward-bound course, Mr Dennis had fixed it for me to be on the first ever Community Service Programme, leading a team of kids building an adventure playground in Bethnal Green.

At the end of the two months the Community Service Programme was over. After living in London and having my own money and responsibilities, it was impossible to consider living with my parents again, but I had nowhere else to go. Also, the results of the O levels I'd taken in borstal had come through – I'd got all six. The thought of being something called a 'student' began to seem very attractive. To be a student in the 1970s meant political activity, squatting and being anti-establishment. (Unlike today where 'student' means 'binge drinker' and university means 'training camp for *The X Factor*'.)

Chapter 13

MUM FUSSED ROUND the table while Dad sat upright, his thick, stocky, milk-white arms crossed.

'So what are you going to do now, son, eh?'

'I'm going to be a student.'

'What does that mean, eh?'

'It means I'm going to do my A levels in Swansea.'

Dad looked smug. 'Oh yes? And how can you afford to do that?'

'I'll get a grant.'

Even A-level students got grants then. This seemed to pacify him. Besides, being a student suited me well. It seemed like a way of doing nothing and getting paid for it.

The local authority gave me a grant to study and I topped up my wages with a holiday job at the water board where Dad worked, and waitering at the weekend at the Copper Grill where Mum worked.

The Copper Grill, on Swansea High Street, was run by an Italian called Mr Minetti, an ex-Italian POW. Dad drove Mum into work on Friday and Saturday nights and befriended Mr Minetti, who obviously appreciated my parents' work ethic – who wouldn't? Soon my father was employed as the greeter and floor manager at the Copper Grill on Friday and Saturday nights. Mr Minetti let Dad work the tills. This was a sign of great trust – no one else was allowed to do it. Dad got me in there as a waiter on Saturday nights, and so it was that the Allen family served steak pizzaiola to the good people of Swansea.

It was interesting watching my mum at work. In those days working-class people used to leave the tip underneath a plate – out of view. Mum would wipe the table and go round looking under plates and cups. If she found something she'd smile at the people as they left, come over to me and say, 'Lovely people ...'

However, if there was no tip, her face would become severe. The exiting people would be followed by a stare as she muttered under her breath, 'Bastards ...'

I had the chance to observe my father too. One evening we both stood outside the restaurant having a cigarette when a crowd of rowdy young men rolled up. That day Wales were playing Scotland and these kids were pissed-up Scottish fans having a good time. I watched my dad's jaw tighten as they approached. I saw how strongly he disapproved of them, how they violated his every ethical standard. It seemed to me then that the gap between us had never been wider.

And so it was that I enrolled in Ty Coch College of Further Education in 1972 to study English, economic history and psychology. I chose English because I was good at it, I've got no idea why I chose economic history and I chose psychology because on enrolment day I'd seen a gaggle of good-looking Welsh girls in the queue.

To an eighteen- going on nineteen-year-old working-class lad, 'why people did things' was the most ludicrous question in the world. It's common sense: if you're happy you do good things and if you're unhappy you fuck things up. Why did we need two whole years to postulate over why Mrs Jones had a third bowl of cornflakes? Er, because she's a greedy cow?

Psychology and economic history were quickly consigned to the bin marked 'complete waste of time'. But English was like nothing I'd ever experienced. First because I was good at it and second because I had a brilliant teacher.

David Williams was Welsh. Now, some say that the Welsh are descended from Scots who couldn't swim. (The Irish being descended from those who could.) Others, more romantically inclined, believe the Welsh to be the direct descendants of the lost tribe of Israel. If David was anything to go by, I'd plump for the second. Short, with troubled, deep-brown eyes, you'd swear blind he was Jewish. He would arrive clean-shaven for his nine o'clock lecture and by lunchtime would have a five o'clock shadow. And he hated Arabs. He would sit in the canteen at lunchtime and vent his spleen at our intake of overseas students.

There was a reason for this. He was working-class, very intelligent and overqualified for village life. He lived in a tiny village called Alltwen, perched on the side of a mountain outside Pontardawe, ten miles from Swansea. His mother, a prostitute, abandoned him as a child; his father was a fairground boxer who had long since disappeared. He was brought up by his Auntie Gladys, and as a lad taught himself how to read music and play the guitar.

I was to find out later* that he also suffered from epilepsy and asthma. As a kid he couldn't do normal stuff so he buried himself in education. Age eighteen he went to study at the Welsh College of Music and Drama, with a view to getting a drama degree.

David believed very strongly in pulling oneself up by the bootstraps, and because he'd done it he loathed and resented rich students, and he didn't like teaching kids who weren't interested in learning. Back to his hatred of Arabs, as well as being a great teacher who loved holding the older female students in his thrall as he talked about romantic literature, he was an incorrigible shagger. He used to frequent and play at the jazz clubs of Tiger Bay. At that time Swansea was full of Arabs, and David would see the self-same female students who mooned over him on the arms of the Arab men who splashed their cash around to pull the girls.

The sound of jazz emanated from David Williams' flat. I'd been invited over – which I saw as a great honour since he was a lecturer and about twenty-nine and I was a spotty student. He snatched open the door with a flourish and welcomed me in, tripping over papers, guitars and books. He pulled out a bottle and a corkscrew. Wine? I really was moving up the social classes now. Dad would be proud.

'You mind red? Make yourself at home.'

Or maybe Dad wouldn't be so proud. David's flat was a filthy shit-hole. But it was an intellectual shit-hole, born out of creativity rather

*When I buried him, twenty years after we first met.

than sloth. And besides, he didn't seem to care. He downed his glass of wine in one and grabbed his jacket.

'Drink up. We're going out.'

We got in his clapped-out van and drove to a jazz club in Swansea. David introduced me to his colleagues and musicians and made me feel mature and sophisticated. Instead of hanging out with kids, I was surrounded by adults having intelligent conversations. I played the part well, enjoying the role of a grown-up.

David had learnt his trade in Cardiff jazz clubs in the early sixties from a jazz guitarist called Ray Norman. The Tiger Bay dock area was full of jazz clubs (and Arabs) because of its history as a port and stop-off point for trade and all sorts of people. David introduced me to Ray, whom I could see he revered. Ray was tall and handsome with a big nose – and was an Arab. But this didn't stop David hating all the others for the aforementioned reason of them nicking the pretty students he had his eye on.

We became great friends and inseparable. We created two characters called Dai and Yanto, two Welsh hillfolk, and we'd stay in these characters for hours, observing the other punters and taking the piss. As Dai and Yanto we'd spend long nights in the Rock in Alltwen. I was accepted as an honorary villager and some nights when David's hovel was too awful to contemplate I'd stay at Fatty Phil's mum's house. (Fatty Phil, later to become a staple part of my various bands, was twelve at the time and David was teaching him guitar.)

In traditional alpha-male bonding style, David and I cemented our friendship with a fight. With some Arabs, of course, in a bar called the Top Spot in Tiger Bay. I can't remember clearly what was said but one minute David and I were discussing the day's book of choice, and three drinks later we were cussing Arabs. Dave picked a fight with one of them, glass was thrown and we all took it outside where I (quite rightly) got a bottle over the head.

The Rock was David's own jazz club, and it was his energy and skill as a musician that convinced me that a musician was what I wanted to be. When he wasn't running his own club, he'd be in various permutations of the David Williams Sound, David Williams Fusion, DW Heartbeats and even an outfit called Flip Side. He was known in the Amman Valley as Dai Banjo, but a more apt moniker would have been 'Dai Lock up your wives and daughters Williams'.

He liked to call his club the Amman Valley Divorcee Club. To the divorcees, not only was he clever – 'Oooh, he's got O levels an' everythin',' they'd purr to each other, eyeing him up from the bar, 'speaks lovely, mind ' – but he also had those mournful sad eyes that encouraged women to want to mother him – 'Oooh and he was abandoned as a child, you know …'

Add to all this the fact he was a brilliant guitarist who could play any request thrown at him, and he could pretty much take his pick of them.

So it was that he introduced me to the Divorcee Club and it became my home for the next eighteen months. And it was filthy. Not the kind of filth I was to indulge in a few years later in Soho House and the Groucho, staggering from one ladies' toilet to another attached to the business end of a bag of Charlie and a chef's wife or two. No, this was an honest, more early kind of filth conducted in darkness under God's own sky.

Many a pub carpark between Morriston and Neath, Pontardawe and Port Talbot has had its gravel rearranged as a result of young Allen's urgings.

'Come on, love,' she purred, all thick make-up and croaky voice, 'we'll have to be quick, he'll wonder where I am.' (Which I doubted, as after falling over and twisting the night away on at least fifteen pints of lager I wondered if their menfolk knew where they were themselves.)

She pushed my head downwards but I struggled against her grip. (Not easy – her muscles were set from years splicing sheep carcasses.)

'I thought you said you were divorced.'

She pushes me down again. 'Did I say that?'

Word must have got round that young Allen – with firm buttocks and boundless enthusiasm – was worth a ride.

'Hang on, love – let me get it wet for you.'

She spat on her hand, pulled down her tights and rubbed spittle into her powdered pussy.

'Put yer fingers in, love – oh come on – put another two in, what's wrong with you, man?'

Up to my wrist in prime Welsh fanny, it did occur to me that if the Allen mitt was what was required for satisfaction, what chance did the much smaller Allen cock have?

'Oooh, let me have your cock, love. I'll wank you off into my hand.'

As my cock spat the Allen life cordial over their experienced motherly hands, I came to realise that – like Mallory who'd climbed Everest 'because it was there' – these women let me into their pleasure dome because I was there.

Not for them the guilt-ridden trudge into pointless marriage-threatening affairs. There were no illusions, no self-delusion, not even a hint of latent nymphomania. It was just a bit of fun, a bit naughty, no real risk and an opportunity to have an eighteen-year-old's fingers stuck inside you for all of five minutes while you let him come in your hands.

'Oh thanks for that, love, it was fucking great, just what the doctor ordered. If I see you inside I'll get you a pint.'

Oh happy days …

My college work went on the back burner. Even David knew not to chastise me for my essay on *Wuthering Heights* – I'd been shagging in his house instead of writing it. My higher education took second place to my new-found interest in lower education.

But this all stopped when I fell in love with an older woman, another lecturer at college. I came to understand the concept of love as opposed to sex. She continued my education between the sheets and beyond. She even took me to see my first play.

The actual play passed me by, I was so fascinated with the set. They'd constructed a whole room on a stage and it looked so real … Then when the actors walked on, I couldn't believe my eyes. I leant over and whispered in Elaine's ear.

'It's him off the telly.'

To see someone 'off the telly' in Wales in the seventies was like seeing a god. I was awestruck. After the show we went to the bar for a drink.

'What did you think of the play?'

'The what?'

'You know, the play.'

'I liked the pipe.'

'The pipe?'

'Yeah, I liked the way they built the whole set round the central heating system of the theatre.'

'No, Keith, that was part of the set.'

Not that impressed with the width of my thinking, it didn't seem to put her off me. Wonder why? (Unless my thinking wasn't what she was after.) One morning I woke to find her staring at me.

'I'm pregnant.'

My heart thumped against my chest. 'My God. That's brilliant. I love you. I'm going to get a job and buy an old farmhouse and we're going to do it up.'

She removed my wandering hand and got up. 'Oh yeah? And how are we going to live?'

'I'll get a job, as a binman – anything.'

I think she was probably envisaging, in horror, life with a nineteen-year-old binman, while I was basking in the glory of my masculinity. I'd got her pregnant. I was a man.

David set me straight later that night over a bottle of wine. 'Don't ever trust a woman, Keith,' he said drunkenly. We'd come to a jazz club in Cardiff for the night and I'd poured my heart out.

'But I love her. I want her to have the baby and I'll look after her.'

'Don't be stupid.'

She started to avoid me and then later she came into the lecture hall and passed me a note. It read: 'I've had an abortion.' She told me that we'd had a lucky escape and that it was best to end the affair.

'What about all our plans? The farmhouse? Kids?'

'Your plans, Keith. Not mine.'

Thereafter I threw myself into learning to play the drums, a good outlet for the pain of heartbreak. (I'm not sure the neighbours at home on my parents' estate thought so during the next holidays when I'd bought myself a drum kit and beat seven shades of merry hell out of it after my parents went to work.)

I convinced David that I was ready for a gig, but no offers came, until one night he was desperate after someone had dropped out of David Williams Fusion and he was due to play a wedding.

'I'll do it.' How hard could it be? My beats were coming along well.

'Great,' said David, imagining a competent drummer. 'It's low key, just a three-piece, me, you and bass guitar.'

On the way to the gig in a little pub near Saundersfoot, the words 'three-piece' re-emerged in my mind. Oh shit. There was nowhere to hide. We set up and didn't have time for a warm-up.

'One, two, three, four …'

David started to play and I tried to play along. I could tell by his furtive then angry glances that I was dragging the combo all over the place, which at that moment sounded like it was made up of David, a bass player and an epileptic dwarf. I reminded myself at that moment of something a jazz-drummer had once said: that the mark of a great drummer is not what you play but what you *don't* play.

Taking this as my direction, I decided not to play at all. I just hit the bass drum every twelve bars, nodding my head like a pro.

The Allen Dictionary definition of 'acting' read: 'A combination of drinking, smoking and having sex and being paid for it.'

After I'd seen my first play, David directed the Christmas Gang Show at Ty Coch. He complimented me on my ability as an impressionist (glad to see the long nights as Dai and Yanto hadn't gone to waste) and suggested I take part. It's true – I was brilliant at characters, and it turned out I was the star of the show. The artistic director of the Swansea Little Theatre saw the gang show and offered me a part in his coming production of Sheridan's *The Rivals* alongside Sean Mathias – another actor who was also a fellow waiter at the Copper Grill. (Small world – Sean went to on to become a director at the National Theatre.)

An actor? This was news to me … but I had noticed the admiring glances from young ladies during the gang show so perhaps this was an avenue worth pursuing. I went along for the read-through and was immediately alerted to the ratio of married and unmarried women to men. I signed up.

Fantastic. Apart from this, it was all Dutch to me. These people called 'actors' busied themselves shouting things like 'darling' and 'the show must go on' and speaking in a sort of emotional morse code punctuated with kisses and hugs. If someone was having a bad day they had to be held, nurtured and coddled. Everyone was kind to me because I was 'part of the company'. In the world of industrial Wales, 'companies' produced things like frozen meats or paper clips. All this company seemed to produce were loud-voiced, melodramatic old queens.

On the opening night I was given a dressing room and I changed into my costume. I was playing the part of Acres and tried to remember my lines.

'Keith, darling, we're ready for you.'

'I was just, er, going for a cig.'

'No time, lovely.'

Sitting in the front row were a couple of women in their late twenties. One of them had her legs folded and I could see some way up her skirt. The thought of forgetting my lines in front of two such babes filled me with horror.

All of a sudden I saw the point of the theatre. Admiration, sexual power and congratulation was a heady mixture to a young lad. Soon I was throwing myself into the roles, all the while sleeping with my new fans wherever possible, marvelling at the effect that three yards of elevated stage had on my desirability.

I may have been dragged kicking and screaming onto the stage but at heart I was still a lad. Shakespeare and Sheridan couldn't compare with raw working-class holiday resorts with their booze, brawls and birds. Tenby, with its easy sex and commercial opportunities, still held an allure for me, and instead of revising for my A levels I decided to spend the summer working the mackerel boats.

Although I ignored the revising, I dutifully caught the train back to Swansea to sit my exams. My tutor looked surprised to see me.

'What are you doing here? The exams don't start till next week.'

'Why didn't you tell me?'

'We did. You'll have to stay here till then.'

But I didn't stay and I didn't return the next week. It seemed that lies could do just as well as a piece of paper. To me a lie was an exploration of this elusive thing called 'truth', and as you know I never thought about 'consequences', which helped me enormously in my pursuit of enjoyment. I returned to Alltwen at the end of the summer to pack my things. David leant in the door with a glass of wine.

'So what are you going to do now?'

'Dunno. Go back to Tenby, I suppose.'

'Don't be stupid. Get yourself a degree.'

'Ha! In what?'

'Drama. You can act, Keith. Use it. I've got contacts at the Welsh College in Cardiff. I'll fix it so you get an audition.'

Getting a grant, drinking beer and shagging girls seemed like an ideal occupation for a lazy cunt like myself. Exploring the theory of 'Living in the Truthfulness of the Moment' was merely a side show, and the thought of actually *becoming* an actor was a dot on my horizon. Not to my father, of course, whose reaction to my chosen career was like a tidal wave raging towards the shore.

'Stanis– who?'

'Stanislavski. He was an actor.'

'What you bloody talking about actors for?'

'I'm going to be one.'

'I don't know, son. I really don't. Why can't you just settle down?'

Prancing round on stage in tight pants was not what he had in mind for me. It wasn't a proper job.

The college sent me audition pieces to learn and in a turret high up in Cardiff Castle it was time for me to stand and be counted. On this occasion it was on a coffee table. The drama tutor, Raymond Edwards, paced the room. The castle was his eyrie. I'd like to say he was a proud eagle, but he wasn't. He looked like an overstuffed owl as he waved his arms in the direction of his coffee table.

'Get up, get up.'

'What?'

'Get on the table. I want you to pretend you're lost in a very rough sea, clinging to life, surrounded by sea serpents.'

'Why?'

'It's called *improvisation* …'

I sighed, scratching my head in embarrassment. The only improvising I wanted to do was of a man who wanted to run as far away as possible from his current situation.

'Now get up there.'

My 'lost at sea' routine was more like a rendition of the Hokey Cokey. Mind you, a couple of Jaffa cakes over the eyes and the odd 'woo woo' would probably impress a man who saw sea serpents round his coffee table. I fucked off back to Tenby thinking that was the last time the turrets of Cardiff castle would be party to my acting skills.

To my amazement they offered me a place to start immediately in what was the inaugural year of the new college building, 1974. (Suffice to say they were trawling with a very fine net in those days – taking anyone who expressed an interest.)

I equated acting with lifestyle, not career prospects. I'd never met people before who really wanted to be actors. Anyway, they were all overblown poofs as far as I was concerned. The third-years treated us like shit, so I decided to try and get as many up on them as possible. (This included covering their snack Welsh cakes in pepper before their big performance. It worked – they sneezed all the way through.)

A couple of them were OK: Sheila and her boyfriend Pete Garvey. Pete was effeminate, tall and ginger-haired, and was into David Bowie (I didn't make the connection yet). Sheila was massive with big tits and full lips. She didn't want to be an actor but a drama teacher. They were earthy and worthy and from the north-east.

Our college was affiliated with UIST, the University of Science and Technology, whose campus was just across the road, and unlike us poofy thesps they had a bar. Thus my home for the next eighteen months became the UIST union drinking hole, where I was quickly accepted into the first eleven football team, joined the card school and met Anna, my first proper girlfriend.

*

'Meet me outside at eight o'clock.' I stared at her as though my life depended on it.

She looked at me and laughed. 'I don't think that's a very good idea.'

'Of course it's not a good idea.'

We'd never spoken before but we understood each other perfectly. Hopelessly in love would have been the understatement of the year. A few moments earlier Anna Bootle, all lips, tits and hair, had kissed her boyfriend as I watched from the other side of the bar. Then he went to the toilet. I drained my pint and went over. My whole body shook. I was drained by fear but also by my destiny. She had to be mine.

'OK then,' she replied hastily as her boyfriend approached and I exited myself.

I whisked her to a jazz club with no intention of giving her back.

'Can I buy you a drink?'

'Yeah, OK. I'll have a pint.'

A pint drinker? This was a new one on me. The other girls drank halves of lager because it was more ladylike. Anna didn't have to worry about whether she was ladylike or not. She just was.

Within a week we were holed up in her student house being kept awake by the anguished wailing of the jilted ex. One night the bedroom door opened and he stood looking at us, a knife pressed against the skin of his wrist.

'I'm going to do it, Anna. If you don't leave him, I'll do it.'

I laughed out loud. There was more chance of him doing his own laundry than taking his own life, a fact I was quick to point out.

'Turn the knife over the other way, you idiot. It's sharper.'

Nightclub, Cardiff. Dark. Sweaty students. Music. Lights. Noise. Booze.

'Keep a lookout, call down if anyone comes ...'

I crept down the stairs to the lower bar, which was closed, with a view to purloining some free drinks – even though I was a student with a grant and prospects! Toby, one of the UIST card school, nodded. It was bravado and sheer stupidity that led me to do it. The drinks, I didn't think was stealing, just a bit of below decks horseplay – the open till with the evening's float … well … As I got my hands in the till, two bouncers appeared. Toby had fucked off to the toilet.

There was no point in running – there was nowhere to run. One of them stayed with me while the other went to fetch the manager. I knew that the manager would want to call the police and that with my record I'd be looking at going back inside. This was inconceivable. My heart nearly burst out of my jacket. I really didn't want to get into trouble again. The bouncer who stayed with me was a nice old geezer.

'What d'you do it for, eh, son? You're a student, got a future ahead of you, eh?'

I appealed to his good nature 'Let me go, mate.'

'Sorry, son. I can't. I'd lose my job, see.'

So I smashed a stool over his head. Why, you ask? Panic, sheer panic at what a fucking stupid and perilous situation I'd placed myself in for no good reason. I just wanted to get away. As he lay on the floor clutching his head, the other bouncer returned, this time with three colleagues. Now one thing you never did was hit a bouncer, because the other bouncers would have no qualms in kicking the merry shit out of you. And so it was.

I was dragged out the back and seriously fucked over. My head and face were covered in blood and my guts were smashed in. Then they left me there. All I could think of was that I wasn't going to be arrested. The relief was massive. I felt guilty about hitting the nice one, but it had all worked out OK. Apart from the fact that in the process of being kicked in the gut I'd shit myself. As I got up and wandered down the alley to the front of the club, I neither knew this nor how badly beaten I was. My only intention, instead of running away, was to remonstrate with the bouncers for beating me up.

'Oi' – I banged on the front door of the club – 'come out, you fuckers.'

The people in the queue turned away after noticing I'd crapped myself and that my face looked like I'd done ten rounds with Ali. Even the bouncers, after coming out and having a look, escorted me away from the club and advised me to go home.

After passing out fully clothed on Toby's bed (poor Toby), I woke to find myself being undressed by two students with clothes pegs on their noses. My eyes were so swollen they looked like cheeks with two lines across. I had to hide out for two weeks.

On my return to college I bowled into improvisation class. The first thing I wanted was a pint. The last thing I wanted was to 'live in the truthfulness of the moment'.

The teacher clapped her hands. 'Today I want you all to imagine six squares on the floor. Right there in front of you. I want you to move from one square to the next, taking on the emotion of that square …'

The squares were Loneliness, Anxiety, Concern, Sadness, Shame and Happiness.

Sadly my improvisation was solely focused on the 'happiness square' – the square mile of Cardiff city centre that included the Quebec pub, the football field and the union bar.

Anna and I teamed up with Peter Garvey and his girlfriend Sheila to rent a three-bedroom semi-detached house in a suburb. It had a garden and we lived like proper grown-ups. My parents would have been proud of me, living the bourgeois dream.

Anna got a job as a waitress in an Italian restaurant. Jealousy is a dreadful thing but my love for her was so obsessive that she is the only woman I've ever been faithful to. The problem was whether she was faithful to me. At the restaurant she started meeting a rich businessman. She denied anything was going on but I knew that Pete and Sheila were covering for her. She always got a lift home but wouldn't say who from.

One night I challenged Pete. He refused to tell so I waited at the window until I saw a brown Rolls-Royce stop at the bottom of the hill. I stormed out of the house and down the hill. Pete followed and tried to stop me so I threw him over the garden fence. He landed with a howl. In my mind he deserved it for keeping something from me. Anna got out of the Roller, which was driven by some older man. She smiled back at him. It was all the proof I needed.

'What the FUCK do you think you're doing?'

They stared over at me.

'What the hell are *you* doing?' said Anna.

'What the hell do you think I'm doing? Catching you at it.'

'I'm not "at" anything. Mr Stevens is just a friend.'

'Oh yeah. Well Mr Stevens can take his Roller and fuck off.'

My keys flashed along the paintwork of the car, leaving a long gash. I gripped Anna firmly and pulled her towards the house, listening to Mr Stevens ranting. She swore there was nothing going on, but I was convinced that the owners of the restaurant had been encouraging the relationship and covering for her by lying to me.

'There's nothing going on. He's an interesting man, that's all.'

'*Interesting*? Ha! You mean rich.'

Next day we discovered that Pete had seriously damaged his knee when I'd thrown him. He had just decided he wanted to be a professional dancer as well. That put paid to it. (Later he did go on to dance but was told by the Ballet Rambert that his knee was too weak for him to go all the way.)

Whether I liked to admit it or not, there was a trail of destruction in my wake. When Keith Allen blew into town, more often than not something else blew out. On this occasion it was Peter's cartilage.

In the holidays Anna took me home to her house to meet her family. She lived in an old vicarage in the countryside outside Liverpool. Her father, Stan, was a professional computer geek and part-time folk song writer who wrote 'Oh You Are A Mucky Kid' which was sung by Cilla Black. They were middle-class and bohemian. The house was full of music and noise and leather sandals. Everyone had holes in their jumpers despite the size of the house. These people were not poor. They had fashionable bread and expensive cutlery. And their surname was not really Bootle. In line with their middle-class penchant for siding with the proletariat, they changed it to match a rundown area of Liverpool. Still, their house was a fantastic place. Anna's three sisters were all artists and they adopted me and treated me as part of the family. It was the kind of rowdy family upbringing I'd yearned for.

Then I took her to my house. Convinced we were going to be together for life, I introduced her to my parents. We stayed there for the summer and got work at the local frozen-food factory in Gorseinon. My job was to slice chicken on a bandsaw while Anna worked in the office. It was here that she struck up another 'friendship', with the owner of Chucky's Frozen Chicken. She told me that she was working late and instead she went out for dinner with him.

'I'm not sure about her, son.'

Eddie paced the kitchen while I waited for her to return from 'working late'.

'Carrying on like this. She's after something.'

I shot him a look and went to bed. She claimed it was totally innocent and told me off for being jealous. Hmmmmm.

Chapter 14

1976. VICTORIA PALACE Theatre, London. *Singalongamax* with Max Bygraves.

La la la la … My cock dangled this way and that as I ran round the stage in front of a gobsmacked Max Bygraves. The line of go-go dancers dressed as wartime WRAFs high-kicked furiously, all desperately trying to carry on as normal. The audience were rolling in the aisles, clearly thinking my impromptu streak was the funniest thing they'd seen all night … Max stormed off stage.

Oh shit. At the age of twenty-two, my career appeared to have ended before it had started.

A few months earlier, after being suspended from the Royal Welsh College for parking my car in the drama tutor's parking bay and then removing the tyres so I couldn't be moved, I had decided that I was misunderstood and maligned, and I should take my talents along to the Royal Shakespeare Company where they would be better appreciated.

So off to Stratford we went, me and Pete Garvey. Needless to say, I didn't hear anything back from them. So, ready to be a mature, wage-earning adult, I headed for London. Anna was going to come with me but at the last minute decided to opt for another year and do a degree course. Looking back, I think she'd met someone else, but I was not prepared to entertain such a thought at the time. So we embarked upon that mythical entity, 'the long-distance relationship'.

The suburban hinterland of Charlton and Brockley was my destination after one of the students gave me an address of a mate there.

Except someone forgot to tell me that Charlton and Brockley are about as far from 'London' as fucking Cardiff is. (I might as well have commuted from Wales. I'm sure that it would have been faster than the number 9 stopping service from Brockley via Orpington to Victoria.)

To sub my student grant, I'd worked at the Cardiff New Theatre doing 'get-ins' and 'get-outs' for the various shows. All the blokes in the Charlton flat worked as stagehands and lighting techs and one of them introduced me to Nigel, who did the lighting board at the Victoria Palace Theatre.

Nigel had the typical pallor of a theatre technician, wore a lot of black, had lank greasy hair and smoked deathly strong skunk weed. He pulled on a joint; I watched him hopefully.

'Any jobs going?'

'Nope.'

'Come on, man … you must need something doing. I'm starving … look at me.' I pulled in my stomach and sucked in my cheeks. He looked implacable. But inside something must have given.

'I suppose I could do with some help setting lights.'

He introduced me to Harpo: 'Stick with him, he'll teach you what to do.' Harpo was a tall thin lad from Battersea, who had yet to ruin himself with heroin – he became my mate and partner in crime.*

So it was that I started on the *Singalongamax* show with Max Bygraves, as a lighting assistant and stagehand. I had to move out of the Charlton flat because I couldn't afford to pay rent, so Nigel offered me his sofa. Obviously we had long days to fill before the show, which suited me very well. I discovered this thing called 'cricket', which went very well with this other thing called 'lying in the park'.

It was the summer of 1976 and blisteringly hot, which was fine by me. I found a radio in Nigel's flat and, having loved radio ever since listening to *The Goon Show* in Malta, it became my passion once again. Lying on your back in a suburban park with a little portable radio, the world seemed an uncomplicated place. Everything good was free. The gentle

---

* He died of a drug overdose a couple of years ago.

thud of leather on willow followed by hearty clapping as England drove straight leg for another boundary.

Test cricket is like chess, so many things to take into account. Like becoming an adult, from the outside it looks pretty simple. (Bat and ball and runs, the most runs wins.) But then you discover the rules, and on top of the rules are the tactics, and then – just when you've got it all taped – the fucking weather comes along and takes it all out of your hands, like fate does with life.

I pondered this conundrum, thanking God that I was very much from the 'fuck it live for today' school of existentialism, as a woman jogged by and stopped to do some sit-ups. She was wearing a headband and some of those new aerobic tights and a leotard thing that went straight up her bum. Every so often she'd bend over specifically to show me her arse. The radio crackled away with another England boundary. I clapped along.

'Oh bravo, boys, bravo.'

Miss Aerobics looked over and laughed. I turned over to lie on my front since my rasper was growing. It was now burrowing its way through the earth's surface. Could life be so easy as simply making people laugh?

Through my long hours of unemployment and my new attachment to the portable, I discovered Capital Radio. The Breakfast Show was hosted by a bloke called Chris Tarrant. It fascinated me how one geezer could unite the whole of London. Arrested by his charms, I decided that I would become 'a Londoner'.

'You can't bum around all summer lying in the park and chatting up strange women.'

Nigel was eating spaghetti from the tin, pissed off because the myriad of buses he used to get himself home had all failed to arrive and he'd had to walk most of the way, only to find me flat out on his sofa, exhausted from a long afternoon's sunbathing.

'Change the channel, will you, Nige. I can't move, it's my back, it's playing up again.'

Nigel's jaw dropped, exasperated. The least I could have done was to budge over and let him sit down. Better still, make him a cuppa.

'And you need to find yourself somewhere to live. I want my sofa back.'

My tendency to get bored easily meant it wasn't long before the evenings in the wings ate away at my brain. One of the regular drag acts in the show was Hope and Keen. Their act consisted of Hope dressed as the air vice marshall inspecting a chorus line of showgirls dressed as WRAFs, except that one of the showgirls was in fact Keen in drag. Ha ha. Between the matinee and the evening show the crew would go to watch a free concert in Hyde Park, drinking beer and smoking spliff to nullify the effects of Max Bygraves. Then we'd retire to the Stage Door, which was opposite the stage door of Vic Palace, to have another few pints before the show. One night, an old geezer came up to us, looking lost.

'Know where I can find Max Bygraves?' he said hopefully. 'I'm just up for the night to see his show. Wanted to say hello to him, see. Used to work with him, see.'

Turned out this old geezer had been the foreman on a building site where Max had worked. They were old friends.

'Yeah, mate, he usually walks past here on his way to the show in the evenings,' I said and took him outside. Max had a penthouse in Westminster and strolled round to the theatre each night about half an hour before curtain up. When Max appeared, the old geezer rushed over the road to say hello. We watched the touching scene. Well, it could have been. In fact, Max didn't even seem to recognise him let alone break stride. The old geezer was devastated. Goes without saying that the words 'What a cunt' resounded backstage.

It was at that moment that I decided I'd ruin his show. I waited till the show started, then stood in the wings and removed my clothes. In the lighting box Nigel was busy trying to stay awake on top of several spliffs. When the cue caller was safely on the other side of the stage, I saw that my cock had a serious case of stage fright and had hidden its usual abundant mass. I hastily massaged it to restore some semblance of normality. The cue caller noticed and stared at me aghast.

There was no going back now ... as soon as the chorus line started to sing, I dashed onto the stage and joined the girls in the line, high-kicking with the best of them.

The girl at the end of the line looked sideways at me and my nakedness as if this was a new part of the act she hadn't been told about. I winked at her.

Pandemonium reigned backstage as the stage manager and cue caller tried to coax me off but I evaded capture and danced a jig, tackle flying, in front of a fuming Max Bygraves, his usual serial-killer smile, bouffant hair and frilly shirt all oddly ruffled.

In the lighting box Nigel was laughing so much he missed all the usual lighting cues and the drummer in the music pit fell off his stool. The audience, full of day-trippers, appreciated the spontaneity. Safe to say Max didn't.

He retired to his dressing room and I didn't see him again. It was the front-of-house manager who threw me and my clothes out of the stage door (me first, my clothes later) with the words: 'Max said you'll never work in the theatre again.'

My act had belittled everything he stood for. I had taken the piss out of the holy grail – 'Good Ol'-Fashioned Entertainment'. Entertainment that was good and wholesome and came from the best place in the heart. This was worse than stealing or being unfaithful. It was the most ungracious of sins, especially as it came from within 'the family'.

The next morning the *Sunday Mirror* had it on page four under the title 'Streak A Long A Max'. At home in Wales, apparently, my brother Kevin proudly showed it to Dad, who gave him the customary clip round the ear. Well – I wasn't there, was I?

Now that I'd lost my job and my low-rent opportunity on Nigel's sofa, my need for accommodation became urgent. I decided to search for a solution to this problem at the bar of the Stage Door. Just so happened that Harpo, still employed at the Palace, nipped over for a quick one.

'Look like you've taken root there, mate ...' He tittered.

'Ha ha, yes, very good ...'

I nodded at the barmaid to bring another pint. She was getting on a bit but still sexy in a timeworn way.

'Listen. An opportunity has come my way. I've found a squat.'

'Great. Where?'

'115 Eaton Square.'

Her arms were a bit flabby but her tits were good enough.

'Keith. Did you hear me?'

'Eaton Square my arse.'

If I did the barmaid it would probably save me paying my tab. Unlike the time of my encounter with Half-a-Crown Rose, I was now *very* familiar with the word prostitute, usually applied to myself.

'I'm not messing about. It's Bernie Cornfield's gaff in Belgravia. You know, the geezer that's been done for fraud.'

I started to take notice. 'Bernie Cornfield is on the run ...'

'Exactly. The gaff's completely empty. One of the stagehands has broken in.'

Harpo had pumped this stagehand for information about his new squat and he'd told all, and Harpo passed it along to me. That's how things worked in the world of theatre crew. Most of us were actors and artists in waiting and always on the lookout for free accommodation.

Without further ado, me and Harpo went round there to case the joint. Harpo disappeared round the back and for a while nothing happened until the front door opened and he stood there grinning at me.

'Welcome to your new palace, sir.'

We wandered from room to room open-mouthed. The ballroom alone was bigger than every house I'd ever lived in put together.

'You reckon we'll get away with it?'

'Course we will. Squatters' rights, innit? We'll have the party to end all parties. We'll open a nightclub in the basement.'

I initiated a fast bowl down the middle of the ballroom, taking out the middle stump of the ornate fireplace.

Word spread like lightning and soon we had a house full of stagehands and lighting technicians. Even Nigel moved in. The other residents of Eaton Square did their damnedest to have us evicted but Bernie Cornfield wasn't about to bust his cover by turning up and serving us notice.

How *not* to impress your girlfriend:

a) Take her on a romantic holiday that involves work (grape picking).

b) Substitute the luxury hotel with a rubbish tip near Béziers.

c) Adopt a stinky donkey and invite it to dine with you.
d) Begin to enjoy living on a rubbish tip and washing up in the local public toilets.

Well, a lad can try to save a relationship, can't he? Anna came up from Cardiff and we decided to go on holiday. We didn't have any money, so grape picking in France seemed the perfect answer. A romantic vision of Anna in floaty skirts smiling in a comely fashion, grapes in one hand and basket on hip, was rudely interrupted by one big problem. We arrived in the South of France just as the last grapes had been crushed.

We plotted up in Béziers and rolled out our sleeping bags on the beach.

'Keith, maybe we should go home …'

'Not yet. I'm going to find us somewhere to live.'

Anne curled up in her bag and stared at the sunset. No way were we going back. I had a fantasy of how the trip was going to be and therefore it *would* happen.

On my way to the public toilets I came upon a rubbish tip and an idea sprang to mind. Here were all the raw materials needed to make a house. I got to work and made walls out of breeze blocks and finished it off with plastic sheeting.

Anna appeared, curious as to what had kept me away so long.

'Ta da … what do you think?'

She smiled. 'I think you're a genius.'

We lived on the rubbish tip for a week. Anna collected all the old tin cans and washed them out in the public toilet that doubled as our bathroom. We made a proper fire and used the tins as cooking pots. Food consisted of the old vegetables the market traders threw away at the end of each day. We even had pets. A donkey and a tame magpie, who ate supper with us. The four of us made an odd family, but a happy one.

At the end of the sixth day of lazing around and sunbathing on the beach by our palace, Anne jogged me awake.

'Don't you think we should try and get a job?'

'I thought you loved living on the rubbish tip.'

'Yeah er, it's just, well, is this it?'

I sulked for a bit and she packed our stuff. (Which I had to carry.) We tried farm after farm, but no one was hiring. After walking about ten miles, we stopped in a place called San Antonio. Anna cried.

'I want to go home.'

'OK, let's go home.'

I went into a shop and bought a tin of pâté. It was all we were going to have for some time. As we sat in the square and tucked in, a scruffy-looking man came over and stared at us.

'You two, what are you doing?' His gravelly voice was gruff rather than inquisitive.

'Trying to get a job.'

'Hah. Je m'appelle Monsieur Limon. Come wiz me.'

Not knowing what to expect, we dutifully climbed in the back of his Citroën 2CV. He took us half an hour down a farm track and into a field full of grapevines bursting with fruit. He stopped the van in front of a rundown cottage under a huge fig tree. It was the most beautiful house I'd ever seen.

'You two live 'ere, you pick grapes, I pay you.'

The cottage had two rooms: a bedroom complete with mosquito nets, and a living room with a massive sink. (For Anna to do the washing and the cooking.) The farmer took out a wad of notes and stuffed some in my hand as an advance on our wages. For the next three weeks we lived an idyllic life and at one point, overcome by the romance of it, we decided to get married.

'Oi! Monsieur Limon.'

He stuck his head out of the window. We were standing outside his house, pissed on cheap red wine.

'Est-ce que possible pour vous de marier us?' (My pidgin French struggled hopelessly before refusing to fly.)

'Je ne comprends pas. Go away, it is past le minuit.' With that the window slammed shut.

Well … it was just an idea. When the work ran out we made our way home, without ever being married. The romance bubble popped as soon as we saw the low terraces of Dover in the rain, and the nail was firmly in the coffin of our relationship. It had been so all-consuming at one point that I think it consumed itself. Anna went back to Cardiff to complete her last term and I went back to Eaton Square, now full of new faces. Some of the boys were scene painters at the ICA and got me some casual work there, whitewashing walls and mounting exhibitions.

'How to Use Printing as a Means of Communication.' Me, a scene painter, and Bob and Ken, house printers at the ICA, sipped our pints at the Two Chairmen pub in St James's as we pondered this dilemma. It was the night before the opening of a landmark new show at the ICA, featuring work from Man Ray, Ernst and Penrose, the cutting edge of the Surrealist art movement, and it was the brainchild of ICA arts programmer Norman Rosenthal.

We sipped some more of our pints – the battle lines were drawn. On one side there was me, Bob, Ken and Ted Little, the artistic director, who all belonged to the school of 'low-concept' art – art that belonged to the people, i.e., anything could be art, and art could be made out of rubbish.

On the other side was Norman Rosenthal, who believed in high-concept art and disagreed with his artistic director, Little, on the direction of the ICA. This exhibition was Norman's big moment. His pièce de résistance.

Bob and Ken had taken me under their wing. They were in their late twenties and both had doctorates in genetics and biology (unlike me) and ran a silk-screen printing business to boot. Bob was married and lived in Camberwell; Ken was unmarried and lived under his printing press in the ICA.

I already loved the atmosphere of the ICA. It was a whole new world to me and was to formulate my already working-class left-wing sense of injustice into proper political beliefs. It also educated me in modern art, cutting-edge performance and music to boot. It was 1976 and I was growing up ... or was I?

Hmm. I sipped some more of my pint. It was around eight in the evening; we were about to put in an all-nighter, whitewashing the walls in preparation for the exhibition the next day. We'd been in the pub for an hour and were well on the way to being trashed. The conversation had got round to Bob and Ken postulating about their silk-screen printing business, which they saw as ground-breaking art. It was – they were to pioneer poster printing for the punk bands of the late seventies and saw poster art as a way of communicating political ideas direct to a mass market.

We all tried to think of a new way to use printing as a form of communication. I drained my pint and got up to go back to the ICA and get started. Bob and Ken had another pint. An hour or so later Ken burst into the exhibition hall, where I was painting away halfway up a wall. Bob had gone home to Camberwell.

'I've got it,' said Ken. He set about daubing on my freshly painted white walls.

I stepped back to look. He certainly had come up with a new way to use printing as a form of communication.

A couple of bottles of Thunderbird wine later and the job was done – we stood back and admired the handiwork before waiting for Norman to arrive. In the morning, Coldstream Guards were seen falling off their horses on the Mall as a result of the screams coming from within the ICA. Norman had walked in to be confronted by six-foot-tall black letters on his white walls spelling: NORMAN ROSENTHAL IS A CUNT.

Ken managed to stop Norman going to the police and admitted, with some glee, that it was him. Norman insisted Ken *and* Bob be sacked, so Bob arrived at work to find out he'd lost his job.

While the two dismissed men went to the pub, I worked hard with another member of staff at covering up the damage. Four coats of white emulsion later and I thought we were off the hook. At 7pm Ken and Bob returned from the Two Chairmen pissed, just as the great and the good started arriving to see the exhibition. I grabbed a glass of champagne from the passing waiter and supped away, spitting it out almost immediately as I watched the words 'NORMAN ROSENTHAL IS A CUNT' slowly becoming visible, seeping through the white paint on top. I was no expert but I felt this was far more surreal than anything Penrose and Man Ray could offer. Particularly because Lady Penrose, who was keen on a glass or two, thought it was hilarious, and she and I sat on the stair together and laughed.

As Ken and Bob continued to drink and enjoy the evening, Norman became increasingly apoplectic, finally disappearing into the office in the bowels of the building, followed by Ken and Bob, and me. Here Bob landed a punch on Norman's nose, sending blood splattering over the wall.*

The following day, Ken and Bob were arrested for assault. After apologising to Norman, I got let off the hook.

'You're on your last warning,' he said.**

Ted Little brought in a bloke called Mike Laye to run the theatre. Mike was a politico from Birmingham University who was heavily into revolutionary politics and a member of this thing called the Workers Revolutionary Party. Mike had a massive wart on his head. Some people cringe at the sound of nails on a blackboard; I used to cringe watching Mike comb his hair in case he sliced off his wart. He wore a cord jacket with a multi-coloured scarf, and rode a motorbike with a small sidecar attached, in which to cart about his bag of contradictions. (Although a card-carrying member of the WRP, he used to love 'indoctrinating' posh white middle-class girls back at his flat.)

Through Mike I started to become politicised as opposed to simply police-hating. Mike let the WRP come into the ICA and sell the *News Line*, in the vain hope that the middle-class fops who hung around smoking Gauloise would join their attempt to free the masses. (But even from a distance I could see there was more chance of the fops starting a revolution if they didn't get chocolate on the top of their cappuccinos.)

Taking my lead from the ICA's 'Art as a Representation of Self', I decided to give it a try. I brought in my dirty laundry and pinned it up on a clothes line across the foyer. Mike Laye watched with interest.

'Keith, why are you pegging your pants and socks out in the ICA?'

'*You* might see pants and socks, but I see it as an expression of the working man's struggle.'

Visitors stared curiously at the stains on my hanging garments and

---

* The stain is still there, protected by Perspex and labelled 'This is Norman Rosenthal's blood'.

** Years later I saw Norman at the Royal Academy and we laughed about the incident. I think that both Time and his time fumbling in men's pants with a bag of bum spanners had softened his attitude.

pondered what it all meant. What it *meant* was being too bone idle to go to the launderette.

In 1977 Mike offered me the job as theatre stage manager. I'd gone from casual labourer to position of power and influence (or that's how I saw it). He was into politically orientated theatre and instituted a policy that touring fringe companies from all over the country could bring their shows to the ICA and therefore get a West End billing. The shows changed every week, plus a special Saturday lunchtime show and cabaret. He also gave space to new punk bands like The Clash and The Nips. Mike was connected to the music industry through his ex-girlfriend, an actress called Diana Patrick, who was going out with the then manager of The Clash. It was at this time that I first met Joe Strummer. After their gig we said hello and nodded at each other. He was a face on the scene and I wasn't, but I knew this musical movement was the place to be.

In the space of a couple of years I saw some fantastic theatre, from *The House of Usher* to Genesis P-Orridge. I became friends with a gay theatre troupe called The Gay Sweatshop; in fact, the first play I saw there was a lunchtime piece they put on called *Mr X*. The fact that the ICA also had a bar made it a very dangerous place to work, a giant private 'arts club' with people getting pissed all the time.

After a performance of The Gay Sweatshop's, Pete, my mate from the Royal Welsh College, turned up in the bar with some friends, an oddly shifty couple.

'Keith, this is Colin and Sarah. They've got, er, a pet lion and they need somewhere, er, large to stay for a couple of days.'

'Just till we can get transport to take him to France. We've got work for 'im there.' Colin wiped his nose on the back of his hand and Lisa smiled and shrugged her shoulders as if indicating a fait accompli.

'Any chance of them staying at Eaton Square, Keith? Clyde's very tame.'

'Clyde? What type of name is that for a lion?'

'Wait till you see him. It really suits him,' Sarah added helpfully.

'Er, well … OK then. Bring him round later.'

Clyde arrived at Eaton Square in the back of a white van. We put him in the ballroom and shut the door. He was a huge motherfucker. Sarah and Colin buggered off to bed. They were obviously a couple of chancers who didn't know anything about lions but thought they could make some money out of him. Peter and I listened to him pad about, sniffing under the door.

'Excuse my ignorance, Pete, but Colin and Sarah don't look much like lion-tamers to me.'

'Don't worry.' Peter buttered some bread and ate it. 'He's a pussy really.'

'A fucking big one.'

The next morning Colin woke me up at 6am. 'Keith, I've got to get Clyde some food.'

'What does Clyde eat then? Apart from children.'

'Raw chicken mainly.'

I drove him to Smithfield meat market and we stocked up on chickens. Colin taught me how to throw them to Clyde without getting your hand bitten off. He was, as they said, a bit of a pussy and I began to enjoy having a lion for a pet.

After two days Colin and Sarah had a row and Sarah left. Then Colin left me a note saying he had something to sort out and would be back in a few days. Suddenly I was alone with Clyde and no back-up. It seemed cruel leaving him locked up in the ballroom, so for exercise we'd have games of football. I went to Smithfield and bought about thirty chickens and filled the fridge with them.

'I think I'll take him for a walk.'

'You what?' Peter nearly choked on his sausage sarnie.

'Why not? He seems tame enough.'

We found a length of chain in the garden and fastened it round Clyde's neck. Holding tight with one hand, I walked him out into Eaton Square. Not really thinking about the effect it might have on passers-by (who mainly screamed and ran away), I ambled into the communal garden, found a bench and sat down. Ten minutes later the police arrived and set up a cordon about three hundred metres away. None of them dared come near.

'Is that your lion, sir?'

'What, you mean this lion?'

'That's right, sir.'

'Well, it fucking looks like it, doesn't it, officer?'

Lord Boothby, a friend of the Kray twins and a notorious old screamer, emerged from his house to see what all the fuss was about. He was overjoyed to see such a sight and joined me for a wander round the garden.

'Marvellous, wonderful sight, very exotic, dear chap ... you know, I once knew a lion-tamer, Russian chap, *very* muscular.'

A more bizarre sight there never was, police everywhere while Lord Boothby and I strolled carelessly round the square. After much debate the police took down the cordon and fucked off. Concerned they may have been, but not enough to have a lion in the back of their van.

Clyde liked watching television, particularly *Sale of the Century* with Nicholas Parsons. The two of us would lie next to each other and try to guess the prizes. My party trick was to stick my thumb in his mouth and he would suck it like a baby.

A day or so later a journalist and photographer turned up.

'We'd like to do a piece on you and your, er, pet.'

And so there appeared a photograph of me and Clyde on the steps of 115 Eaton Square in the *Evening Standard*. The headline read: 'King of the Squatters'. Greatly amused, I sent the article home to Kevin, who proudly showed it to my father. This was an error. Another clip round the ear for Kevin. The only times he ever got a clip from my dad was because of me.

'You think it's funny? Your brother's dragging this family's name through the mud and all you can do is laugh.'

Relations between me and my father were at an all-time low, but that was no guarantee that they wouldn't get lower.

Call it the devil in me but I decided that Clyde should come with me to work and make the acquaintance of The Gay Sweatshop. We had a communal van at the squat and Clyde fitted snugly in the back. There was an official permit-holder's parking bay right outside the door of the ICA, so I parked up and shipped Clyde out.

Once in the theatre Clyde padded about, exploring his new space. I climbed into the lighting box to wait for The Gay Sweatshop to arrive.

Ten minutes later Gordon, the leader of The Gay Sweatshop, arrived. He stood stock still and stared before setting his coffee down and making kissy noises to Clyde.

'Oooh ah saaaay. You're a big boy, aarn't yeee?'

I swear I saw fear on Clyde's face as Gordon knelt down to stroke him lovingly before calmly calling out, 'Mike? There appears tae be a lion in the theatre.'

I was quite shocked that a lion in the ICA didn't cause more of a stir, but I suppose it was just another day on the frontline of cutting-edge culture. My party trick over, I loaded Clyde back into the van. It was a lesbian Gay Sweatshop show that day and the girls arrived just in time to admire my pussy. One of them came up to me.

'So you like cats then?'

'Yeah, I suppose I do.'

'Well, my girlfriend's got some kittens to give away. You want one?'

'Yeah all right.'

As I drove up the Mall towards Buckingham Palace, Clyde started to growl. The growl became a roar and he lashed out. In one movement I was out, leaving the van with Clyde in it to trundle up a kerb and come to a stop in a group of Japanese tourists, who screamed and scattered. The Mall was the most heavily guarded road in the country so it was only a matter of time before the police arrived to arrest me and take Clyde to the zoo. Except they didn't turn up. After a while Clyde calmed down and I examined the van, looking for what made him flip.

Turned out the air vent was open. Poor Clyde had been getting an eyeful of air. Anyone who has a dog or a cat will know how much animals hate it when you blow in their eyes. With Clyde safely back in the ballroom, I went back to work to collect my altogether more teensy pet, a kitten I named Tea Cake.

Dad had a saying: 'Tell you what, son, you'll be laughing tea cakes after this.' I didn't know what it meant, and I'd never bothered to ask, but I felt it was a fittingly surreal name for a cat. I introduced Tea Cake to Clyde by opening the door of the ballroom just a bit and dangling him invitingly round the corner. Thinking this was dessert, Clyde roared over and Tea Cake's four legs stuck out sideways. The little cat hissed and mewed with his hair on end like a cartoon creature. Poor Tea Cake never fully recovered from the trauma. He probably suffered some kind of nervous breakdown, thinking he was supposed to be Clyde when he grew up.

Colin reappeared and took Clyde to the South of France. The next thing I heard was that he was starring in a commercial for British Airways.

In between stints at the ICA, my income was supplemented by film-extra work, which was an endless opportunity to buy knocked-off goods. All the other extras were small-time crooks for whom breaks in filming were a car boot sale for light-fingered East-enders.

'Yeah, I was in that *Lawrence of Arabia* flick, third soldier from the left. What about a lovely clock for yer old mum?'

'Do me a favour.'

My nonchalant routine always got the price down.

'All right then, what about a floral duvet cover?'

'Stop it.'

'All right, Keef. Look, I've got two hundred Bensons, yours for the price of a little horse, know what I mean.'

'No.'

'Pony, mate. Yours for a pony.'

One of the films I did was *The Slipper and the Rose* starring Richard Chamberlain, in which I played a ballroom dancer. Walking down Tottenham Court Road a few months later with a couple of friends, I nearly choked on my kebab.

'What is it, Keith?'

My hand pointed to a movie poster advertising *The Slipper and the Rose*. There, behind darling Richard Chamberlain, was yours truly.

'It's ME! I've made it! I'm on the poster!'

Nigel and Adam peered closely at the poster.

'Where?'

'Behind Richard Chamberlain's hair, you can see half my face.'

Adam and Nigel tutted and walked on, leaving me in paroxysms of joy. Surely now the big time beckoned?

No such luck. The next week I was back at Pinewood underneath six tons of chainmail playing one of the English invading army busily burning Joan of Arc at the stake. Sweat was pouring off me. For want of a more elegant phrase, I stank.

Glenda Jackson was being Sarah Bernhardt being the Joan being burnt. (Got it?) As she writhed atop a flaming pile, Glenda nearly fainted at the stench of me. Afterwards, politely covering her nose with a hanky, she kindly said, 'Did you know that if you are made to stand within twelve feet of a naked flame on set you are entitled to more money?'

With that I was straight into the personnel office demanding my cut.

The extra work was shit boring but good money, and the ICA was vice versa. I needed a new direction.

Chapter 15

THE NEW DIRECTION I took was in the form of a pretty artist named Mavis Taylor.

She was a set designer with The Gay Sweatshop at the ICA, and we also saw each other at Bob and Ken's studio, which they'd now set up at Butler's Wharf. I asked her out for a drink and she ordered a pint. She held it in paint-stained hands and drank it fast, her Nana Mouskouri-style long black hair hanging like curtains down to her multi-coloured scarf and velvet jacket.

'Don't you ever wear skirts?' I asked hopefully, noticing that she was wearing jeans again. She'd worn jeans every day when she came to work, painting the set for the play.

She shook her head. 'Why should I?'

Mavis was an enigma. She interested me; like other artists there was a hint of madness there. As well as designing sets for The Gay Sweatshop at the ICA, Mavis worked a lot with another designer called Bill Drummond. I'd seen her around the ICA but never got to know her. I stared into her eyes. Staring is my speciality. There's a way to look at a woman, long and direct, most effective in penetrating her inner psyche (which if I'm not mistaken is where the vagina is to be found).

'Because it would make it easier for me to fuck you.'

We drained our pints and rushed back to her place. She lived above the Nat West bank in King's Road. After frantic undressing (her fucking jeans), I got inside her.

'Don't move,' she ordered. I froze, thinking something was wrong. 'Just be still. I want to explore the stillness.'

We lay there, exploring the stillness, which was a new one on me. My understanding of sex was a cross between a bouncing bean and two puppies fighting in a sack. In fact, we explored the stillness to such an extent that Mavis nodded off. But it did work, the stillness. I think she saw me as an exercise; she wanted me to realise my potential, which as far as I could see meant painting her sets and moving her furniture.

Mike Laye was involved in the evolution of Rock Against Racism and put on late-night cabaret shows with the bands that were at the forefront of the new political rock movement, like Shane McGowan of The Nips, and The Clash. He also continued to indoctrinate me, and under his guidance I joined the WRP. I moved into a flat with Mike in Colville Terrace, West London.

It was a great time. I felt right in the thick of it. Portobello Road was *the* place to be. Not just for left-wing politicos like us, it also was a multi-cultural melting pot, ska and reggae spilt out of windows next to punk, and white Cockney market traders next to afros and hippy beads.

The flat – which was Mike's; I was his tenant – was straight out of the movie *Performance*. It was all peeling walls and damp. My bedroom was at the back and featured a bed on top of some scaffolding, which I erected. As usual I didn't have any possessions to speak of. I hadn't got round to accumulating anything. Mike, however, was busy making the place home, and among the things he was amassing were huge stacks of *News Line*, the official paper of the workers, who used it as insulation against the shouts of public schoolboys banging at their door to call them to arms. The only call to arms the working-class man was interested in was the call of the armchair during *Match of the Day*.

The WRP membership consisted of middle-class blokes rebelling against Daddy. It was Daddy's fault that they had nice houses and pet ponies when all they'd ever wanted was to be commies and live in draughty council flats. I don't think so. I loved the way these blokes blamed their fathers for turning them into twats. (You'd never catch me doing that.)

Norman Rosenthal brought in a new creative director, Paul Taylor. He disagreed with the left-wing slant of the ICA, and particularly with Mike. The two rowed and naturally I sided with my landlord. Paul responded by sacking us both.

Part of living with Mike meant observing his posh-tottie patter at first hand. It went something like this.

'You see, darling, it's not your fault. You've been born into the system. It's the system that needs to be crushed.'

'Oh ya ya. Sounds absolutely *fascinating*. Where's the bathroom? I simply must pee.'

Mike joined me on the sofa and stared at the TV while 'Ophelia' relieved herself.

'Why do you only sleep with posh girls if you've sworn an oath against the middle classes?'

'Ah well, you see … if you want to change people's opinions you've got to start from the inside.'

I pulled on the end of a butt, nagged at by my newly agitated social conscience. 'Yeah but I didn't think you meant *literally*.'

On top of his penchant for posh tottie, Mike's contradictions extended to supporting the emergence of a black underclass, his entire darkroom furnished with stolen camera equipment bought from the Jamaican kids in Powis Square. He burst in one day with a new camera, hastily loading film and fitting a special lens.

'Keith! It's started.'

He was standing in front of the television just as *Coronation Street* came on.

'I know it has, and you're fucking standing in front of it.'

'Not the bloody soap, Keith, the revolution.'

The patriotism of the Silver Jubilee in 1977 was matched by a similarly fervent bout of violent unpatriotism against it. It was a time of social disturbance in West London, where the Notting Hill riot took place, and inspired the lyrics for the Clash song, 'White Riot'. It was around this time that I started to drink in the Warwick Castle, a pub also frequented by Joe Strummer, and we shared the occasional joke or fag.

The Notting Hill Carnival came right round Powis Square and we would hang out of the flat windows, drinking cheap red wine and smoking, as the sound of steel drums and the smell of freshly cooked curried goat and Jamaican patties floated upwards. On the last day of the carnival, large groups of youths gathered on street corners round Portobello Road, the air heavy with pent-up aggression.

'There's gonna be a riot outside this very door,' said Mike.

Mike turned the channel over to the news and, sure enough, it was beaming back pictures of clashes between the police and youths that were taking place not two hundred and fifty yards from my sofa.

'Wow, great.' I settled down to watch.

Mike kicked me. 'Get out there! Do your bit. Rage against the capitalist filth.'

'No.'

'You haven't moved for about a week. Look at that sofa, you've fossilised it.'

'Oh all right then.' I sat up. 'It's just one social revolution after another with you, Mike, it really is.'

Sighing loudly, I dragged my arse out into the fray and was confronted by the sight of a hundred youths standing on the corner of All Saints Road and Westbourne Grove. Someone threw a bottle at the police and it all kicked off. All at once the malaise left me and I was in the thick of it. The coppers didn't have riot shields but had to make do with dustbin lids while missiles rained down on them. Then a shout went up: 'Let's do the fucking Co-op.'

Now, my nan swore by the Co-op, which existed to give people some kind of premium. She used to send me down there to get her dividends and stamps. I felt guilty about taking the revolution to the shelves of reasonably priced tinned peas and cheap bacon. (Who said revolution helped the oppressed?) Nevertheless I was in there with the best of them and helped an old black lady fill her trolley.

'Could you pass me da Coco Pops please, young man,' she said calmly, looking at her shopping list. 'And de Shredded Wheat. Don'tcha forget dat.'

On the way out, ignoring the tinned peaches, I made straight for the tobacco counter and loaded my shirt with Golden Virginia. After dumping my loot back in the flat, I went back for more.

The riot was now in full flow and a hot-dog and ice-cream trolley had gone over, spilling lumps of ice all over the road. I picked one up and hurled it at a huddle of four policemen, who promptly charged me, knocked me to the floor and stood on me while they waited for a van to arrive. I was bundled in the back and made to lie down in the aisle where they stood on me some more.

The van stopped at some lights and a black woman stuck her head in the window, clearly in distress.

'Please help me … I can't find me daughter.'

The policemen smiled sadistically at her. 'Well, you should keep the little nigger off the street then,' said one of them.

This was standard for the police. They were brutalised cunts and everybody in the country hated them. They were the centre and focus of all protest. I spent a night in a cell at Paddington Green. Listening to the tramps singing amid the piss-drenched holding cells, I was a happy man. I'd done my bit.

In the morning they had me up in front of the magistrates and served a fifty quid fine for being a naughty chap and lobbing ice at the fuzz.

Back at home the geezer from the flat above was sharing riot stories with Mike. His name was Colin Bennett;* he had swept-back hair and a ponytail. From the side he looked like he was straight out of a country and western festival and from the front he looked like a librarian. Like Mike, he was another bag of contradictions, but I'd much rather be talking to him about science fiction than Mike about class struggle. Colin was obsessed with inanimate objects, like German tank metal. Where Mike saw political struggle, Colin would see the supernatural at work. Where Mike would see a workforce being laid off, Colin would hear the anguished cries of Gaia.

So I got home from my night in a cell at Paddington Green to find Mike and Colin hard at it, arguing the class war. Funny that the only one

---

* Colin is now a playwright who writes about UFOs and has a massive knowledge of the drugs/arms axis.

at the sharp end of this war was Keith Allen, who after spending a night in the cells for 'the cause' was roundly ignored at the expense of another hour of useless extemporising. I didn't even get a cup of fucking tea. The phone rang just in time to stop me killing them.

It was Paul Bassett Davis. What was interesting about Paul was you wouldn't notice him in a crowd. Physically he was utterly unremarkable in every way. Mentally, he was a very interesting man.

'Fancy doing some performing, Keith?'

'Not half. Where?'

'Bristol.'

Without further ado I packed a bag and went. Paul had a performance theatre company called the Crystal Theatre of the Saint and we'd met when he brought a show to the ICA. I'd really liked their stuff – brilliantly obscure performance art whose mantra was 'Ideas are Animals'. Their performance pieces spanned the range from conventional to bizarre.

I got to their performance space in Bristol, the Crystal Warehouse, a replica of the Flatiron Building in New York, and Paul told me I could kip in the office for the time being. All I could think about was that I was going to be part of the Crystal Theatre in a show that would, if it was good enough, get on at the ICA.

Paul was doing this show about a very bad comedian/ventriloquist who would tell jokes and then descend into madness and his dummy would come to life. This dummy was to be played by a tiny skinny midget but they had no one to play the ventriloquist. So, if I could come up with a script, the part was mine.

'You want the job, Keith?'

Paul Bassett Davis looked up from what he was reading in the office of the Crystal Warehouse. I was messing about with two little ruffians who were trying to get a football off me with little success. I pushed the littlest one over. He was only about eleven and he kicked my shin.

''koff, mister.'

'Oi! Watch your mouth.'

His mate put the V sign up and ran off before I could get him. They were always hanging around the theatre playing up.* My attention turned back to Paul, who had been expecting a response. It was a habit of mine to put off answering a question until I had time to think it through, which made people think I was either rude or deaf.

'No problem.'

'You have to write a comedy routine.'

'No problem.'

It was a fucking problem. I was shitting myself. I'd never done a comedy routine before. So I did the only thing I knew how. I cheated. I bought four joke books from WH Smith and took the worst ones and worked them into a routine. The show was called Radio Beelzebub and the idea was to start with standard jokes and make them increasingly surreal, at which point the ventriloquist's dummy would be replaced by the dwarf and come to life.

The show went well and it did transfer to the ICA, but not with me in it – with some other actor who'd been promised the role if it transferred. Nothing more came of it but I had gained a lot of confidence. The freedom that the 'bad comedian' role had given me was immense, and I enjoyed playing with the 'descent into madness' bit and making up my own surreal jokes.

Now, before I go on, there is a collection of three stories from this time that I need to tell:

1) Milkveg Arts Festival in Amsterdam.
2) Fake Vicar.
3) Jubilee Clips.

First, they're all true. They may seem to you like the actions of a silly cunt who wastes every opportunity he gets. Not so. Or yes, maybe. But the reason is this. About this time my brother Kevin showed up at Colville Terrace and informed me he was enrolling in drama college. He wanted to be an actor. Soon he was hanging round with me and my friends. Not to put too fine a point on it, at the time I was living in ignorance of my

---

* Their names were Nellee Hooper and Dom Thrupp, and they came to London a few years later to make their fortune in the music industry.

family. And here was my brother, a constant reminder of everything I was trying to get away from.

Whatever I was doing, I was doing it on my own. Therefore I spent some time away, on my own, becoming even more extreme and destructive in what I did to make fucking sure he didn't or couldn't copy me. I didn't want anything or anybody slowing me down. Please bear that in mind when you read the following stories.

1: Milkveg Arts Festival

I wanted to stay involved in the Crystal Theatre and I asked Paul for a job. Each year Crystal took a show to the Milkveg Arts Festival at the Milkveg Centre in Amsterdam, and Paul got me a job running drama workshops at the festival. Two months' rent free in Amsterdam sounded genius and I packed with great excitement before realising that there was a problem: no passport.

'Paul, it's Keith. Listen. I can't find my passport.'

'What do you mean?'

'I mean I haven't got one.'

'Well, get down to the sodding Post Office and get a temporary one. You've got to be there tomorrow to start teaching.'

'I know, I know. Don't worry, I won't let you down.'

'You better not.'

In my infinite wisdom, for my temporary passport I used a picture of me pulling a face, which my mate who worked in the Post Office duly stamped.

The ferry arrived in Rotterdam and I handed over my passport to the customs officer. First he looked at the photograph, and when he looked back at me I was pulling the same face with one eye bulging and tongue poking out the side of my mouth. Expressionless, he motioned for me to stand to one side, where he handed the passport to his equally expressionless boss.

'You think this is funny?'

They stood over me. A third now perused my passport under a forgery machine.

'Well, yes, as a matter of fact I do.'

'We don't think this is so funny.'

No one had told me that humour didn't travel the distance between Harwich and the Hook of Holland. They put me in a holding cell and let me phone Paul, who was already in Amsterdam.

'Listen, er, there's been a problem.'

He sighed down the phone.

'They, er, don't believe I am who I say I am. I need you to phone Llanelli and get a copy of my birth certificate faxed over.'

Twelve hours of nightmare organisation later, Paul and I had all the necessary paperwork to prove my identity. The chief customs officer came in – the kind of Dutchman who spent a century terrorising the Africans.

'We are sending you home now.'

'But why? Look, you've got my birth certificate and everything you need.'

'Yes but this is about breaking the law. You must pay the price.'

They put me in a cell on the ferry back and handed me over to the English customs in Harwich, who, having a healthy disregard for their opposite number, looked on me sympathetically.

'What did they nick you for then?'

'Pulling a stupid face.'

'That all? Wankers. Don't worry, son. We'll have one of theirs.'

They went off to look for a suitable victim to send back to Holland. Suddenly I was overcome with guilt that some little backpacker was at that moment being deported because of me.

2: Fake Vicar

I needed to hitch to Bristol to do the onstage intro for some friends in a gig. So I bought a grey suit in a charity shop for fifty pence and made myself a dog collar. I also bought a Teasmade and an old suitcase. The Teasmade and extension cord went in the old suitcase and I went in the suit. The final piece of my outfit was a tin with a slit in the top and a piece of paper stuck on which read: 'Church Roof Repair Fund – Please

Give Generously'. Next to it I drew a thermometer with only the very bottom bit coloured in.

After I'd stood for about ten minutes at the side of the road, a white van pulled over.

'Jump in, Father.'

'Thank you so very much.'

Eric, an electrical engineer, was glad to take me as far as Swindon. I gazed peacefully out of the window, revelling in the awkward silence as guilt seeped out of his beer gut.

'I'm, er, you know, not much of a churchgoer.'

'Oh not to worry, the Lord smiles on everyone.'

'I didn't know they had vicars so young.'

'Yes, well, it's a myth that the Church is old and stuffy. Us Presbyterian ministers are very modern.'

'Really? Presbyterian, are you?'

'Oh yes. Tell me, what football team do you support?'

'Swindon, as it happens, Father.'

'What a bag of shite they are.'

Eric looked at me in shock before I replied matter-of-factly, 'Oh yes, we all swear, us churchmen. That's another, ahem, myth about the Church.'

Eric pulled over and signalled that it was his turn-off. I shook the tin at him and he put his hand in his pocket and reluctantly pulled out two quid.

'The Lord thanks you, Eric.'

No sooner had he disappeared than a Morris 1000 pulled over. This vicar shit really worked.

'Where are you going, Father?'

'Oh, wherever the Lord's work takes me. Er, Bristol town centre, actually.'

A rather straight-looking bloke ushered me into the back of the car and his mousy wife smiled deferentially.

'We're going to visit our daughter in hospital. She's paraplegic,' he said.

I buried the tin deep in my suit. 'I'm so sorry. What are the chances of her recovery?'

'There aren't any. She's paraplegic.'

'I wish there was something I could say to make it better for you both.'

The woman, silent up to now, turned round to look at me, this queer unshaven vicar in a wonky dog collar with a battered suitcase.

'Er, you could say a prayer for her, Father.'

'Of course, why don't you pull over and we'll pray together?'

There in a layby, squashed in the back of a Morris 1000, hands clasped together, we prayed.

'What would you like to ask the Lord?'

'Well, actually, we could do with a bungalow since my daughter can't use the stairs.'

They stared at me earnestly.

'Dear Lord, please be gracious and provide this couple with a bungalow for …'

The mother prompted me. 'Janine. Her name's Janine.'

Two more lifts and a bagful more lies later I arrived in Bristol and headed for the university. At the lodge a grim-faced porter stared at me.

'Ahem, could you tell me where the gig is on tonight? You see, I've come from a parish outside Bristol and want to spread the word among the younger folk.'

'Of course, Father.'

The porter turned and shouted at an equally grim-faced colleague. 'Tommy! Take the father to the union bar, will you?'

It was five o'clock and the bar was starting to fill up with the first sportsmen finishing their rugby and football games and ready to start a bender. There was plenty of time to kill before the gig. The barman looked at me with interest.

'Can I get you something?'

'Oh no, no, nothing alcoholic anyway. I'm here to, er, collect for the church fund.'

'Oh really? Well, give the tin over here and I'll pass it round the lads.' He was clearly in with all the sporty types, and went over to a group of thickset rugby lads. 'The vicar here is collecting. Put your hands in your pockets, lads.'

I sensed trouble. The barman was too worldly-wise for my liking.

'Come on, let me get you a drink, Father.'

'Well, just half a Guinness then.'

The bar filled and the Guinness started to have an effect. A young woman at the bar looked aghast as I belched and downed another half.

'Now, young lady, when do you think the Lord will give up on you? Will it be this term or next term?'

She ran away so I went up to another group of girls. 'Don't be afraid … have you got a boyfriend? Do your parents know you're sleeping with him?'

'Er, no.'

'Don't worry, the Lord will forgive you. Would you like to buy some dope?'

They looked at each other in astonishment. 'Did he just ask us if we wanted any dope?'

I took the suitcase and opened it to reveal the Teasmade.

The barman watched suspiciously. 'What's that, Father?'

'Oh this is holy water from Lourdes. If you just plug in this extension for me, I'm going to make some holy tea.'

'Holy tea.'

'Yeah, fifty pence a cup. A small price to pay for salvation.'

I stood in the middle of the student union flogging holy tea for fifty pence.

'Come on, don't be scared, it won't kill you. In fact, it will save you. Make you virgins again.'

Mr Avuncular eyed me mercilessly from behind the bar. 'Are you sure you wouldn't like another drink, "Father"?'

'Oh go on then. I'll have a double whisky and a pint of Guinness.'

He poured my whisky and slammed it down, palm open to receive money.

'That'll be a quid, please.'

Sighing loudly, I pulled out a tin opener and proceeded to open the Church Roof Repair fund. I poured the money out onto the bar.

'Take it out of that and use the rest to buy everyone a drink.'

With that I picked up my pint and made off to watch the gig. Some may see this act as deception, others as entertainment. I suppose this will depend on whether or not one has a large rod stuck up one's arse.

3: Jubilee Clips

Me and Paul Bassett Davis took the train to Brighton. When we got there we went to a thrift store in The Lanes, where I bought a leather attaché case and fastened a small Union Jack flag into the lid. Then we went to the ironmonger's.

'You want what?'

'All of your jubilee clips, please.'

A jubilee clip, as it is known in the plumbing trade, is a round chrome ring that comes in various sizes and is used to fasten pipes to walls or to each other. The housewife or gardener knows it as that little ring you put round the end of a hose to secure it to your tap. Each clip comes with the word 'Jubilee' on it, and since it was the year of our esteemed Queen's Jubilee, we thought we'd have some fun.

On the seafront I set up my stall, opening my case to display the jubilee clips. The place was a mass of foreign tourists, in particular German and Dutch. With a smile and a wink to the girls, I warmed up.

'Come on, ladies, get your lovely jubbly Jubilee jewellery here, lovely silver Jubilee clips. I've got small ones, I've got big ones … I've got rings and necklaces. Just put 'em on a piece of string and you've got a lovely necklace …'

The girls stopped and looked at the clips curiously, at which point I'd take out a screwdriver and adjust them to fit their fingers.

'Come on, girls, only ten pound for a necklace.'

As the crowds swelled, the other stallholders got suspicious and tried to warn the tourists. 'Don't listen to him, he's a spiv, tryin' to do you …'

At that moment Paul came up in his corduroy shorts and rucksack, pretending to be a Dutchman.

'Vat iz zees? Jubilee clips, yah? How much?' He winked and I took his lead.

'Only a fiver for a ring, sir, special for the Jubilee. Look, it says "Jubilee" on it.'

'Oh, yah, I vill have two of zeez lovely clips.'

Encouraged by his willingness to buy, several Swiss girls opened their purses. As Paul handed me a pile of Dutch guilders, an irate stallholder intervened.

'Listen, mate, it's a con. These are Jubilee clips, not souvenirs. From an ironmonger's.'

'Yah, Jubilee clips, yah? What iz ze ironmonger's? Is it another English king?'

'No, mate. It's a shop where you buy Jubilee clips.'

'Yah, zis good thing, yah? I give you all my money, you take it all.'

We moved along the beach away from the other sellers and set up the same routine again. Not only was it a laugh, we also sold all the Jubilee clips.

Christmas 1977 was a strange time for me. Everyone had gone home to their families and London was empty. Only in Chinatown was there a semblance of bustling normality, the eager Asians trying to make as much money as they could out of the sad fuckers like me with nowhere to go. My family would be all together in Wales, probably with Nan. It was too late for me to join them. We'd drifted so far apart that the Severn Bridge would have struggled to reunite us.

A wizened old waiter bore down on me, his eyes a continuation of his smile.

'You wan ordah?'

'I think I better had, otherwise I'll be pissed as a cunt.'

The menu was a mass of little houses so I ignored it.

'Mixed meat, fried noodles, please.'

As I ate, bits of noodle fell onto the pages of my book, staining it with blobs of monosodium glutamate. There was nowhere to go so I ordered more sake and read on. At 6am on Christmas morning the waiter came back.

'Solly, mista, you have to go, we crosing.'

Still wide awake, I decided to walk through Hyde Park and then through Notting Hill to see Colin Bennett, the only other sad fucker I knew who wouldn't be celebrating, due to the fact that he was Jewish.

He opened his door and Tea Cake rushed out to greet me, rubbing herself on my leg.

'Happy Christmas, Col. Got any pork sausages?'

Naturally, he didn't. From behind my back I produced a packet of Wall's bangers. 'Good job I have, then. Let me in. It's sausage sandwiches for Christmas lunch.'

I fried the sausages and wafted the pan in the direction of the lounge. I wanted to break him. To me religion was a manifestation of insecurity, a pathetic attempt to engender community spirit. Why not be nice to each other because we want to instead of because we're told to? Eventually the combined aroma of melted butter and fried pork fat did for him. Penniless writers are easy prey for conversion and he bit voraciously into the bread.

'Jesus Christ, this is heaven.'

'See … I told you that you'd accept Christ in the end.'

Chapter 16

AT THE BEGINNING of 1978 Mike wanted me out of Colville Terrace so he could rent it to someone who could afford to call himself a tenant. Moving from sofa to sofa wasn't good for Tea Cake, who was possibly still traumatised over the encounter with Clyde, and since she had spent the majority of her time upstairs in the company of Colin Bennett and his cat Copernicus, it was decided that she should stay there.

When it was time to say goodbye, she came and sat on my head, staring out of the window at a bird pecking at a squashed Jamaican patty.

Faster than we could shout, 'No, Tea Cake, no! Don't do it!' she was out the window and flying through the air. We ran down to scoop her up, expecting to find her dead, but she was very much alive, mewing wildly with her back leg sticking out sideways. She remained this way for the rest of her life.

Bob and Ken offered me a job screen printing for them at their studio in Butler's Wharf. Through the ICA and Mike Laye they had come into contact with Miles Copeland, who managed all the cool new rock bands like The Police, Squeeze and Generation X. Now that Miles had commissioned Bob and Ken to do all the posters for his bands, they were getting so much work they needed someone to print while they designed. I jumped at the chance. It was an exciting time to be at Butler's Wharf, which was turning into a bohemian community. Artists such as Andrew Logan had a studio there.

All Bob and Ken's work was done by hand on old-fashioned silk-screen machines and they had built all the printing tables themselves. My father would have been proud of their 'no waste' ethos. For counter-weights, for example, they'd used nuts and bolts.

I set up home under the printing table at Butler's Wharf. It was a measly place, furnished only with a sleeping bag and a stack of left-wing magazines. As you know, I didn't really care about material possessions. As long there was a packet of Marlboro Red close to hand, I could survive almost anywhere.

However, the industrial no-man's-land around London Bridge opened up a wealth of opportunity for establishing a new squat. The regeneration of the area hadn't started, and the Docklands was still dying, which meant there were many abandoned buildings. In nearby Gainsford Street was a row of three early Victorian workers' houses. The rest of the street had been bombed out during the war. Over three floors there were four or five bedrooms, an upstairs parlour, a small kitchen and an outside loo. This became home to seven bohemian squatters. Again it was the stagehands and set painters who moved in, all men; there was always someone coming or going.

Funnily enough I was happiest in the kitchen, which had a little fireplace, cooking breakfast for everyone. (I love the feel of a houseful of people, and have always sought that out.) Bob and Ken came to visit me in my new place and we sat down to my speciality – the humble fry-up. People think the fry-up is easy, but it's an art form. Beans on first, then the bacon, then the mushrooms and lastly the eggs. Then, of course, the jewel in the crown: the bubble. Bob popped a portion into his mouth.

'Tell you what, Keith, you cook a mean bubble.'

'The best,' said Ken.

'You should start a café.'

Ken nodded vigorously, spitting a molecule of egg into my eye.

'And call it Keith's Lovely Bubbly Café.'

The word spread among all their artist mates at Butler's Wharf and soon people were dropping in daily for my Great British Bubble and Squeak. At the back, in a disused factory, I found all the furniture I needed to turn the first-floor parlour into a café. I broke into the factory and emptied it of a canteen of formica tables, even a display cabinet for fancies. I took it very seriously, fetching the redtops from the newsagent every day and filling the display cabinet with Twix and Dundee cake. It was all going very well until Susan, my long-lost sister, decided to drop in out of the blue.

'All right, little brother.'

The serving spatula in my hand fell into the pan and pierced the egg that one of my customers had been careful to tell me not to break. Susan was probably the last person in the world I expected to walk into my squat. There was more chance of my father dropping in. The last time I'd seen her was in Singapore or somewhere else in my childhood.

'What the fuck are you doing here?'

She looked older, a bit messy; she was with another woman in a short skirt. They were both wearing too much make-up. Susan looked at me, as if regretting everything, then smiled and squeezed my cheek.

'That's a nice way to greet your sister. You got a fag?'

Turned out she was working in some club or other up the West End. The mate, whose name was Dawn (she certainly looked like she'd seen it come up a few too many times), was a little more forthcoming.

'I'm a stripper,' she said. 'We've come to London to seek our fortune.'

The way she said this was supposed to be a joke. It certainly was.

'Give us a fag then, Keith.'

Susan stretched out her arm to reach the cigarette and her shirtsleeve rode up, revealing a tattoo that read 'All Coppers are Bastards'. Ah, what had happened to Susan to turn her from a Shirley Temple lookalike who got the Best in Class award into this woman with tattoos? Well, she didn't say anything, but I knew enough about prison life to recognise her tattoos as the ones you gave yourself inside.

'So, nice place you've got here …'

I could see she was in a spot. She must have been to come and find me after all this time.

'You can, er, stay if you like. For a bit.'

'What? Here? Me? No, don't be silly. You don't want me here.'

She was right, I didn't.

'I'm not being silly. You can have a room. I'll kick Tony out. His feet stink anyway.'

'Cheers, Keith.'

She looked genuinely pleased. I didn't ask too many questions. There was desperation in her laughter, in the way she smoked, in the way she looked. Also her wardrobe didn't sit pretty in the 'boho' artist crowd and ICA theatre tech crowd. Her cheap perfume and miniskirts made it hit home how much of a stranger she was. If I hadn't known her I'd have run a mile. I was relieved when I woke one afternoon to find all the washing-up done and a note that said, 'See you in another five years. Susan, X', along with ten quid and ten Bensons by way of payment.

Why I like swearing:

1) It sounds good. 'Fuck it, you cunt ...'
2) It's in the Oxford English Dictionary.
3) It makes you feel better if you're depressed and directionless.

'Fuck, fuck and fucking cunt again.'

I kicked the printing machine, which had started playing up halfway through a Sex Pistols poster run. It was a bad day. My mood did occasionally get dark. When this happened it was my wont to hide away and not show anybody. When the mist descended, it wasn't me who jumped up and said, 'I'm depressed.'

While all it took was one broken egg yolk to send the middle classes running for the comfort of the psychotherapist's couch, being depressed is not the kind of thing that the working-class man admits to. Much as I enjoyed Keith's Café and silk-screen printing, I was after proper money and knew that cooking breakfast for redundant artists was not going to cut the mustard.

As I attempted to kick the machine back into action, there was no denying that I was down. There was a bigger place for me in the world and my instincts told me that happiness lay in the public gaze. Since arriving in London acting had been something of a sideshow to my desire to LIVE, but now was the time to put it centre stage.

'All right, Keith?'

Colin Bennett popped his head round the door of the print workshop.

'Fancy auditioning for my new play?'

Not half, was the answer, of course. But this meant I had to do an audition. I was developing a pathological hatred of auditions. For me, performing in front of judge and jury was akin to ritual torture.

I struggled through the audition and waited, thinking that, really, there was no point. I'd done a shit audition – as usual. They called me back in and my worst fear was that I was going to have to read again. No, please – anything but that. I walked in and the director smiled and got up to shake my hand.

'Well done, Keith. You've got the part.'

I couldn't believe it. This was fantastic news. I was ecstatic! It was a big part, the lead role. I was finally in a play at the ICA. After all my posturing and messing about, there was actually a chance that, potentially, I had enough talent to make it big.

Rowan moaned with pleasure (well, I think it was pleasure) and rolled on her back. I busied myself with scrabbling back into my jeans. We were at her place, her place that she shared with Bill Nighy, both of whom were my co-stars in *All Along the Watchtower*.

Ahem. I wasn't sure, nor was Rowan, whether or not she and Bill had finished their relationship. But, well, she was up for it and so was I. She was pretty, sexy and unavailable. That made her even more attractive in my eyes.

'See you tomorrow.'

I kissed her and fled, not wanting to run into Bill on the stairs. He was pretty into his drink at the time and I didn't fancy a clout. The play went well. I can't remember a good deal about it apart from enjoying my time in the limelight so much that I got to shag Bill Nighy's girlfriend. I got a couple of good reviews, but when it ended it was back to screen printing and the same routine.

I sometimes stayed with Mavis, who lived in an ACME house in Bow. The ACME was a collective of flats specifically for artists, who lived above their studios. They had an art gallery in Covent Garden where Mavis exhibited her work.

It turned out that her bohemian community included a chapter of Hells Angels led by Pete the Murderer. They lived in a prefabricated estate between Bow and Commercial Road. Despite their appearance they were decent people who just liked a party every night.

'All right? Mavis in?'

Pete stood in the doorway, tall and wiry, sinewy muscles underneath the breasts of a mermaid who was swimming up his arm.

'Upstairs in her studio.'

Mavis certainly had eclectic contacts. Pete the Murderer, Bob Hoskins from *All Along the Watchtower* …

'Anyway, er …'

'It's Keith.' I smiled like a schoolboy, forgiving him for forgetting who I was.

I was already familiar with music festivals, but Reading 1978 was the first one I had a backstage pass for. I only ever went to festivals for the people, not for the bands. That is of course why I loved Glastonbury, which I was to go to again the following year, 1979, but more of that later. Of course, the punk movement sneered at Glastonbury then, which was a small hippy arts and folk festival, but they were missing the point completely.

Miles Copeland took me along to Reading as his plus one and it turned into a memorable weekend. Not one for 'posh drugs' like cocaine, I stuck to paint-stripper and beer. Miles took me aside.

'Listen, Keith. I've been meaning to talk to you about something.' Miles was staring intently at my empty pint glass.

'Don't tell me, you want to buy me a drink.'

We'd been there two days and he still hadn't got a round in. The big cheeses were always the same, last to put their hands in their pockets. One reason I was always skint is that my nasty habit was buying drinks for everyone.

'Nah. I'm being serious. I'm starting a new religion. Based on the thinking behind … dolphins. Well, I mean, they are more intelligent than us and peaceful.'

'Right … and what's this got to do with my pint?'

'Well, I'm looking for a leader, y'know, for the cult, and I thought of you.'

'Me.'

'Yeah, well, fuck all that crap about the meek inheriting the earth. We've got to take it by force.'

Miles's father had been head of the CIA in the Middle East and he went on to bore me with conspiracy theories about corrupt politicians.

'Religion is the only way forward,' he said, finally releasing a five-pound note from the vault that was his back pocket.

After more alcohol, including some 80 per cent proof firewater, everything became a blur, but I remember one thing. In need of a piss, I shinned up a flagpole, took my cock out and rained piss down below, accidentally spraying Cosmo Vinyl, the manager of The Clash. He picked up a bottle and was aiming it at me when an arm appeared, got him in a lock and carted him away. It was none other than Pete the Murderer, who was there doing security. I loved being friends with Pete the Murderer.

An insight into the Allen mind:

Wake up.

Smoke.

Scratch balls.

Go back to sleep for a bit.

Fuck Mavis (quickly).

Get up.

Go to work.

See Ken Campbell.

Think, ah, there's Ken Campbell, the director.

Knock some more nails into the set.

Go for a pint.

See Ken Campbell.

Think, ah, there's Ken Campbell, the director.

Buy Ken Campbell a pint.

Get pissed with Ken Campbell.

Set the world to rights.

Ask Ken Campbell for a part in his new play, *Illuminatus*.

Ken tells me to fuck off.

Go home.

Go to sleep.

Have a dream about walking onstage in a monk's outfit with a goat.

Wake up.

Scratch my balls.

Fuck Mavis (a bit).

Get up.

Fart.

Piss.

Smoke.

Go and steal a monk's outfit from the costume department.

Go and borrow a goat.

Wait for the curtain to go up.

Walk on in monk's outfit with a goat.

1978 was an exciting time. It saw the opening of the Cottesloe, the new stage at the National Theatre, and Bill Drummond, to whom Mavis had introduced me, had got me a job building the set for the first show on the new stage, Ken Campbell's *Illuminatus*. I'd met Ken a couple of times previously, drinking at the ICA when he did a show, and in the Haverstock Pub in Belsize Park, which he lived next door to.

After my walk-on-with-goat appearance in *Illuminatus*, I asked Ken what his next play was to be.

'A sci-fi opera called *The Case of Charles Dexter Ward*.'

'Oh, that sounds ... interesting. Can I have a part?'

'No.'

'Go on.'

'Oh all right then. You can play the waiter.'

'Great! Go on, give me some of his lines.'

'He hasn't got any.'

Mavis secured the job of designing the set for the new show, which was an experimental musical. Ken had found a young musician who had written the music and wanted to give her a chance. Trouble was, the penniless musician (I forget her name) had nowhere to rehearse. It just so happened that the Gainsford Street squat made a good rehearsal space, and so her piano was installed there. Her boyfriend and writing partner, who played the trumpet, came along to rehearse too. Therefore full English breakfast in Keith's Café would now be accompanied by the piano and the pah-pah-pah of trumpets.

This, along with the fact that Mavis and I were building the set for the play at her ACME pad, made me indispensable to the show, and so I kept on at Ken about the role of the waiter – and made sure my part in the play was nailed down for the tour.

We opened at the Matthew Street Theatre in Liverpool, but it wasn't until our first night at the ICA that I finally got to stamp my personality on the role of the (dumb) waiter. All that was required of me was to walk on, deliver some soup and leave, but what the audience got was an epic journey through the whole gamut of human emotions. It took about thirty seconds to get to the table due to the poor downtrodden waiter having a bad back. Once at the table I painstakingly set down the bowl, only to discover that I'd forgotten the spoon. My face took on the agony of a waiter who has failed in his one vocation – a masterstroke of improvisation. I indicated that I would return with the spoon with a series of facial expressions that Marcel Marceau himself would be proud of. My moment was rudely interrupted by Ken's booming voice.

'For fuck's sake, Keith, it's a bowl of soup not the fucking Holy Grail! Get off the fucking stage.'

Disinclined to submit to this pressure, I loaded up my tray and bowed to the audience, at which point the whole theatre went black. Ken had switched the lights off, plunging the stage into darkness.

'Now get the fuck off.'

The next day, Neil Cunningham – one of my fellow actors and a screaming gay – rushed in all of a flutter and shoved the paper in my face.

'They love you, darling! Look,' he gushed.

I read the review, carefully tore it out of the paper and put it in my pocket.

'Well? Say something.'

'I'm going to put it on a T-shirt and wear it in front of Ken every day.'

Neil's face fell. 'Do you think that's a good idea, Keith?'

'Yes, Neil, I think it's a fucking great idea.'

It wasn't, of course, but I did it anyway. I got the entire review, which started 'Keith Allen steals the show', printed on the front of a T-shirt and 'I am Keith Allen' emblazoned on the back. I took great pride in wearing it. Ken and the rest of the cast ignored me for a long time.

Christmas 1978 was spent with Mavis in a Mercedes van given to me by Ken Campbell, which acted as yet another temporary home. Parked in the Devil's Punch Bowl near Haslemere, we tucked into a festive lunch of mackerel.

1979 brought everything to a head with Mavis. She was bipolar, or manic depressive as we called it then. I didn't know how to tackle it. Mavis was a thinker from the deep end of the pool. Me, at that age I was firmly at the shallow end. I wanted to run a mile – sure I got depressed from time to time, but mainly when I wasn't working. I didn't wake up suicidal like Mavis did, even when everything was good. Once I did attempt to help her get things into perspective and took her for a drive.

'Let's go to Gosport for the day.'

'Why would I want to go to Gosport?'

'Well, you think you've got it so bad, come and see the shithole where I grew up. Boring flat soulless lifeless frigging Gosport.'

Mavis went quiet, as if considering what I'd said, then she opened the door and tried to jump out.

'Mavis! What the –'

'I don't want to go to Gosport.'

'OK, fine, just shut the fucking door, you mad woman.'

'I'm not mad. Don't call me mad.'

Her legs were already out of the door and the only thing I could get an anchor on was her hair. We travelled along in this way until I was able to pull over. Clearly things could not go on like this.

When we got back to London she went straight to bed. It was time to extricate myself in the best way for both of us. (Which meant packing my stuff and leaving before she woke up.)

I found room in the squat again. With no Mavis there was a need in my life for companionship – without the liberal dose of psychosis. A pet seemed the obvious answer. But what? Cat? Dog? Tortoise? Pig? Budgie?

Chapter 17

'BULLSEYE ... COME 'ERE, you 'orrible little dog ...' Bill Sykes drains his pitcher and throws it across the tavern at Bullseye. It misses, on purpose, but Bullseye, usually snarling with pent-up aggression, approaches his master whimpering like a puppy. Bill pets Bullseye drunkenly, a tear in his eye.

'You're my only friend, Bullseye ... you know that?'

Oh yes ... There was something *very* romantic about this image: man and dog living outside the law, trudging the streets of London, stopping only to eat and sleep, needing nothing but each other ...

It was with this in mind that I decided to get a dog. During our *Charles Dexter Ward* tour, Ken Campbell's dog, Verner (named after Wernher von Braun, rocket inventor), had had a litter of puppies. I offered to buy one for the price of a pint of Guinness.

So it was that Von Brown (named after his mother) became mine for the princely sum of 32 pence. He was a jet-black mongrel and he came everywhere with me; he knew our patch at Butler's Wharf like the back of his paw. In the morning at about nine I'd open the door of the studio and he'd fuck off for the day – out shagging. Then he'd come back at six for his tea. He had a beautiful black coat that I used to wash and shampoo regularly. If ever I wasn't at the studio he knew to come and find me at the Anchor Tap, my local.

One night at six he didn't come back, so Ken and I, already fairly stupefied in an unventilated workshop full of paint fumes and white spirit, headed for the Anchor Tap and got even more stupefied (remember that Butler's Wharf was ungentrified then and we drank with the old warehousemen). Later that night he still wasn't home, and in the morning when he didn't show up I went to look in all his usual haunts.

The thought that he'd been run over and was dead started to play on my mind, or worse that he was lying injured somewhere. He had a collar with his name on but no address (he didn't need any bitches following him home). I regretted that now as I trudged into Tooley St police station to see if anything had been reported.

It was now Saturday afternoon. Having got nowhere, I went back to the workshop and dejectedly climbed the stairs. At the very top, by my door, lay Von Brown, whimpering. His leg was broken and he had cuts all over. He must have been hit by a car and had lain somewhere for a while before crawling home and all the way up the stairs.

Me and Ken took him to the only place open, a Blue Cross hospital in Acton, and they put a cast on his leg. The bill came to fifty-seven quid. In 1979 that was a lot of money. Still, no doubt Bill would have done the same for Bullseye.

Everything in my life was temporary, except for Von Brown, who showed no more regard for fixed abodes than he did for lamp-posts. Then one day, early in 1979, I got a telephone call at Butler's Wharf.

It was somebody from the Glasgow Citizens' Theatre Company. Apparently, one of their directors, Giles Havergal, had seen me at the ICA in *All Along the Watchtower* and somehow through the ICA and Mike Laye had tracked me down. They were offering me the chance to audition in London for their new production of *Macbeth*. I was speaking to the delightful company secretary, called Lynne, who informed me that I would be required to audition for the company on Friday morning and would I prepare two pieces to read – one modern and one classic?

'Two pieces? Modern! Classic! Audition? The horror, the absolute horror!' I didn't say any of this, however. I thought it. 'Er, no, I can't,' I mumbled.

'What do you mean, you can't?'

In a nano-second I came up with: 'My grandmother's dead and I've got to go to her funeral. It's on Thursday.'

'Oh, Keith, I'm so sorry.' There was genuine concern in her voice. 'That's awful for you.'

'Yeah I know, we were very close.'

'Oh dear, I'm so sorry. You must be so upset.'

'Yeah … yeah, I know. I mean, I might be all right, I don't know …'

'Oh no. Look, if you think you should spend more time with your family then everybody here will understand that. It's just such a shame that it's the last day of auditions on Friday.'

'So you won't be doing any more then?'

'No, no. That's it finished on Friday lunchtime, then the recalls on the Monday.'

Hmmm, I'd dug myself a reasonably sized hole here.

'What I'll do, Keith – I'll put you down last to be seen on Friday. At least it'll give you time to get here if you feel up to it.'

I thanked her and put the phone down. It was Monday lunchtime.

Over the next couple of days I thought about what I'd done and why. I pretended to Ken and Bob and even to myself that I wasn't interested, that it wasn't for me – *fuck that*, etc. As Friday approached I convinced myself that although I didn't want the job it would be silly to miss the opportunity to exploit the situation – so I came up with a plan.

Thursday lunchtime. 'Hello, is that Lynne?'

'Yes.'

'Hi, my name is Paul D'arsay and I'm a journalist working for the *Sunday Mirror*.'

'How can I help you, Paul?'

I explained to Lynne that the *Mirror* were doing a big piece on acting, spread over four weeks, and each weekend we would be covering a different aspect of the profession. One of the areas we thought we should include was the audition process.

'Oh, that sounds really fascinating, but you realise that the auditions will be over by lunchtime tomorrow?'

I asked her what time they'd be finishing today. She replied, 'Five o'clock.'

'Well, do you think it would be possible for me to pop down at about four thirty and maybe meet with the directors so that I could explain what I'm after?'

'I'm sure that'll be fine. I'll tell them to expect you. Sorry, what was your name again?'

'Paul. Paul D'arsay – that's D-apostrophe-A-R-S-A-Y.'

'Oh, right.'

'Yeah, I know, most people think that it's spelt the French way, D-apostrophe-A-R-C-Y, but it isn't.'

'OK, Paul, I'll tell them to expect you at about four thirty.'

I put the phone down and paid a visit to the Dutch artist called Heine Bonger (it's true) in the opposite studio. It's a fact the Dutch have no dress sense.

Having raided Heine's wardrobe, I arrived at the King's Road Theatre at half past four sporting a brown riding jacket, blue denim shirt and a red neckerchief. I looked, for all the world, like the ambitious cub reporter I'd always wanted to be. I introduced myself to the only lady in the foyer. 'Hi, you must be Lynne. Paul, Paul D'Arsay.'

She told me that she had spoken to Giles and he'd agreed to meet me as soon as the auditions had ended for the day. Lynne offered me a cup of tea and biscuits and we chatted about the unusual spelling of my name. My theory was that if we talked about my name she wouldn't press me for a NUJ card, which I of course didn't possess.

As we waited for Giles to appear, it occurred to me that Lynne was pleased to have my company. She'd spent the last few days on her own out in the foyer – a lone breakwater around which a forever moving, bobbing tide of young boys came and went, time only for themselves and their immediate future in British Theatre.

Giles thought the piece for the *Mirror* was fascinating, really interesting, and *of course* I could come along tomorrow and interview the actors. He was sure they'd love to talk about themselves.

The next morning, I arrived early hoping to catch the directors on their way in. Lynne made me a lovely cup of tea and as we waited I suggested interviewing her. She didn't think she would be of any use, but she agreed. The night before I'd got Heine's wife, who understood these things, to fill up about thirty pages of a notebook with shorthand. Now we sat there, chatting away, me pretending to make the occasional note, sipping tea, getting on famously. I asked how many actors were being interviewed.

'There's supposed to be twelve but I don't think one of the actors is going to show up.'

'Oh really – why not?'

'His grandmother died and they were really close. He buried her yesterday and I think he's too upset to make it.'

'Will he get another chance?'

'No, he won't – but I've put him up last, so fingers crossed he'll get here.'

Giles sashayed in and asked why I had a copy of Shakespeare's plays and sonnets with me. We talked about the production, and with a bit of prompting he went on to describe exactly the kind of actor they were looking for. I asked him if they took into consideration the fact that some actors just weren't at their best in the audition environment. He said of course they did; they were looking for something deeper than just good audition technique.

'Would it be possible for me to sit in and watch the auditions?' I asked and, bless him, he replied: 'No, out of the question. It's hard enough as it is without anyone who isn't necessary being there.'

I said I thought it would be a good idea if, as well as interviewing the actors, maybe I could get up on stage at the end and read a sonnet, and write about that experience for my readers. Giles thought that was a terrific hoot. He then suggested I join him and the other directors for a spot of lunch after the auditions. This was getting better by the second.

The morning sailed past, blown by the combined pantings of expectant young actors explaining to Mr D'arsay what theatre meant, how terrifying the audition process was, how much they loved Shakespeare, etc. It was getting closer to midday and the final actor went in. I declined another cup of Lynne's delightful tea, but asked her if she'd heard anything from the missing actor, whose name I'd learnt was Keith Allen. Was there any chance he'd turn up?

'No, he hasn't phoned so I think that's it. Such a shame.'

At that point the foyer door opened and three actresses and an actor poured in, full of the joys of spring. They were present and past members of the Glasgow Citz. Unlike the auditioning actors, this lot were relaxed, open, and when they were told by Lynne that I was a journalist doing a huge piece on acting, they were very interested in me.

I pretended to interview them and even went so far as to suggest to the male actor that since we needed a picture for the piece, why didn't he allow us to photograph him at the Irish Club in Eaton Square the following Tuesday? I took his number.

The last actor came out and Lynne went in to tell the directors that Keith Allen hadn't been able to make it.

I followed her in, and walked slowly down the auditorium towards the stage. The directors Philip Prowse, Ian Macdonald and Giles were relaxing after a hard morning's work. Lynne was explaining the unfortunate circumstances regarding Keith Allen's non-appearance.

'Ah, Paul, has it been a good morning for you?' asked Giles.

I replied that it had been fascinating and that I had more than enough material. As we chatted I could see that Philip Prowse was fingering a pile of photographs. He kept looking up at me slightly suspiciously. Giles explained that he'd agreed to allow me on stage to read a sonnet and asked if the others would mind. Philip Prowse suddenly held up a photo and waved it at me. Before he could open his mouth, I said, 'Actually, the reason I wanted to get up on stage is because my name is Keith Allen. I am him.'

Silence. Huge silence. The sort of silence in which big decisions are made.

'I don't understand why,' Giles said slowly.

I began to explain my reasons. As I talked I was painfully aware of Lynne walking out. Her head was lowered, eyes down-turned. She walked very slowly.

I got on stage and read a sonnet of their choice. They must have seen something in me because they invited me back the following week for a recall. They told me to arrange a time with Lynne on the way out.

I walked out into the foyer. Another terrible silence. The actors all looked at me as I approached. Lynne now sat in the box office. Not a word was spoken.

'They told me to tell you that I've been recalled on Monday.'

'Fine.' She wrote down a time. 'If you could be here at 10.30am.'

'I'm, er, sorry ...'

She stopped writing, stepped out of the box office, and, as she passed me, but without looking in my direction, she asked: 'How's your grand-mother?'

I got the part. Until that moment it hadn't occurred to me that having duped these people into taking me on, I now had to work with them for three months.

I flew up to Glasgow with great trepidation. First off, I stopped in George Square to get some breakfast. I have to say I recognised the egg and the chips, but not the oblong block that purported to be a sausage. And the vinegar was white. This was a foreign land indeed.

I walked from there all the way to the theatre, which was on a council estate in the middle of the Gorbals. They found me digs in a lovely family house, a stone 'villa' of the kind inhabited by merchants in the time of the industrial boom. There I met my fellow actors: Kieran Hines, Danny Webb and a lot of the young turks who were the future of British Theatre.

I was playing Lady Macduff and the production was seen as cutting edge, no sets and no costumes, but all of us playing women had to wear a rehearsal skirt (I certainly hadn't trained for *this* at my Welsh school).

The fuck-ups came thick and fast. After a late-night game of poker with the other actors, things got a bit rowdy and drunken and I fell down a flight of stairs and broke my leg. It was too late to recast for my part so I continued to rehearse, but now wearing a cast from the knee down. As you can imagine, this was slightly problematic with my rehearsal skirt. Anyway, so it was that the limping Lady Macduff took the stage.

After being inspired by all the theatre I saw at the ICA, this experience in Glasgow did the opposite. Never a more appropriate phrase had been uttered than this.

Pretentious middle-class bollocks.

And, what was worse than having to be in the play was that we weren't allowed to leave the stage. So we had to watch the fucking thing as well. Because there was no set, the 'playing area' on the stage was marked by two white lines, so when you weren't in a scene, you had to leave the 'playing area' and sit at the other side of the white line. Usually, in the time-honoured tradition of acting, I'd have been straight next door for a half in between scenes, but instead, Lady Macduff spent her down time itching furiously. Not to get onstage, I assure you, but at her plaster cast with a knitting needle.

I was very lucky to get on stage at all. The second fuck-up was potentially catastrophic. During lunch I chatted with Giles, the director, while eating my cottage pie. (A more apt dish you couldn't have wished for since the Glasgow Citizens' Theatre Company was largely gay.)

'So, when do I get my Equity card, Giles?' I shovelled in another mouthful.

Giles's fork hovered just in front of his now quivering lips. Peas fell onto his plate. 'You mean you don't have one?' he whispered.

'No.' I shovelled in some more, sensing I'd said the wrong thing. 'I thought that was part of the deal.'

My whole reason for doing this show was to get myself an Equity card, without which, in those days, you couldn't work. (Therein lay the problem ...)

Giles looked exasperated, then said, 'I did not hear that,' before finishing his meal in silence.

I looked for a way round the problem. Three weeks earlier when a call had gone round the company for an Equity manager it had fallen on deaf ears. Now I saw an opportunity. I decided to become the Equity manager and enthusiastically collected the subscriptions. I signed the list with an illegible scrawl, of course omitting my own name from the cast list. Clever, I thought. Very clever.

Four days before we were due to open, a tannoy announcement said: 'Could Keith Allen please come to the stage door.'

I upped crutches and hobbled off the stage, to be met by a po-faced man from Equity.

'Are you the company Equity manager?'

'Yes.'

'Is this your signature?'

'Yes.'

'And who are you supposed to be?'

I mumbled, 'Keith Allen.'

He scribbled something down and said, 'I want to see the director.'

I hobbled back towards the stage where Giles was rehearsing.

'Er, Giles, the Equity man wants to see you.'

Giles said, 'I'm not here,' and dashed off the stage.

There began a chase round the building by me and the Equity man, looking for Giles. Eventually there was nowhere else for Giles to go: he was cornered. The truth was out. I explained that I had never intended to get the production into trouble. After deliberation, Scottish Equity granted me a temporary card.

At the end of the run I returned to London, still without an Equity card.*

---

* I eventually got the Equity card of a piano-bar performer from Manchester called Keith Allen, who paid my dues for six months even though he was dead.

Chapter 18

I RETURNED TO Notting Hill. At Glasgow Citz I'd left behind my plaster cast, rehearsal skirts and any desire I may have had to become an actor. It wasn't for me; well, not in that form. Anyway, there were other things to occupy my mind. Notting Hill at the time – this was pre-gentrification – was probably the most exciting place to be in London.

Within a mile of my local, the Warwick Castle on Portobello Road, there were three amazing music pubs: the Chippenham, the Elgin and the Windsor Castle. Pub rock was at its most vibrant and on any given night you could call in and watch up to four or five bands. The Vincent Units, The Slits, pragVEC, The Raincoats, The Derelicts (later to become The Passions) were all West London bands who were playing and drinking in the area.

The new Rough Trade record shop was an occasional employer of most of the above and also served as a meeting place for hopeful musicians. You were likely to meet any of The Clash, The Damned or even Vic Godard, as well as me rifling through the bins looking for tunes.

This was post-punk, so everybody wanted to be in a band. I was no exception. I had moved back in with Mike temporarily so I set about finding somewhere to squat.

There was a knock on the door.

'Who is it?'

'Kevin!'

Fuck me, my brother. I hadn't heard from him for about a year. The last time I'd seen Kevin was at the beginning of the previous summer when he appeared in Notting Hill, having been expelled from the Rose Bruford acting college in North London. Hardly surprising. He'd been of the opinion that the principal was a cunt, and his chosen medium to communicate this observation with the rest of the world was spray paint. All down the side of the college wall.

The principal wasn't the only cunt in Kevin's life. I was determined to maintain my 'families don't mean anything' position and the last thing I wanted was a reminder that actually they probably did. I told Kevin that he'd have to make his own way without any help from me.

'Don't get any ideas about moving into the area and hanging out with me – it isn't going to happen,' I told him.

He'd spent the past six months down in the South of France working in a boatyard looking after rich people's boats, and, by all accounts, their daughters.

'All right, so what are you doing here?' I said.

'I've found a squat.'

'Really, where?'

'Off the Harrow Road.'

'*Really* … ?'

The particular area off the Harrow Road that Kevin had squatted was less than half a mile from Colville Terrace. It still counted as W11. It was perfect. We stopped off at the Golborne Road end of Portobello Market and bought a pound's worth of mattress. We struggled homeward, my position on families having shifted slightly, you understand.

I moved into Albion Road with Kevin and a paranoid schizophrenic whose name the day I moved in was John. He changed it every three days and made us laugh.

Going to see gigs every night was bound to have an effect.

'Photeos what?'

'Photeos D'mitriou!' he shouted above the din. We were in the Windsor Castle on the Harrow Road. I'd seen him at almost all the other gigs I'd been to in the last week but this was the first time I'd spoken to him. He was quite wonderful was Photeos. You've probably established that he was Greek. I was to find out that he was a lithographic printer (it's a small world) and lived with his mum and dad in Willesden. He also rode a Kawasaki 250.

By chucking-out time we'd got very pissed and had exhausted our 'all corporate music is shit' conversation when something amazing happened – we decided to do something about it ...

Believe me, there was something in the air. The Labour government of the time had made lots of enemies. The unions hated them because of their contribution to the slow decline of British manufacturing. They had in place a police force that was as vicious as anything seen since the miners' and general strike of 1926, and they had had plenty of opportunity to flex their muscles in the latter part of the seventies. The 'Troops out of Ireland' marches, combined with the anti-Nazi and anti-BNP rallies, were seen as a great opportunity to acquaint the left with their boots and truncheons. If you had a problem with Sus laws and voiced an opinion or went on a 'Rock against Racism' march you were considered the enemy. There was a definite 'them and us' mentality sweeping the country and this was as keenly felt in W11 as anywhere.

You should know this was not the Notting Hill that Richard Curtis shat onto our screens five years ago. This Notting Hill had *black* people in it, and lots of them. Most of the working-class white populations could trace their ancestry back to Ireland. All Saints Road was new black front line. Anarcho-Punk poets rubbed shoulders with Rude Boys and lesbian separatists. The Angry Brigade shopped in Portobello Road. You could see why Rough Trade set up shop here, why Christine Keeler dropped into the Mangrove on All Saints Road. The people of W11 had a real history of oppression. In the late seventies it was the place to be. It pulsated...

I was sitting in Photeos's mum and dad's home in Willesden. We were there because there was a piano in the front room. Photeos's mum hovered in the hallway, I presume to ensure I didn't step off the two-foot-wide plastic sheeting that connected the door and the three-piece suite. This seemed a bit belt-and-braces to me. We'd taken our shoes off in the kitchen. Maybe it was a precaution against carpet wear, although it didn't seem like the type of house that did any entertaining.

I noticed there was no plastic pathway to the piano. I had an idea for a song that would incorporate my loathing of Max Bygraves and maybe comment upon his contribution to entertainment, which us post-punk punks were trying to replace. It was called 'Max Bygraves Killed My Mother'. My unique contribution to music is to play the drum parts of a song on the piano, i.e., I can't play. But the order of the day was 'So what, this is punk ... just *mean* it.' I hammered out three notes which I thought was ample to carry the weight of the song, G, C and D, and settled on a simple reggae beat.

Photeos lovingly removed his new guitar from its case. His mother slowly shook her head and shuffled back to the kitchen. Her look seemed to say that she had been dreading this day for some time. Her only son, the son who had flatly refused to go into the family business, a Greek restaurant in Harlesden, was about to be lost to rock 'n' roll.

No such luck ...

Maybe I'd misheard him with all the din in the Windsor Castle, or maybe he said he owned a rhythm guitar, because he sure as fuck couldn't play an electric one.

He took out the guitar, strapped it on, plugged it into his mini amp, set the volume level and then pulled out a book.

'Oh, what's that?'

Indignant, nervous, defensive, Photeos mumbled, 'Book of chords.'

Photeos was one angry young Greek man brought up in the stifling environment of a traditional Greek family, who had religiously reminded him of their expectations for him since he was a small child. To be in a punk band, for Photeos, was as big a 'fuck you' as he could ever have dreamed of. Who was I to stand in his way?

'Fair enough ... four bars of G, two of C and D, then back to G.'

Photeos's one eyebrow samba-ed above his fierce staring eyes as he silently accused the chord-shape of taking the piss. The three fingers required to create the chord hovered above their respective string then moved agonisingly slowly into position. He strummed the guitar – it was definitely a C. Things that just don't work together: chalk and cheese, crème brûlée and trifle, me and monogamy – add to that list Greeks and reggae.

The concept of the off beat was an alien one as far as Photeos was concerned. Jamaica and its music might as well have been on the moon.

I went in search of additional band members.

1979 was a momentous year for me. I became famous for the first time, admittedly in a limited field, but famous all the same, and I also got tattooed.

Tony Allen, a well-known street performer/anarchist and stalwart of Speakers' Corner, squatted four houses down in Albion Road. Over a cup of tea one morning he pointed out a piece in London's *Evening Standard*. It was a review of a haphazard evening's entertainment in a strip club in Soho. Apparently, people could just get up on stage and have a go at being funny. They could stay on until either they finished their act or were gonged off at the audience's request. Bit like Caesar's thumbs at the Colosseum.

Tony immediately spotted the potential, and the political implications. By making a few calls Tony could load a show with funny people from street and fringe theatre and hijack it away from the 'my mother-in-law' crowd. You must remember: this was 1979 and the comic fare of the day consisted mostly of the likes of Lennie Bennett and Lenny Henry playing working men's clubs and the new super entertainment clubs that were springing up all over England. Comedy for people of my generation was nowhere to be found on the cultural map.

The following Sunday, Tony wandered into my house.

'You've got to get down there tonight.' He'd been the night before, the Saturday. 'You can do whatever you want. The acts are just shit apart from one bloke, the compere Alexei Sayle.'

And so my comedy career started on a Sunday night with an impression of Max Bygraves. Max Bygraves doing cabaret in Bahrain. He's got pissed and he's been caught trying to steal someone's wallet. This is my impression of Max Bygraves waking up in his bathroom. 'You need – haaaaagh!'

As I say, early days.

It was at the Comedy Store, as it became known, where I discovered that the most energising time you can experience is when you've got nothing to lose. When you have nothing to lose, you have no fear. An incredible freedom comes from operating outside the normal field of expectations. I loved being on stage without the constraints of either a recognisable act or the disciplines of a script. I could do anything – and, believe me, I did. Remember, reader, I was blessed with an extraordinary ability to think on my feet, honed to perfection by the lies I told as a child to try to get myself out of trouble. Very early on in my career as a stand-up comic I learnt not to think about what I was going to say next.

I developed a reputation for dealing with hecklers. Sometimes I would piss on them, other times pour their drinks over them. At one gig, at the Royal College of Art, I performed in the union bar. They were pretty rowdy and the last thing they wanted was to be entertained by *moi*. I started performing and was continually heckled. After a short while I stopped. I told them I had three surefire ways of stopping hecklers and if they carried on, I'd use them. I produced a set of darts and continued in what I thought was now respectful silence … but there's always one. No sooner had he said whatever it was he said than the audience came to know I was a man of my word. If he hadn't ducked there's every chance I would have spent part of the eighties inside charged with malicious wounding.

Oh, and another thing – by the time I'd done two weekends as the undoubted star of new-wave comedy we'd waved goodbye to Old Labour and ushered in a new form of Conservatism as exemplified by one Mrs Margaret Thatcher.

If the left thought it had been bad under Labour, they were in for a massive shock under the one who was to become the 'Iron Lady'. But for the non-voting, disaffected, performing underclasses, this was manna from heaven. She was exactly what was needed – a distinct enemy, a target…

My experience of the Glasgow Citz (negative) coupled with performing at the Comedy Store (positive) made me think about performance and what I wanted to do with it. I hadn't realised it then, but my first love was situationism. There was something a little too obvious about 'spectacle', so I set about looking for a suitable 'situation' where I could perform.

The answer came one night in a pub on North Pole Road called, interestingly enough, the North Pole. I'd popped in there for a pint with Sue Gogan and John Studholm, original members of The Derelicts who were now going out as pragVEC. I'd been trying to convince them that they should join my band, The Atoms. I was still rehearsing with Photeos but by now I was of the opinion that he had more chance getting rhythm out of a root vegetable.

John and Sue wanted nothing to do with it. They were a well-respected band in their own right; John Peel had spoken about them and they'd released records on Rough Trade. Why would they join me and Photeos? The answer was just about to reveal itself.

As we chatted, I'd noticed a chap setting up a rudimentary PA system. Apparently, we'd wandered into a brewery-sponsored talent contest. If you had strolled into this pretty pokey pub, you would have seen a few fairly ancient regulars staring into their pints trying to ignore a group of QPR fans playing darts. If you'd stayed long enough, you'd have seen them joined by friends and family of the hopeful contestants. What I was looking at, however, was an audience … and, even better, an audience with no expectations.

Perfect.

I shared my views about performance and audience with John and Sue, and convinced them to become Atoms with a view to performing only at talent contests. They were perverse enough to recognise this could be fun, and pissed enough to enter the talent contest. Sue's unaccompanied rendition of 'Danny Boy' didn't trouble the judges …

Meanwhile, back at the Comedy Store I was developing my pretty wild stream-of-consciousness routine. Tony had been urging plenty of left-wing performers from the fringe circuit to pack the place. At this point, the Comedy Store hadn't become an entry point into television and most of the acts were either left wing or barking mad. The safer, more middle-class kind of comedy of Rik Mayall, Ade Edmondson, French and Saunders *et al* had yet to find its way to the Store.

Tony Allen had called a meeting of comics at the West London Media Workshop with a view to setting up some kind of organisation that could represent this new-wave comedy movement. Those present, besides Tony Allen, were Alexei Sayle, Pauline Quirke, Andy de la Tour, Jim Barclay and me. Apart from Alexei, I don't think any of the others seriously considered comedy as a career. They were there because they believed they could set up a loose sort of organisation that could provide comics and develop venues as an alternative to what was on offer. And so 'alternative comedy' was born.

I wanted nothing to do with it, of course. My argument was I didn't want to be alternative to anything. I wished them well and got on a train to Swansea. I was heading west in order to borrow £500.

I'd talked Roy Dodds, a session drummer, into drumming for The Atoms, and we were joined by David James, a performance-art-type musician I'd seen play at the ICA. We'd had one rehearsal, which was all it took to master the two classics I'd written. It was also all that was required for the rest of the band to realise Photeos couldn't play. Sue, rather cleverly I thought, suggested that she play the wasp synthesiser to beef up the sound. It perfectly masked the sound of Photeos's wayward strumming.

Our first gig at the North Pole had been a triumph. We were only allowed to play one song ('Max Bygraves Killed My Mother'), but it was enough. I'm not sure that the judges would have placed us but the QPR fans let it be known that we should win, so we went on to the semi-finals, where we played the other song in our repertoire, 'Beatle Jacket', a furious, three-minute, three-chord punk epic about my father not letting me wear a Beatle jacket. This struck a chord with the QPR fans, who had now swelled in numbers and, when we were declared the winners, insisted we play both our songs again.

I was on the train to Swansea when I realised I'd have to disband the band after the finals. Our QPR following kind of flew in the face of not playing to people's expectations, so we thought it fitting that we should bow out by making a record.

The Copper Grill Restaurant, Swansea. A small place decorated for tourists serving Italian food and steaks. Brass ornaments, cushioned menus and dinky-dos. It was a Saturday morning before opening. Dad was there with Mum.

'Why didn't you ask us?'

'Because, Mum, you would have said no.'

I'd met up with Tony Minetti, the restaurant owner's son, and had asked him to lend me £500 so I could make a record. Astonishingly, he agreed. Cue utter consternation from Mum and Dad. They could see that my failure to repay the loan would be another stain on the Allen family name. They were also concerned that this would affect their relationship with the Minettis, who were now family friends.

I arrived back in London determined not to let Tony or my family down.

Nowadays, if you want to make a record you can access anything you need on your laptop – Garageband, Pro Tools, Logic, whatever – and when you've finished creating, pop in a CD and, hey presto, out it comes and you have it in your hand. Things were different back then.

For a start, you had to go and record in a studio. As I walked into the little basement studio in Shepherd's Bush I felt like Elvis Presley walking into the Sun Studios in Memphis. By the time I got into the vocal booth at the end of the day, I thought I was Jimmy Page.

Your first time in a recording studio is up there with your first fag, your first fuck. To be able to say truthfully, 'I can't, I'm in the studio tomorrow', is life-enhancing. It's up there with the first time you say 'I'm a student' – it was for me anyway. I looked at Photeos. If he'd died right then he'd have been the happiest man in the world. He was in a band, for fuck's sake. One minute he's in the pub, a printer, four weeks later he's in a band in a recording studio making a fucking record! At the end of the session, Keith 'Can I have a bit of reverb on the vocal' Allen paid the recording costs – it was an hourly rate so we were out by nine – and we retired to the Bush pub with the now disbanded Atoms, where we all got well and truly pissed. Happy days.

My brother and Ray 'Rougher' Jones had started a cricket team with Peter Donne from Rough Trade. We were called the Old Roughians. It was our first match and we'd managed to hire a pitch in Regent's Park. Back at the Warwick Castle, when bored we'd invented this game called Amyl Darts. Pretty self-explanatory – snort of amyl, wait until your head went red, then throw. Closest to the wall won. Amyl Pool was even funnier.

As we stood in the slips, I passed Kevin a bottle of amyl. We took a snort and spent most of the afternoon in hysterics. One of the opposing batsmen asked us what it was. We told him. He asked for a snort. We gave it to him.

Peter Donne sent down a screamer, which under normal circumstances any batsman would have left alone. This one, however, in a fit of giggles, managed to walk straight into it. It hit him on the top of his forehead, seam first. There was a lot of blood. He was immediately driven to hospital to have his head stitched.

On the way back to West London, Pete asked why I'd disbanded The Atoms. I explained that we'd served our purpose. We'd got to the final of the talent contest and come third. We'd lost to a fourteen-year-old Irish girl singer and a fifty-year-old comedian. Our QPR following had wrecked the pub.

He said he needed record racks built in the downstairs of Rough Trade and would me and Paul Durdan, a friend of mine, be interested in the job? I was doing only occasional work at Butler's Wharf so the money would come in handy but that wasn't the only reason I agreed to do it. The extension was to accommodate Rough Trade's move into distribution and I couldn't think of a better place to be able to put my case for Rough Trade to distribute my 2,000 copies of 'Max Bygraves Killed My Mother'.

After a day's amateur carpentry at Rough Trade, I'd borrow Photeos's Kawasaki and ride over to Butler's Wharf to print the front and back covers and the labels.

I'd got Mike to take a picture of Von Brown and the hole in the middle of the label was significantly placed in the centre of Von Brown's head. I printed on red 'blood' so as to give the impression he'd been shot through the head.

There had been a long-running court case involving Liberal leader Jeremy Thorpe's alleged homosexual affair with Norman Scott. Jeremy Thorpe stood accused of conspiracy to murder. In evidence, Scott mentioned that a certain Gino Newton, a carpet salesman from Cardiff, had arrived at his house in Devon and, as a warning to keep quiet, had shot his dog, a Great Dane called Rinka, through the head. I was lying in bed listening to the radio when news broke that the verdict had been returned. It was not guilty. I thought it stank of the establishment closing ranks. I leapt out of bed, outraged, and headed off to find a tattooist.

Years later I was explaining the story to a well-known actress who was later to become a dame. She rubbed her finger over the tattoo of the dog's head with the name 'Rinka' underneath.

'That's such a wonderful story,' she sighed.

An hour later we were in her bedroom snorting amyl nitrate; her with a pair of headphones on, listening to opera, and me with my tongue about two inches up her magnificent bottom. (No, it wasn't Judi Dench.) 'Max Bygraves Killed My Mother' was released on Rinka Records, distributed by Rough Trade and sold 2,000 copies. I paid back the £500 loan. I'd sent a copy to John Peel, and he played it three times. Photeos was around my squat the first time and he cried when he heard it.

One upside of The Atoms was meeting Sue Gogan's sister Barbara, who was lead singer in The Passions. This brief but appropriately passionate love affair coincided with me opening a new squat in Talbot Road. A council block had been thrown up but was still empty after being deemed too damp to put families into. Kevin and I opened it up for a squatting organisation from Kensington called the Ruff Tuff Housing Association. My new abode was a brand-new three-bedroom council flat in which to indulge in wild lovemaking with Babs.

I was on a roll. I'd been in, and then disbanded, a situationist band, I'd recorded a single that had been played by John Peel, and I'd had an affair with a popstar … what next?

THE EIGHTIES

Chapter 19

A VERY PRETTY young black girl hung about my table, looking at me curiously.

'You're famous, innit? Can you get me in a band?'

'No.'

'All right den, can I come back to yours?'

'Yes.'

I'd had my first write-up in the *Daily Mirror*. They did a feature proclaiming me as the 'Punk Comedian – new face of stand-up' and I was beginning to be that thing called 'famous'. This particular night, after a disastrous gig in downtrodden Kings Lynn with Alexei Sayle and a bunch of others from the Comedy Store, I went back to Ladbroke Grove to seek comfort in an after-hours blues. A blues is an illegal party, usually in a seedy basement or flat. My face was starting to get around and that meant extra attention from women – who didn't know what I did, but knew my face.

This woman, or more like girl, because I found out she was eighteen, flirted with me unashamedly. I suppose I loved it. I was the older man, and one that perhaps could offer her something, even if it was only a story to tell her mates. So we went back to my place. She was from the area, born and bred West London, second or third generation Afro Caribbean. We fucked and that was it. Ten weeks later she came and found me in my local boozer.

'I'm pregnant,' she announced coolly.

'Oh. Er, shit. What are you going to do?'

'Have it.'

'Oh. I mean, if you want I'll give you some money to, er, you know, if that's what you want.'

'No. I want this baby. I'm having it. Don't worry, I won't ask you for anything.'

This brief union resulted in the birth of my son Kevin. She was eighteen and wanted a child; I was twenty-seven and didn't. She knew I didn't want a baby with her, but it was her choice, what she wanted. She'd taken the decision, but by the same merit she'd taken the decision away from *me*. That wasn't particularly fair. So the compromise was that it was to be her child, not mine. After that I neither saw nor heard from her. She got on with her life and I got on with mine.

A wall went up against the memory. Getting rid of a sense of responsibility is easy when you refuse it as a concept. If it doesn't exist, it can't affect you. Also, by the time Kevin was born, I was living in South Kensington – not a million miles I know. But it might as well have been.

'Do you think I should give it up?'

I sucked on my post-coital cigarette. 'What would you do?'

'Well, I've trained as a teacher. Guess I'd go back to that.'

Her self-doubt was a result of a not very good gig she and her partner had performed that night in Norwich. I'd stepped into the breach as compere for the night due to Alexei Sayle's illness. Her tastes had yet to include black comedians and Terry's Chocolate Oranges, so on that particular night I would have to do.

'If I was you, Dawn, I'd go back to teaching. At least it's rewarding.'

The rest, as they say, is history.

I'd virtually stopped performing at the Comedy Store. Two reasons a) the audience were coming to expect me to be insulting and outrageous and b) the Store was now so successful it was a recognisable entry point into TV, so the madness and anarchy of the first six months were being replaced by a more structured career-orientated act. The likes of Rik Mayall, Ade Edmondson, Peter Richardson, Nigel Planer, Dawn and Jennifer were now playing weekly and it was becoming boring. They were usually doing the same act week in week out. Paul Jackson, a BBC producer, had been down and realised that the comedy from the Store was now ripe for television.

A mate of mine called Peter Rosengard let me crash in his pad in Cranley Gardens, South Ken. He was the brain that brought the concept of the Comedy Store to England, and whose claim to fame was being in the Guinness Book of Records for selling the most insurance in one day. Later he would manage a band called Curiosity Killed The Cat fronted by a fop in an oversized tea cosy. A wet blokes' band.

Peter was greasier than an oil slick and reckoned he could teach me a thing or two about pulling women. Although my technique was similar to a wrecking ball through a plate-glass window, I didn't need lessons from a man whose trousers didn't meet his shoes and who tucked his jumper into his jeans.

One day he offered to take me for a cruise through South Kensington in his open-top Porsche looking for skirt. Peter was lovely guy but he could get on your nerves. No doubt he felt the same about me leaving a hundredweight of dirty washing on his smart sofa. We pulled up at some lights in South Kensington, level with some good-looking stupid women.

'Watch this, Keith.'

He got out and leant into their car, palms flat against the roof.

'Hi, gals. Fancy coming along for a drink with me and my pal? Yeah. That's him in the Porsche over there ...'

As he pointed in my direction, I slid over into the driver's seat, released the handbrake and drove off, leaving him stranded in the middle of the road. Falling over myself with laughter, I drove to Ladbroke Grove and parked up outside my mate Paul Durdan's house.

'Nice car, who'd you nick it from?'

'Peter Rosengard.'

'Fancy coming to a party?'

We drove to a party in Acton. This woman I'd seen around at the Comedy Store opened the door.

'Welcome to my house.'

After a few hours my flirting had gone from Level Five: No Threat to

Level Two: Clear and Present Danger. The hostess was ripe for the picking.

'Fancy coming back to my place?'

'I can't, it's my party.'

'So?'

'Well, I kind of should be here, really, shouldn't I?'

One look at me must have told her she was asking the wrong man about 'correct practice'. She grabbed a coat and followed me. She told me she had a child but he was being babysat somewhere, so back we went and spent the night at Cranley Gardens, where another child was conceived. A few weeks later she got in touch.

'I'm pregnant.'

'Oh, er, well, what do you want me to do? Pay for an abortion?'

'No. It's fine, I wanted another child and I'm having the baby.'

'Oh. Right.'

What was becoming blindingly obvious was that my sperm had their own set of bollocks and could surf a tsunami and still have time to fertilise a few stray females on the way. Grace, my daughter, was born eight months later, and although her mother told me about her arrival, nothing changed and she was never part of my life.

Now it may come as a surprise to you that I didn't respond emotionally to the news that I had impregnated two women. That's because it didn't worry me – they were both a result of one-night stands. I would like to say that my time was taken up considering the future of these children, but the truth is, it wasn't.

In Grace's case her mother made it absolutely clear that she wanted Grace as company for her son Philip. I don't feel I have anything to answer for with Grace but I do feel guilty about Kevin. His mum was a single mother with a young boy (who would soon be joined by a sister by another man). I wasn't sure if there was another guy floating around, but if there was, it wasn't a good scene.

My stints at the Comedy Store had got me noticed by the new middle-class working-class-loving journos who were setting up Channel Four. What was happening there was the incorporation of the 'anarchy of punk' in a new television channel for the purpose of engaging the youth. The mission statement was to offer a 'radical alternative to mainstream TV' and they invited me to front their first youth magazine show, called *Whatever You Want*.

The fact that twenty-five years later Channel Four is about as alternative or radical as a portion of chips and a round of white sliced has a hint of irony about it. Its slavish adherence to reality television makes a mockery of its mission statement.

My very first television appearance was on a show called *Boom Boom ... Out Go the Lights*, commissioned by Paul Jackson and featuring all the – dare I say it – good 'alternative' comedians coming out of the Comedy Store. I was fucking terrible. My style of comedy didn't translate onto TV, which just couldn't capture the edginess of my performance. (Like Freddie Starr, who was never as good on TV as in real life.)

So with that debut on my mind, I hoped that presenting *Whatever You Want* would be different. It was. I quickly discovered that nothing on TV is as it appears to be – you have the capacity to cut and go again and everything is edited to create whatever illusion you want. As well as that, I could decide the content and write the sketches.

I presented the show from the ACE, a live venue in Brixton. It was a big-money operation with OB vans and all the best bands like The Undertones, Jesus and Mary Chain and Nick Cave. The first show featured a sketch with the legendary newsreader Reginald Bosanquet. I went to film him at his house. He lived above Malcolm McLaren on the King's Road and he was drinking sherry out of a pewter goblet. Anyway, the purpose of the sketch was to deconstruct newsreading.

The rest of the first show went off with a bang as I had decided that, after introducing the band The Dead Kennedys, I would dive into the audience. The producer and director went mad, not knowing if and when I'd re-emerge to present the next link. Fucking brilliant. For the first time in my life I had a production crew around me and revelled in it. They allowed me to be chaotic, then they would shape it and make it all fit together.

Channel Four spent their large budget for *WYW* going round the country finding out what topics mattered most to young people and we would feature whichever topic was hottest. It was called 'access television'. One week we featured Arlington House, a homeless shelter in Camden owned by a rich property developer, who was charging unfair rent. The residents were unable to protest because their homeless, unemployed status meant they were denied union membership. My researchers/runners on this show were a couple of low-achievers called Jonathan Ross and Michael Caton-Jones. (Obviously their future success came from watching such a master of media at work. Ahem.)

Thatcher didn't like the way Channel Four were going, and told them to clean up or get off the air. It was in this spirit of the times that I decided to present the whole of *Whatever You Want* stark bollock naked, singing all my introductions opera-style. I was having Fun on a grand scale. It was all about having a laugh.

Then I hit the destruct button. The production company wanted to pull a piece because of its politically sensitive content; I wanted it to stay. The next morning two letters crossed London in the first-class mail. One from Channel Four to me said: 'You are sacked.' The other from me to Channel Four said: 'I resign.' The minute life became too serious, something inside fell away and exposed the ordinariness of Keith. The ability to stand out was what defined me.

Now, by way of explaining how I got to be the warm-up gig for The Clash, I need to acquaint you a bit better with a few people. First, Paul Durdan, a tough left-wing lad from Swansea who was a big mate of Ian Bone's, who set up Class War. Paul and Ian brought about the downfall of a couple of corrupt councillors in Swansea by publishing a leaflet that in turn became a broadsheet story. We all met at Rough Trade Records when I was making shelves there with Mike Laye. Paul became my best mate and we'd drink, of course, in the Warwick Castle, where we got chatting to Bernie Rhodes, The Clash's manager. At the time Paul was managing a band called The Rocking Sikh.

I knew Bernie through Mike Laye. At that time Paul Simonon was running Billy Idol a very close second for the most-handsome-man-in-punk title. I'd go down and watch them rehearse in a room in Camden Market; Mike Laye was taking all the photos for Bernie Rhodes. Bernie used to come round the flat and talk about the dignity of labour till two in the morning. But at the time I was actually much more into a band called Vic Godard and the Subway Sect, who had a dry, witty, miserabilist approach to life with bizarre phrasing. A precursor to Morrissey, methinks.

Bernie called a few days later and invited me to open for The Clash in Bristol. Of course I said yes and jumped on the train before realising I didn't know what 'warm-up act' involved. So as usual, on the day of the gig, I wandered round Bristol looking for divine inspiration. It came, of course, in the form of the title of the Clash tour, 'Combat Rock'.

'All right, Bristol.'

I took the stage in front of a large and baying crowd. In contrast to Joe Strummer and Paul Simonon's chiselled cheekbones and artily torn combats, I looked like an extra from It Ain't Half Hot Mum. I'd gone to an army surplus store and found a tin hat etc, and kitted myself out. I was followed onstage by Rocking Sikh, who were wearing nothing but loincloths, after Joe had given the lead singer a bottle of whisky. Oh, the days of artistic freedom.

The final act on the warm-up menu that night in Bristol was the Singing Vicar. He was a unionist, a Presbyterian preacher who sang country and western tunes. You'd have thought he'd found a fancy-dress costume but it was for real. He re-enters my life a couple of years later (you'll find out why ...).

I got to meet television drama writer and producer Stephen Frears, who was directing the Joe Orton film Prick Up Your Ears and was serious about considering me to play Orton. I think Stephen saw some of Joe's charming wickedness in me. (As well as us both being provocative, outspoken and anti-establishment.)

I really wanted the part and went all out to get it. Me and Mike Laye decided to recreate the famous photograph of Orton in a deckchair to convince them I was the man for the job. We shaved off all my chest hair and covered me in early fake tan. I had the audition and was recalled. It was all going according to plan. I remember very clearly rollerskating from Notting Hill up Oxford Street to meet the financial backers of the film. (It wasn't such a gay thing then – rollerskating.) Then I was invited to Elstree to do a screen test with Ian Charleson (pre-*Chariots of Fire*); he was to play Joe's lover Halliwell.

The next stage was to meet the writers, the great Alan Bennett and John Lahr. I went to Alan's house and was amazed to see a rusting caravan perched out front. In it lived the old tramp lady he wrote about so often.

'Morning,' she said cheerily.

'Afternoon,' I returned.

I rang the doorbell. Alan answered the door and invited me in. I remembered *That Was The Week That Was* from my youth and didn't really know what to say to him because I was slightly overawed. Stephen Frears and John Lahr were also there. I must have been impressed by Alan's front room because years later I was to decorate my council flat the same way. He'd left the plasterwork exposed and covered it in a green wash and then sealed it, to give a faux rustic look.

Alan came into the room holding an Evening Standard Drama Award – a big gold thing.

'Thanks very much, but I haven't done anything yet,' I said.

'That's Joe Orton's Evening Standard Drama Award. If you wouldn't mind, I'd like you to give us Joe's acceptance speech, in character.'

I got the part. The role seemed to be made for me and I couldn't wait to get started. Then the production date started to slip. Apparently the way Joe's relationship with his lover Halliwell was told in the script too closely resembled that between John Lahr and his wife Victoria. Amid accusations of plagiarism and slander, the production date was put back two years, in which time my reputation as a hell-raiser had infiltrated the film and television world and I was shelved in favour of the safer option, a certain Gary Oldman.

I pretended I didn't mind and got on with my life, which wasn't uneventful.

Around about this time, I went to New York for the first time. It was an interesting experience.

The first night we were there, me and Mike Laye went round the corner from the Gramercy Park Hotel to have a drink in a nearby bar. On the way we passed what I thought was a second-hand shop. It appeared to be selling police uniforms and badges, and little else besides. We arrived at the bar to discover it was the local bar for the cops from the nearby precinct, most of whom were Irish or Italian. It was St Patrick's Day, so the place was in full riotous swing, given an extra significance because the owner's son, a NY cop, had been privileged enough to lead an Irish Wolfhound at the head of the Fifth Avenue Parade.

I asked about this shop round the corner selling police stuff. I discovered it wasn't second-hand stuff, it was new. The NY cops were given a standard uniform and they had to buy the rest themselves. Bullet-proof vests, badges, belts, all had to be paid for by the cops themselves. I found this astonishing.

'See this jacket?' The cop took off his leather jacket and handed it to me. 'Make me an offer.'

'Eh?'

'Make me an offer. I gotta sell.'

He explained that the leather jackets were no longer official NY cop uniform. They all had to replace the leather ones with the new down-filled, lightweight, manmade-fibre jackets. And they had to buy them.

The leather jackets were iconic. They weighed about two and a half kilos and had a removable fleece lining.

I offered him $30 – we agreed on $35.

'Hey, bud, you want more of these things?' a tall young Italian cop asked.

I said I'd take as many as he could get. He suggested I meet him the next day at the precinct.

We spent the evening in their company. It was an amazing experience, to be in a bar where detectives would wander in and hand their guns in at the bar. It was noisy, raucous. I saw two fights, but I didn't once feel threatened. I imagined what it would have been like for an American punk drinking in a coppers' pub in London. Back home, all coppers were cunts. They protected and carried out a government's laws that enabled greedy multinationals to buy into the health service, nationalised industry, education and transport. The overtly anti-union Thatcher government used this reactionary bunch of cunts to ensure their laws were enforced. And how they loved it! So how come I was here in America having a great time with American police, who carried out the laws of government and whose Keynesian market-led free-enterprise economy the Thatcher government was using as the template to govern England? Capitalism market forces, that's how. Unlike in England, where most policemen were eager to jump into a uniform and beat people up for very little money, people became cops in America because the money was good. They saw it simply as a well-paid job. It meant that your average American cop was a worker, much like any other, unlike in England where their main delight was kicking the shit out of workers. It meant I could view them as human beings first and cops second.

I met Tony the Italian cop the next day as arranged, at the precinct. He introduced me to Molly, the woman who put out the calls to patrol cars. He explained that I was interested in buying jackets and asked Molly to put out a call.

That evening I returned to find five jackets, with the linings but minus badges, ready for me to pick. By the end of my stay, I'd bought fifteen, and had to buy two large suitcases to get them back to England.

On the plane journey home, me and Mike sat in silence. We weren't talking because we'd had a massive fight on the streets of NY the night before. He'd accused me of being a selfish cunt because I'd spent the previous two nights with a sex-mad Puerto Rican I'd been introduced to by my cop friends.

I'd been living back at Mike's but things were tricky after the American flight, and that, coupled with my dislike of his new girlfriend, meant I was in need of somewhere to stay.

The fickle finger of fate was about to point …

The phone rang.

'Keith, it's John Turner, we've had a show pull out – do you want to do a month of Thursdays, Fridays, Saturdays and Sundays?'

John ran the Albany Empire in Deptford, and through a number of in-house shows I'd done and various benefits, I'd got a pretty good reputation in SE London.

I said I'd do it but on one condition.

'What is it?'

'That I live in the theatre.'

Sometimes necessity really is the mother of invention. I had nowhere to stay so my reasoning was that this would give me a month to find somewhere else. I moved my possessions in: bed, Baby Belling (a squatter's best friend), table, chair and small freestanding kitchen cabinet. I set them up on a small stage, and started thinking up a new show.

Whatever Happened to the AA Man's Salute? opened on a Thursday night and with an interval ran for two and a half hours. I built two other small stages. On one I put a robot I'd made out of a trouser press, whose head was a nine-inch speaker. On the other I constructed a slash curtain through which I'd appear in the second half and do a stand-up act.

The lights came up on what looked like a small bedsit. I lay under the duvet for half an hour while the auditorium filled. The show started with me having a nightmare. I'd connected the robot up to a small switch in the bed and I'd toss and turn, then start shouting, 'No! No! You can't do that!', press the switch and robot would say: 'Course you can, you know you want to.'

'I can't – I can't. Comedy has changed.'

'Fuck off. They're just jokes.'

'No, *argh*! We've moved forward.'

'Why do black people have big lips?'

'Stop it! Stop it!'

'So they can stick the kids on the window when shopping in Tesco's.'

Off Robot would go. Nobody escaped. Jews, gays, the Irish, everybody. Pure sexist, racist gags that really shouldn't be told in public. It was brilliant. I'd do five minutes, unseen. And the audience were laughing, albeit guiltily. But it was fine – it was ironic, wasn't it?

I would then wake up from the nightmare and leap out of bed, naked. I'd be on stage for an hour or so, pottering about. If I was hungry I'd cook bacon and eggs, make a coffee, sit down, eat and drink and talk about anything that came to mind.

During the interval I'd change into a suit and appear in the second half on the little performing stage where I'd do an hour's stand-up. It was a sort of 'day in the life of' affair. I think I managed to capture a sense of a passing life, because I received some pretty fantastic reviews. The following week I was sat in John Turner's office, watching the crowds gather outside, when I saw my dad wander past. I rushed out into the foyer.

'Dad, what are you doing here?'

'What do you think we're doing here? We've come to see you.'

'We? What do you mean *we*?'

'Your mother and Auntie Ethnie.'

Fuck me. Auntie Ethnie! 'Dad, I swear to you, this isn't something you want to see.'

'What're you on about? Everyone says it's brilliant – we read the reviews.'

'Dad, it's pretty heavy. The language is really, really strong.'

'Son, I was in the fucking navy for twenty-five years.'

'Yes, I know – but – I'm naked for most of it.'

'Me and your mum brought you up. You think we haven't seen you naked?'

'What about Auntie Ethnie?'

'Just get on with it, and listen – don't change anything just cos we're here.' He held out his hand. 'Have a great one, son.'

As I lay under the bed, I really was having a nightmare.

I leapt out of bed, naked, and moved to the front of the stage. Second row, three seats bang in the middle. Oh God …

The show was going well. I could see Mum and Dad and Auntie Ethnie from the stage. So far, so good; they were clearly enjoying themselves.

I cooked some bacon and eggs, sat at the table to eat it and chatted away about American actors and their obsession with eating while acting. How they felt their on-screen masticating would somehow make them more real. And then I did something, the reason for which I still don't know to this day.

I stood up and spooned some instant coffee into a cup, walked to the front of the stage and, while chatting away about navel fluff, filled the cup with piss. As one, the audience let out a huge *Urghhhh!* I carried on talking and placed the cup on the table.

It was like a ticking time-bomb. All eyes were on the cup. Eventually I lifted the cup to my lips. Three times it went up and twice it went down again. Each time: 'No, he's not!', 'Oh no, he can't!', 'He's going to do it!', 'No, he won't!'…

The third time I finished what I was saying and, in one, drank the lot.

The audience stared in disbelief. Auntie Ethnie was in a state of mild shock. Dad was looking at me – he didn't give anything away. In between them was Mum. Absolutely priceless. She was telling anyone who'd listen: 'That's my son – oh, he's naughty! It's my boy!' I swear to you she not only looked proud, she really was. Only mothers …

I said, 'If it was good enough for Gandhi, it's good enough for me.'

Around about that time of my life I think my parents could see some sort of future for me. I was becoming successful, maybe things would be all right. For me it meant I'd got some sort of recognition and that maybe I was not as useless as I 'secretly' thought I might be. Maybe now I could stop blaming my parents, tell my dad I'd got through the 'hate your parents' bit, have it out with him and get on with developing an adult, loving relationship with him … No such luck.

They loved the show, by the way.

The Church hated them, the Tory government despised them, their mere existence drove the police to apoplexy, and most young kids of an Afro-Caribbean persuasion were disgusted by them; I speak, of course, of homosexuals.

Don't be too surprised. This was a time when most football managers were of the opinion that black footballers couldn't play in winter conditions. 'Good footwork on firm ground, but no stamina in the wet.' Prejudice reigned supreme.

These were the perfect conditions for my kind of performing. The eighties reinforced my position as outsider.

I signed a deal with Charisma Records to make an album; the same week as Malcolm McLaren and Billy Bragg. Pete Jenner, the guy who signed me, handed me over to Glen Coulson to look after. Glen was a former part-time drummer with the Bonzo Dog Doo Dah Band. I think he had a problem at one time with paranoia and dope and instead of snorting for Colombia with his contemporaries was now in charge of the post at Charisma Records in Wardour Street. I didn't hold out much hope. I hadn't even been offered an advance.

Two weeks later me and Glen walked back into Peter Jenner's office.

'I'd like you to stump up the money for a pirate radio station,' I said.

'A what?'

'A pirate radio station.'

I thought an album of a recorded gig was, well, a bit boring really, so I hit on the idea of doing the album as a pirate radio broadcast. It would give me a chance to present my gay characters to a wider audience.

I think Pete Jenner had misunderstood me. 'So why do you want us to buy equipment? Just go in the studio and record!'

'No, I don't want to pretend it is a pirate radio station. I want to set up a real pirate radio station.'

Pete stared at me. 'What a great idea.'

And so Breakfast Pirate Radio was born.

We transmitted on Sunday morning between eleven and one, on 235 MW. We chose medium wave because we didn't want to get busted as most pirates on FM seemed to be doing. Our theory was the Post Office and the police would be far too busy worrying about London's youth being corrupted by FM transmission to even consider looking at the MW spectrum, which was, after all, the home of Radios 3 and 4. And we were right next to Radio 3 on the dial. I would have loved to see the Radio 3 listeners' faces had they strayed past Radio 3 with their tuning knob. They would have heard Tommy Cross (Cross by name not by nature), the station's gay main presenter, encouraging people to send in more names of bent coppers. Or Gerry Arkwright, the northern industrial gay.

Gerry was on his way down to London, to lead a march in protest against Thatcher's cutbacks in government expenditure and the closure of British heavy industry. Gerry hated the gay movement; he thought it was a 'southern poof conspiracy'.

'There is a marvellous tradition of male-on-male working-man sex in the north and I'm here to defend it! That bitch Thatcher is closing down the workplace, the place where a man could work up a sweat, where his loins would gyrate to rhythmic pounding of heavy industry, his oily skin tingling in the white heat of industrial furnaces. Where was a man supposed to fuck? In a fucking call-centre? And I'm not gay. I'm a working man who likes four pounds of beef shoved up his arse on a regular basis. And believe me, love, there's lots of us.'

We transmitted from a tall tree right next door to the London Police Training College. (Charisma passed up on the album, but we repackaged it and sold it through Rough Trade as a three-cassette package called BPR.)

I first met Alison at the Apollo on All Saints Road. The gigs there every Sunday brought the girls flocking in, particularly the trustafarians like Rose Boyt, who had got in with the trendy rock set while at London University. She borrowed somebody's kid and pretended it was hers, parading this cute little girl round the pub like she was this 'happening earth mother' type. Her seduction technique worked on me.

Rose started to bring her mates from London Uni to the gigs every Sunday. One of them was this punk girl who had a Mohican with pink bits in. She seemed impossibly small apart from the most enormous pair of tits. She stared at me all the way through the gig. The last drum roll sounded and she struck up the applause while I got on to plug my new Breakfast Pirate Radio.

Rose Boyt brought the punk girl over and introduced her.

'This is Alison. It was her kid I borrowed to get you into bed,' Rose said carelessly, already heading back to the bar to join the party. Alison smiled apologetically. She had arrived at university from Portsmouth already pregnant and had Sarah in her first term. All the posh girls at the university like Rose, Bella Freud and Lucy Astor adopted her and through them she started to hang out in the posh/trendy West London scene.

I sucked a peanut out of my teeth and concentrated on her cleavage.

'I'd like to get involved in your pirate radio station. I think your show is really good.'

'Yeah?'

'Yeah.'

A free researcher was very appealing to a lazy cunt like me. 'In that case go and find out everything you can about Ken Livingstone. I want to do a show about him.'

Alison's intelligence manifested itself in many ways. The first was that she spent her entire freshers term joining every single society from the netball to the geographical club and applying for maternity grants from all of them. Thus she managed to get a three-bedroom flat in Bury Place opposite the British Museum in which she lived with her daughter Sarah. Her intelligence was manifested in my direction in the shape of an eighty-page dossier on Ken Livingstone that she turned up with a week later.

Flicking through the pages I did wonder if her ulterior motive was to impress me and whether that meant she expected me to make a pass at her.

'Thanks for this.'

She hung round and drank coffee.

'Want me to get you a cab?'

'Thing is, I've got a terrible headache. Would you mind if I just lay down for a bit?'

That old chestnut. In her case it was a very bloody big pair of chestnuts.

'Well, I've only got one bed but you're welcome to it.'

She undressed apart from a Sex Pistols shirt that only covered a tiny portion of bosom. A couple more cigarettes and a respectable twenty minutes later, I joined her. I felt a primeval need to protect *her* from me. In the morning I'd send her away clean, both of us unscathed by the bitty seething sexual minestrone that was fucking.

Chapter 20

AS THE MORNING light streamed in, no one was more surprised than me that I'd managed to keep my word. Alison was already awake.

'Pass me some water, will you?' She nudged me.

'Mmmmmm.'

'The water, it's by you.'

'I can't.'

One of my fatal flaws is being too lazy to do what is asked of me. The trouble it gets me into is untold.

'Fine. I'll get it myself then.'

Alison leaned over me to get the water glass just by my head. Suddenly the heady perfume of flesh and a sizeable portion of ripe young breast fell in my face. My eye opened.

'Oh God … nipple at ten o'clock … incoming.'

It was too much. My hands clamped the proffered breast and there was no going back. All the good intentions were no match for a woman on a mission.

Later, lying like a satiated lion, fat from devouring its prey, she pulled on a cigarette and shook her head rapidly in the way that women do.

'I didn't want to do that.'

I nearly fell off the bed with the temerity of it.

'You what? You put your titties in my face.'

'I was *trying* to find the water.'

'Well, I've heard of loads of things tits are good for but that's the first time I've heard of their water-divining powers.'

'I've got to pick up my daughter.'

'Oh yeah. I'd forgotten you had one of those.'

'Does it make any difference?'

Actually it didn't. It made her more attractive. Alison provoked in me a masculine urge to protect and provide, which didn't happen very often, but when it did shook me to my foundations like a new burst of energy, a new reason to do new stuff.

I would occasionally take Gerry Arkwright (I should mention I played most of the parts on BPR) out to do live gigs. I would shape my facial hair into a sort of Edwardian mutton-chop affair avec moustache, put on a leather biker's cap, a pair of turned-down Wellingtons and a black leatherette posing pouch, and march on stage holding a 48-inch stilson spanner. I'd squeeze body oil over myself from a Fairy Liquid bottle. I opened for New Order at the Royal Festival Hall like this, doing a benefit for the miners.

Peter Hook had to walk on stage to stop security throwing me off halfway through my epic poem:

You soft southern bastards
You cultural pigs
I've come wi' a tale from up north
I'm an industrial gay
And I like it that way
Fist fucking on the Firth of Forth
The time has come for the north to rise
In a welter of leather and sweat
I've come down south looking for big boys
And I haven't met a big one yet …

Gerry opened for The Stranglers at Wembley, and was responsible for the abysmal Simon Fanshawe fleeing from the stage at the Comedy Store, crying.

My personal favourite, though, was Sex Boots Dread. By now I was living in All Saints Road, next door to the Mangrove, and had a recording studio in the basement of my flat. Living on the front line in 1982 meant I was perfectly placed to canvass local opinion about homosexuality. It didn't make pretty listening. The black youth I'd spent years defending by

going on anti-Sus law marches were in no way going to return the cour-
tesy by going on pro-gay marches. I had the technology (the studio and
the radio station), so I thought it right I did my bit to encourage debate.
Me and Glen lifted a couple of studio dub plates, added a bit of keyboard
and vocals and pressed 1,000 white label twelve-inch singles. The two
songs were 'Tickle Tune' and 'Pentel'.

I used to pre-record the pirate radio show in the studio on All Saints
Road, then transfer it to cassette ready to be played Sunday lunchtimes. As
Tommy Cross I was interviewing some youth brothers off the front line
about the injustices being meted out by the local Old Bill. I listened to them
while looking through the window to my small back garden. As I said, I lived
next door to the Mangrove, and I'd noticed that of a morning after a busy
weekend, my small back garden would yield an astonishing crop of empty
wallets, purses, key-rings, bus passes and the occasional jacket. At carnival
weekend, I could quite easily have opened a second-hand accessory stall on
Portobello market and lived off the proceeds. I'd spoken to Frank, the owner
of the Mangrove, about this and assured him that although I didn't condone
robbery, I liked where I lived and I wasn't a grass so could young men
possibly throw the discarded fruit of their labour over somebody else's wall?

I casually asked the brothers if they'd heard of Sex Boots Dread. They
hadn't, so I explained that he was a reggae artist who sang about sexual liberation and repression. I played them the second of the two tracks. The first,
'Tickle Tune', I had premiered in Rough Trade the previous Saturday. Pete
Donne had put it on in the shop, very loudly, just as it started to fill with
black youth on the hunt for the latest twelve-inch import from Jamaica.

The eight-bar intro was greeted with knowing looks and barely
perceptible nods by the attendant youth. This was praise of the highest
order. Then Sex Boots sang. Oops.

I take it in the mouth
and I jam it in me pants
I like a big man with
fuck all romance
cos me homosexual
yes me a homosexual

If I'd run in with a well-greased dildo and bum-fucked them there and then, the response I guess would have been the same. Absolute mayhem.

There were cries for the single's instant removal from play. A shame, because if we'd managed to get to the chorus: 'North, south, east and west / Sexual freedom always the best', there's every chance a healthy discussion would have ensued. We live in hope. The track I was now playing was a far more deliverable piece. A love song, a story of forbidden romance. It was called 'Pentel'.

Pentel is my boyfriend's name
He comes from Acton Town
Me always meet him Saturday
'Im never let me down.

I watched as they strained to hear the lyrics – were they really hearing this? Confusion slowly spread across their faces.

I'm not flash and I'm not fly
And I'm not 'ard and ting
But, when he beat me fucking arse
It really fucking sting.

Confusion quickly followed by disgust. The song had finished.

'Nah, man, that's … not … Nah, that's just wrong, man.'

I explained that Sex Boots Dread was a gay Rastafarian.

'A gay Rasta? You are joking, man.'

I said I wasn't and as a gay man myself (remember I was interviewing them as Tommy Cross) I found it incredibly moving that Sex Boots had the courage to sing about his love for an Indian kid who worked in his parents' corner shop.

'What, the other one's Indian?'

'Yes, that's what the song is about. Sexual liberation and freedom in a multicultural society.'

'Ah, right.'

'What do you mean?' I asked.

'If it was a black-on-black man, I tell you that would be disgusting, but now I understand that he's an Indian.'

'What?'

'Well, they're just different. They're not like us, they're dirty.'

I broadcast the whole interview on BPR. People wrote in, thinking it was a sick joke ...

The record became a collector's item in England and it went on to sell 8,000 in San Francisco, where it became a massive underground club hit in the mid-eighties.

As was often the case, my totally unconscious knack of 'getting it wrong' at just the right moment was about to strike again. Dressed in a red Harrington jacket, combat trousers and Doc Marten boots, I turned up at the front line of an anti-fascist march and fell into step with Alison. She looked at me with horror.

'Oh God, what have you come as?'

'This is a great look. What are you talking about?'

'You look like a neo-Nazi.'

'So?'

'So – they're the Nazis over there ...'

She indicated the rows of passing skinheads, dressed, ironically enough, just like me. Except they were racist bigots and I wasn't. One of them spotted me and shouted, 'Oi! Brother! What you doing with the nigger lovers? Get over here?'

That was the signal for us to storm their ranks. In the following mêlée the police intervened and hauled a few of us towards the waiting banks of Black Marias.

As the doors clinked shut we all looked at each other. We were all skinheads. I knocked on the partition between us and the police at the front and asked to be let out, suggesting that they'd made a mistake.

'Sit down, sonny. You're off to Holborn nick with the rest of your skinhead mates.'

At the station a couple of coppers listened sympathetically to my story before proceeding to book me.

'Name.'

'Er.'

The booking officer looked up from his paperwork, then screwed his eyes tight.

'Wait a minute, don't I know you?'

My heart jumped. I had an outstanding charge for a motoring offence in Cardiff so I didn't want them to find out who I was.

'Er … no.'

He pointed his pen and smiled. 'You're that bloke off the telly, aren't you? What was it called? *Boom Boom … Out Go the Lights*, weren't it?'

I swallowed, then closed my eyes and smiled in acceptance. 'Yeah, you got me.' I nodded. 'I'm Rik Mayall.'

To this day I don't know whether Rik knows it or not but he was fined £50 for affray.

About this time I moved in with Alison at her Bury Place address. I had to look after her daughter Sarah, and I loved it, so long as I could fuck off again at a moment's notice.

In the early eighties my dual career strands as 'punk comedian' and television presenter wound together sometimes and apart at others, very much like the structure of DNA. What appealed was variety and the freedom to fuck off at any given moment. When Dexys Midnight Runners offered me a slot on their tour of Britain and Ireland as the comedy warm-up act, there was only one answer. Moving and touring were part of me since the age of sixteen and Geno Washington.

There was little joy in Dexys – busy promoting their young soul rebel earnestness, unlike UB40 on the other side of Birmingham, they forgot to live. Kevin ruled the band with an iron fist. The only fun to be had was watching various members of the band squeezed into small hotel rooms smoking weed, with the window open, in case Kevin smelt it. He enforced a strict no drugs policy. To alienate the boredom, my stage act got more outrageous whilst touring Ireland. One night in Dundalk, I went on stage as a priest. In what I think was a very passable Irish accent I informed them 'That God didn't mind them having fun, even liked music himself, and the Catholic Church as you know is no stranger to a bit of chanting … however, everything must be put into perspective, and you must ask yourself does soul music really concern itself with affairs of the Christian soul …'

I droned on for about ten minutes in complete foot-shuffling silence … Just before leaving: 'Oh and one more thing. I know a lot of you live on farms and keep livestock. So if any of you know the whereabouts of a fine young toothless calf that wouldn't mind ten minutes on the end of my cock, please leave the address at the stage door. And if there's any sheep you know of that might need a bit of arse battering, even better … Good night and God bless.'

Pandemonium. I spent the rest of the night hidden by the Irish promoter, begging me not to ever do it again. I didn't.

Back in the UK Dexys went on a new Saturday morning show called *The Fun Factory*, which was filmed in an old warehouse at the back of Granada studios in Manchester. It featured exactly the kind of false jollity that I despised. Grown men behaving like juveniles and dressed up in loud jumpers talking banal shite. Now *my* type of fun (which was anything that took the piss out of *their* kind of fun) was *much* more fun.

My need to spoil the show originated in my resentment of the idea of 'safe' and 'mainstream'.

So it was that one Saturday morning I carved my name into the annals of 'Best Ever TV Moments'. All the children who made up the audience were organised into groups to sing along to Showaddywaddy and Dexys. They were made to wear fancy dress to make the whole thing more 'fun'. As Kevin pranced round in front of the cameras, I snarled and paced, hating the whole sickeningly 'innocent' experience. One of the adult presenters was a character called 'Uncle Bill' who wore an idiotic jumper bearing the name 'Uncle Bill'.

I hid behind a large fruit (no, not Chris Tarrant – he was on *Tiswas*), a super-size polystyrene strawberry, and waved manically at a little kid.

'Pssst! Oi, laddie, come over here …'

An eight-year-old shuffled over doubtfully and I put my arm on his shoulder and pointed to Uncle Bill.

'See that man over there.' He nodded. 'I want you to go over and hit him in the bollocks when I give you the signal. OK?'

He nodded again and went over to stand in front of Uncle Bill. The cameras were rolling and just as he was about to hit him, a producer pulled him away. The lad got told off and started crying and pointing in my direction.

'That man over there told me to hit Uncle Bill in the bollocks.'

'Which man? Can you show me?'

The lad nodded and took the producer's hand, pointing in my direction, so I ran and hid until they'd gone. Another kid saw me hiding and came over.

'What are you hiding from?'

'Uncle Bill.'

'Why?'

'Because he's an idiot.'

The kid laughed.

'Do you want to do something funny?'

The kid nodded eagerly.

'Right. On my signal, I want you to go up to Uncle Bill and say Karl Marx is a god.'

'Garl Marx is a cod.'

'Not a cod, a god.'

He practised until he got it right and went straight over to Uncle Bill, who was now in the 'science area' conducting a scientific experiment with a plastic bottle 'submarine', making it move by showing how air displaces water.

It was all recorded live and the camera was rolling. Uncle Bill looked down at the lad and smiled.

'Who've we got here, then? What do you want to ask me, laddie?'

'Karl Marx is a god.'

The producers went white and dragged him away. Not waiting round for the search party I ran into the car park, which was full of huge fibreglass heads, and hid behind a nose. Eventually the first kid spotted me and grassed me up. At which point they unceremoniously ejected me.

'You'll never work in television again,' ranted the executive producer as I mounted the steps of the Dexys tour bus. A few weeks later the 'Karl Marx Is A God' clip was played on *TV's Funniest Moments* for the first of many times.

*

One of my sketches on *Whatever You Want* had been a piss-take of *The Professionals* called 'The Bullshitters'. When Channel Four commissioned the first series of *The Comic Strip Presents*, Peter Richardson, having been in 'The Bullshitters' with me, returned the favour and offered me a few small parts. By series two we decided to write *The Bullshitters* as a full-length Comic Strip episode.

Two o'clock in the morning. Peter Richardson and me lying on the floor at his house, drinking and writing the feature-length version of *The Bullshitters*.

Then Peter's pregnant wife started to go into labour.

'Sorry, Keith, you'll have to stay over. I'll be back.' They rushed off without further ado.

'Shame ...' I muttered, noticing his sister was staying over and that there was a cold bottle of bubbly in the fridge. As you can imagine, me, Peter's sister, cold champagne ... one thing led to another.

In the morning it was smiles all round when Peter got home with another bottle of champagne and we toasted his first-born. I felt very much like part of the Comic Strip family. In fact, I *had* been feeling part of the family. The part of the Comic Strip family I had been feeling was his sister.

Chapter 21

ALISON AND I married at the Unitarian Church in Highbury on 21 July 1984. Despite both of us holding anti-establishment views and aspiring to 'fuck the system', we wanted an excuse for a party.

We didn't have any money and didn't want a religious ceremony so our mate Paul Durdan recommended the Singing Vicar. Gareth was also the resident preacher at the Unitarian Church and was very understanding when we said that we hated religion.

The day started in glorious English sunshine. My uncles stood outside, legs apart, hands thrust deep into their Sunday best when not holding cigarettes, while Peter Richardson handed out lapel flowers and exchanged banter. Peter was now my best mate because of our collaborations on *The Bullshitters* film.

Mum and Dad arrived, Eddie stepping briskly out of the cab making naval adjustments in the groin area, ready to meet the new in-laws. He rocked back on his heels and mock-punched me. Mum looked at me proudly, hanky at the ready. I knew what they were thinking: could this be the (somewhat delayed) start of normality for me? Wife, kids and a semi in Slough? They'd have loved me to live somewhere like that: good roads, plenty of roundabouts and supermarkets.

And on a baking-hot afternoon in July, conforming didn't seem so bad. Love, marriage and children was 'a new high' to throw myself into and explore. The novelty of being bound up with another person brought a natural adrenalin rush.

Fuck it, though, this was my day and an excuse for a right royal piss-up so why should I behave? It was a dream come true. I was the centre of attention without having to work for it, plus all my beloved Welsh family were there and the London posse.

After the 'I do's' (which should probably have been 'I don'ts') we went into the chapel to sign the book. Against my better judgement, it felt good to be doing something to please the folks. Mum grabbed Alison and took her aside, whispering furiously. Mum looked over at me a little too seriously before leaving. I grabbed Alison nervously.

'What was all that about?'

Alison casually brushed her fingers through her hair. 'Oh, she just told me to keep you clean.'

'Keep me *clean*?'

'Yeah.'

'Is that all she's worried about? My bodily odour? What about my happiness?'

'She didn't mention that.'

'Didn't she even give you any cookbooks?'

She shot me a dirty look. If I'd hoped that marriage might bring meat, two veg and freshly ironed handkerchiefs, I probably shouldn't have married a punk anarchist feminist. Still, a man can dream.

We decamped from the communal garden and headed for a pub, the Red Lion (not the one on Upper Street in Islington) where we had a wedding buffet. All the Welsh were most at home among the sausage rolls and egg butties. The air was full of warm alcohol; we were surfing on a wave of laughter. Jimmy Fag came over and slapped me on the back.

'I see you've brought the Welsh Male Voice Choir ... Fancy a singsong?'

Jimmy was a comedian pianist who did a residency at the Red Lion. Joining him on the stage was Alana Peelay (real name Alan), a black transvestite I'd signed up as a regular in the Comic Strip films.

Alison and I listened to the strains of Jimmy and Alana while sunbathing in the pub's adventure playground. Peter Richardson had paid for a honeymoon car to take us to Devon, but as the car waited, the party started to get going. Alison tapped me on the shoulder and suggested we make a move. There was only one thing worse than being dragged away from a party, and that was being dragged away from one's own party because of a stupid tradition that decreed 'husband and wife shalt go and fuck'. It's not as if you haven't got the rest of your life to do it. Why spoil a good party?

Alison and Peter cajoled me away. Shoved in the back of the car I promptly fell asleep. (Had it not been a twelve-pints-of-beer sleep, I might have heard the soft sound of female tears as Alison realised she'd made a terrible mistake.)

As it was, with me safely oblivious to her doubts, we enjoyed a honeymoon picnic in Hope Cove the next morning. Peter had packed a hamper full of fine cheese and French red wine and we made love on the beach. Ever the romantic and buoyed by alcohol, I scooped up the minute pebbles beneath Alison's bare arse and filled the empty wine bottle.

'What are you doing?' Alison stared at me, horrified.

'This is going on our mantelpiece ... so everyone will see the very sand on which we had our first married fuck.'

Alison's face showed vague revulsion. 'I'm not sure I want people to know that.'

'Tough. It's beautiful.'

The bottle did indeed take pride of place on the mantelpiece in Bury Place, and took extra significance when we discovered that our daughter had been conceived there.

We settled down to family life and prepared for the baby. Fatherhood and family stirred strange emotions in me. Yeah, it was what you did when you grew up, and, no, fuck off I'm not ready to grow up. But love got in the way and I wanted Alison to have my baby.

Dutiful and devoted, the man of the house would go every day to the local Price Check supermarket and buy food for the family. The Pakistanis who ran the shop would have a laugh and a joke as they loaded the spaghetti hoops and jammy dodgers for Sarah, Alison's kid.

'How is married life, Mr Keith, eh?' They giggled.

'Fucking brilliant.'

But when a woman is pregnant, a man can do no right. For example, I came home one day with an old-fashioned mangle I'd managed to get hold of.

'Isn't this great?'

Alison looked at me disparagingly, her response something like: 'No. My mother used to have one.'

'Yeah, mine too, isn't it fantastic? Now that's proper, that is. You can use it to do the washing.'

Which was immediately taken with the utmost offence and a reply along the lines of: 'If you hadn't noticed, Keith, women were emancipated in 1911.' With that she waddled into the kitchen and slammed the door.

What was the problem? Living with a pregnant woman was like trying to negotiate Hyde Park Corner on acid.

Filming was about to commence on *A Fistful of Travellers' Cheques* with the Comic Strip. We filmed in San José, a fishing town near Almeria in Spain. I first met Danny Peacock here, who I had to headbutt in the film (which was to become one of the most famous headbutts on TV). I thought that Danny must have a problem with excess thyroid secretions because of his deep voice, massive Adam's apple and even more massive cock (of which I am about to speak). He was, like me, an outsider within the Comic Strip. Also like me he loved drink, drugs and shagging – he was a dirt bag.

Of course, three long weeks' drinking and marauding there led the locals to hate us. They were right too. A group that included Rik Mayall, Ade Edmondson, Danny, Dawn French and me was enough to make anyone puke, let alone a posse of ugly Spanish fishermen who wanted their bar back. This led to tensions being extremely frayed on the last night. We were propping up the bar and things almost came to blows with the locals when I proposed an answer to the problem.

'Right. Why don't we sort this argie bargie out with a cock-measuring contest?'

Remarkably the manager of the bar agreed, while my fellow actors looked at me as if I was insane. It was decided that each side should elect six men to represent them, and rather than collecting all cock sizes (if that were the case we would have been roundly beaten), it was decided (by me) that the side with the man with the biggest cock should win outright.

So the competition got under way and the first two men put their cocks, in turn, on the 'saucer of cock'. This was not a big plate – it was a saucer of a double espresso cup. By this time, the idea of fighting each other had long gone out of the window, replaced by a new atmosphere of uncomfortable excitement. Ade Edmondson dropped it out and that was a fair handful. Then Glyn, our first assistant director, was up against some wizened old Spanish fisherman, who, after the gravitational wear and tear of sixty-odd years, was no match, and we were inching ahead ...

I was up second to last, and much like my Max Bygraves streak, I had to massage it out a bit. In repose there wasn't a great deal to sigh at. In fact, I had great difficulty keeping it on the saucer of cock. (I think the phrase is it's a grower, not a shower.) The competition was neck and neck ...

Then the final young Spaniard came up and took out his manhood and laid it on the saucer of cock. Its end just failed to show over the other side, but it was the biggest so far.

'Right, lads, cop a load of this ...'

Danny was offered the saucer of cock but he refused.

'Pass me that fucking ashtray,' he said.

There were roars of approval from the gathered crowd. Even the clearly now defeated Spaniards were clapping their approval. Where there had been animosity, there was now a shared appreciation. Nestling atop a half-full pewter ashtray was as fine a piece of English meat as ever had been seen on those shores. As he plumped it down on the ashtray, a Vesuvian mass of ash erupted into atmosphere under the weight if it.

(Mind you, the Spaniards should have been glad Robbie Coltrane wasn't there. He would have needed a fire bucket – yes, it is that big. Imagine a small monkey with Tom Jones's head.)

'Get them in, Keith.'

'Why me?'

'Ach, because you don't have to cope with what Ah do,' said Robbie Coltrane.

Peter rolled his eyes at me. Robbie had been bemoaning the pressures of fame again. The three of us were indulging in an afternoon drinking session in The George in Wardour Street.

'Ya doon't undastaaand. Ah can't get down the streeet without bein' bothered.'

His head was resting on the significant wedge of flesh that doorstopped his face and prevented his chin hitting the floor. My sympathy was limited. He was wearing a tartan suit, fluorescent pink socks and red brothel creepers.

'I hate to be a killjoy, Robbie, obvious as it is that you are wallowing in the most enjoyable mud bath of self-pity, but if you didn't go about in a suit that's louder than Iron Maiden you might have a better chance of being ignored by the great unwashed.'

My view on fame is that one gets only the attention one wants. Should you want to be left alone, usually that's what happens. Going about in a big car with a retinue of hangers-on signifies a need to be noticed, but famous people only want to be noticed on *their* terms, which means only when *they* feel like it. For example, when they're drunk (like me).

I dealt with the bullshit of fame by going round in nondescript clothes, eating in greasy spoons and driving decrepit cars. Apart from the odd lout in the pub, and the occasional well-informed media type, people never bothered me. Either the message I gave off was working, or no one knew who I was. I didn't care which it was and I was free to get on with my life.

At last orders Peter extricated himself and said his goodbyes, leaving us to find a new hostelry that could house our massive egos. We headed down Old Compton Street. Robbie stopped outside the Zanzibar Club, a media and celebrity haunt.

'Let's go in here.'

'No fucking way am I drinking in a private members' club.'

'Come on, I'll pay.'

'OK then.'

Installed in a corner with a couple of whiskies, talk turned to family matters.

'How's Alison?'

'Oh. You know. Pregnant.'

'You a changed man?'

'Oh yeah,' I said, rather too enthusiastically. 'I love it. Love it all.'

Robbie looked away with a wry smile, but my head was full of grandiose thoughts. It was all to be loved, all of life. The drinking, eating, fucking, laughing, joking, smoking. That's what life was – the moment.

Soon it was 1am and Robbie got up to leave. I wouldn't let him.

'Have another fucking drink.'

'Shouldn't you go home?'

'Yeah yeah, in a minute.'

Robbie pulled on his coat and threw me a look as he left. I searched for a new drinking partner. At the bar was a woman on a stool stirring a cocktail.

'Mind if I join you?'

She shifted along the bar and made space. 'Not at all.'

The barman looked at me and shook his head severely.

'Sorry, sir, are you a member?'

'I only want one more drink.'

'I'm afraid I can't serve you if you're not a member.'

'You've been serving me all fucking night.'

'Sorry, sir, you'll have to leave.'

The woman looked at me apologetically. Now I was angry and someone was gonna get it. I hated private members' drinking clubs and the elitist bullshit they stood for. To be excluded because you weren't rich or famous enough was to devalue the common man, and since my nightmare days at Brentwood public school all that mattered to me was to be the common man.

I ground my cigarette butt deep into the ashtray and I did some reasoning. What I would have done, before I was a family man, was smash the place up. I removed my jacket and handed it to the woman at the bar.

'Don't worry.' I calmly rolled up my sleeves. 'No one will get hurt.'

I picked up a bar stool and hurled it into the parade of bottles behind the bar. All three barmen ducked as glass flew everywhere. The next stool smashed the tables and the third tore the pictures off the walls.

After the stools I trampled on the tables and picked up a chair and ran it along the rows of empty, clean glasses.

The barmen attempted to get a hold on me but I shrugged them off, holding my hands up to signify that I was finished. The woman at the bar had long gone.

'Don't worry. I'm going.'

They understood that whatever it was I'd needed to do was done and left me alone.

The next morning I was overcome by guilt and remorse, resolving to go first thing and offer to pay for the damage.

'I smashed up the Zanzibar Club last night,' I told Alison.

Alison listened patiently, helping Sarah eat her breakfast cereal. 'Oh. Right.'

'But don't worry, I'm going to offer to pay.'

'Well, that's all right then.'

She hid her despair well. I phoned the owners of the Zanzibar Club and got through to the woman who owned it. I apologised and said I would give them some money, which they accepted. An hour went by, life returned to normal, and then the doorbell rang. It was the police.

'Keith Allen? PC Trevor Holland.'

For some reason he was inordinately pleased with himself. Turned out that they'd done some research, checked the local police station and seen from my last court appearance from my arrest at the Anti-Fascist League March that my address was Bury Place.

'I was called to an incident at the Zanzibar Club, sir. I was wondering if you could come down to the station and answer some questions.'

'Not really. You see, I'm busy. And I've spoken to the club; they're not going to press charges.'

'I'm afraid the police are. You're under arrest.'

PC Trevor Holland took it upon himself to make an example of me and charged me with criminal damage. I was bailed to appear at the magistrates' court three weeks later. The police case rested on the evidence of the woman at the bar, who made a statement that I'd told her no one would get hurt, which proved I was in full possession of my senses at the time of the attack and therefore responsible for my actions.

On the morning of my court appearance I grabbed some toast, kissed Alison and headed for the door.

'See you in a few hours.'

She looked me up and down. 'Are you going like that?'

My jumper and jeans combo had failed the 'Alison' test.

'What's wrong with it?'

'You're not going to make a very good impression dressed like a binman.'

'I'm only going to pay a fucking fine.'

At the court house a collection of ne'er-do-wells and freaks were waiting to be ticked off for stealing cars and forgetting to pay back loans. I took my place alongside a young man with sticking-out hair who was ranting.

'Tiger Tiger burning bright, in the forests of the night, not for daytime are thee so lost in glorious symmetry.'

In the face of obvious insanity the only thing to do was act normally. 'Got a fag?'

He was madder than a badger's hat but he had fags so we sat and chatted. The clerk called my name and I went into court two. The magistrate didn't look up.

'Have you a solicitor, Mr Allen?'

'No. I don't need one. I'm entering a guilty plea and offering to pay for all damage.'

He looked up above his spectacles at me. 'You will be allocated the duty solicitor, Mr Allen, and then your case will be heard.'

'But ...' There wasn't any point because he'd already shut my file and called the next case.

Back in the corridor Mr Mad was busy wiggling his sandalled toes and talking gibberish. 'Come friendly bombs, come fall on Slough, it is not fit for humans now.'

'I agree.'

Then he waved at a messy-looking geezer with grey, wiry, untidy hair and a ragged corduroy jacket. It was Ken Campbell.

'Fuck me ...' I said, hugging him. 'What happened to Mr Certifiable over there?'

'Oh, he's an actor from the Theatre of Brent. He was found wandering round naked on Primrose Hill reciting Robert Blake poetry. Which is no bad thing – but naked at 10am was probably pushing it. I'm here to testify that he's sound of mind.'

'You are?' I said doubtfully.

'What about you, Keith?'

'I smashed up the Zanzibar Club.'

'Well done.'

We caught up on old times while the Theatre of Brent actor gnawed through his arm. The duty solicitor approached somewhat hesitantly.

'Mr Allen.'

I stood up. 'Let's get on with it.'

'I just wanted to say I love *The Comic Strip*. And if it helps, I'm willing to say you're a well-known TV actor of good character.'

'Don't you fucking dare! I don't want you to mention anything about who I am or what I do.'

That week the newspapers had been full of celebrities going off the rails. The actor Stacey Keach had just been jailed in England for drug-related offences, and in England a judge had decided to make an example of George Best and sentenced him to Ford open prison for drink-driving.

When my case was called, Ken sat in the public gallery. I think the judge, who had listened to Ken trying to impress upon the court that his poetry-reading naked friend was sane, may have been influenced by his presence. He does have the maddest eyes and eyebrows.

The solicitor stood up and faced the bench. 'Your honour. I would like to mention that my client is a respected television presenter and well-known public figure of good character ...'

I put my head in my hands.

'He demonstrated great modesty in asking that this was not made known to the bench.'

My heart sank. The judge scribbled madly on the form. I was done for. He threw down his pen and removed his glasses.

'Mr Allen, you are undoubtedly in a position of great responsibility, held up as an example to the general public. Therefore I have no alternative but to sentence you to three months in prison.'

I jumped out of my seat in a state of shock and appealed urgently to the judge. 'This is ridiculous … I offered to pay for all the damage.'

'Are you saying that you made this offer at the time?'

'Yes. And the owners accepted it. Why the fuck should I be sent down for it?'

The judge called the prosecution and defence to the bench. After a period of harsh whispering between the judge and PC Holland, the judge replaced his glasses and addressed the court.

'On the evidence of the police I have no option but to pass a custodial sentence, Mr Allen, but for the record I have to say that since you offered to pay for the damage I see no reason why this case should ever have been brought in front of me. It seems a ludicrous waste of public money. Take him away.'

As the prison officer escorted me to the cells, my only thought was Alison, probably making a stew for tea and wondering what time I'd be back. All that mattered to me was letting her know. The fact that I was going to Pentonville didn't bother me in the slightest. A few thousand recidivists was nothing compared to Alison in full rant.

'Erm, I won't be home for tea.'

'Why the hell not?'

'I'm in Pentonville nick.'

My only solace was that the owners of the Zanzibar, feeling so guilty over me being sent down, offered me life membership to a new club that they were opening up called the Groucho. Presented to me in this way, my attitude towards private members' clubs suddenly softened.

Chapter 22

ALTHOUGH THE REDTOPS got hold of the story the next morning, it completely passed my parents by, or at least I think it did. I certainly wasn't going to bring up the subject of heaping yet more shame and delinquency on the Allen name, and Dad didn't mention it to me. Whether he read about it and chose to delete it from his memory, I'll never know. He probably preferred to pretend that bad things weren't continually happening to his family.

My first night in the cells reminded me of borstal. The smells of cabbage and disinfectant seem to be common to all government institutions: prisons smelt like hospitals smelt like schools. Back in a familiar uniform of blue pinstripe shirt and regulation blue canvas trousers, I lit up, put my hands behind my head and closed my eyes. Adaptability was one of my strong points. Like Gladstone's foreign policy in the 1880s, I believed firmly in 'laisser faire' – leaving things alone and letting them happen. Unfortunately the standards of sanitation and the daily routine in Pentonville didn't appear to have changed since the 1880s, and would try even the most placid temperament. My cellmate gave me a copy of Wal Hannington's diaries, which attested to this. He was a trade-union agitator and was incarcerated in Pentonville in 1926. I was astounded to discover that the daily routine he described was exactly the same as mine more than fifty years later.

Some of my duties included cleaning the toilets and the prison offices. From the office window I could see the buses streaming down Caledonian Road. It was bizarre to see normal life carrying on so close by. The buses would stop and the people on the top deck would look over at the prison, wondering what it was like inside. Far from being free, they looked bored, far away and dead. Perhaps a spell in prison would be good for every citizen every few years, to remind them what it is to be free.

After serving three and a half weeks of my three-month stretch, I was released on parole for good behaviour. One of the screws had tipped off the papers and a few photographers were waiting for me and my plastic bag full of belongings. Unfortunately so were a full complement of Comic Strip actors, including Nigel Planer and Peter Richardson. Alison had organised a Chevrolet and they all arrived dressed as gangsters and molls complete with champagne and cigars. It wasn't sensationalism, it was hedonism.

A few weeks later on 2 May 1985, Alison went into labour. We were at home; I was playing with Sarah and Alison was reading a book.

'I think it's started.'

She didn't even look up from the book. On the other side of the female-male divide all hell was breaking out as I went into panic mode.

'Fuck! Where are my car keys, Alison?'

'I haven't touched your keys.'

'Well, someone has. Sarah?'

Sarah toddled into the room and felt her mum's tummy, and while they calmly cooed my life was disappearing down the swanny.

'Where are my fags! Alison?'

'I haven't touched your fags.'

'Well, someone has. Sarah?'

'She's three. She hasn't started smoking yet. Calm down for God's sake.'

'I can't. I need a fucking cigarette.'

We dropped Sarah with a friend and motored along Euston Road where I cursed and hooted my way through stationary traffic.

'Get out the way, you cunts! My wife's having a baby.'

Finally a passage opened up just enough for me to squeeze through and pull over.

Alison stopped groaning and looked at me. 'Keith, what are you doing?'

'Buying fags. Won't be a minute … want anything?'

'Erm, a hospital.'

I dashed into the newsagent's and grabbed some cigs, a paper and some Revels. Now I was all set. Back on the road the traffic was still hellish but inside the car things were a lot calmer as I puffed away. Alison regarded me stony-faced.

'All you care about is smoking.'

It didn't warrant a reply. Inside my stomach there were half a dozen kittens being born but I couldn't be present at the birth of our first child without twenty Marlboro. It was as simple as that.

At Hammersmith General, Alison settled into bed and continued to read. Out of the window Wormwood Scrubs loomed large in the foreground.

'Keith?'

'Mmmm.'

'I think my waters just broke.'

'Shall I call the plumber?'

'Get a nurse.'

Whatever she was reading must have been good because she barely looked up when the nurse arrived and stuck a hand up her vag.

'Yes! The cervix is dilated to two, no, three inches, no, wait, gosh! That's the head! Quick! Baby's coming.'

All of a sudden the top of Lily's head appeared, all of a rush to get the fuck out of there and get off to some party. They took us into the delivery suite and I tried not to faint. At one point I was distracted by the sight of Wormwood Scrubs and spent the next few minutes looking out of the window trying to locate the exact cell I'd been in all those years before while waiting to be shipped off to borstal.

'There it is! There's my cell! Alison.'

Alison meanwhile was inconveniently indisposed having a baby. One big push later, Lily was born.

'Er, sir.' The nurse handed me this thing. 'Would you like to hold your daughter?'

Overcome with emotion though I was, the honest answer to that question would have been: not really. Lily was idiridescent green, covered in all this white shit. She looked like she was made of marble. I stared at her in wonder, a little concerned that we'd spawned a tadpole. She wasn't saying much either, but I needn't have worried on that front. As soon as she was put on Alison's tit she broke out in a rush of colour, gasping for air as the blood rushed round her body and she found victims for her lungs.

Lily was a beautiful baby, with porcelain skin and lots of dark hair. I spent hours and hours just staring at her.

Apart from the Comic Strip films, I was earning a reputation as a 'proper' actor, getting cameos and bit parts in British movies. One problem I've always had with British movies is that no one wants to see them, apart from the people who make them. Who wants to go and see a film about Grimsby in the rain? The Americans realised pretty quickly that normal people want to go and see movies that take them out of the drudgery of their futile existence, not drive them further towards it. Very occasionally there is an exception, as was the case with Bill Douglas. His documentary *My Ain Folk* was genius, and when he offered me a part in his new movie, *Comrades*, about the Tolpuddle Martyrs, I jumped at it.

The set was an abandoned village near Swanage in Dorset which had been requisitioned in the Second World War by the army and was never given back. It was now used as a tank firing range. The film company had enlisted the help of the brigadier's wife – a certain Sue Roderick Jones, a 'fixer' who used her contacts in the local landowning gentry to find cottages in which all the cast could live. She got all the bored army housewives from the nearby Bovington Camp to cook for us as a way to make a few quid.

Sue was a hurricane of activity with the most wonderful, firm, cashmere-clad breasts. I made a mental note. What really got me was the way she spoke, very clipped and fast, with a cut-glass accent. She wouldn't stand for any nonsense at all but I could see that there was something, a chink in the armour. I could tell she had a sense of humour.

She was the kind of woman I imagined would never buy T-shirts or sleeveless vests because they didn't have sleeves that she could roll up and 'get on with it'. Her piercing blue eyes belied a fabulously witty intelligence, and a month after having met her I would watch them flitting between grilling bacon and the *Daily Telegraph* crossword puzzle.

Filming started in Dorset in autumn 1985. Sue gave me and the other actor Phil Davis a cottage in some woods. Of course there was something incredibly sexy about her starched English manners, and above all I loved a challenge.

'OK, chaps? There will be a char lady who'll come and cook and clean for you, yah.'

'Thank you so much, er?'

'Sue. Sue Roderick Jones.'

'Thank you, Sue. You must come over for dinner with us one night.'

'Oh no, I don't think so, my husband wouldn't approve at all, ha ha.'

I nodded at Phil. 'Bring a friend, and don't worry … We won't bite.'

The next evening she turned up with an equally horsey but much plainer woman who laughed like a gorilla and looked like one too. I cleared plates and dumped them into the kitchen where Phil was spooning something ominous into bowls for dessert.

'Don't fancy yours much,' I tittered.

Phil looked daggers at me.

'You'll never get yours into bed. She's a different class.'

He was right. She didn't look very interested and soon made her excuses to leave.

'Thank you so much for a wonderful evening, rarely rarely wonderful, but I must go. I have to take Veronica back to her car.'

'I'll come with you.'

She looked at me sternly.

'That won't be necessary, Keith, rarely.'

They got into Sue's car and I followed in mine. After waving off Veronica, Sue hit fourth gear all the way through the estate in a bid to shake me off. She pulled up outside the big house and came to knock on the car window.

'Go away, Keith.'

'No. I know your husband is up in town, so why can't I come in?'

'Because you can't.'

'Fine, but if you don't let me in I'll sing. Very loudly.'

'If you don't go I'll call the police,' she retorted.

End of story.

I got a cup of cocoa out of her.

'But, Sue, now I'm here, I might as well stay.'

She put me in the spare room.

End of story.

'Sue, I'm not being funny but I think the spare room's haunted.'

She was reading in bed and laughed. 'Oh don't be so ridiculous.'

Our sex on the first night was amazing. Some people argue that the condition we call love is a chemically induced state whose existence causes those feelings we articulate in order to define it. Others believe the opposite to be true. The feelings cause the chemical reaction. Me? I don't mind either way, to be quite honest. There is, however, one thing of which I'm absolutely certain. You lose intimacy in a relationship – sexual or emotional – and your relationship as conceived is doomed.

This is what I was dealing with here. This woman was being ignored on an industrial scale. Her husband, the youngest brigadier-general in the British Army, was out on manoeuvres not entirely of a military kind.

I'm sure that if she'd really wanted, Sue would have called to a halt my own meticulously executed advances at any time. She had the most wonderful body; she was an expert skier and horsewoman. I too am an expert in certain fields. One of my skills is being able to detect bullshit, weakness and vulnerability. Over the next couple of weeks I came to understand why there was a sadness behind Sue's wonderfully experienced eyes. Not only had she had to contend with the death of her fifteen-year-old daughter in a skiing accident, but she had also told me that her husband was having an affair and that she knew the identity of the woman involved.

The combination of her stoicism and a desire to avoid scandal at any cost (there was a military career to consider) meant that she carried on being a dutiful army wife with her sleeves well and truly rolled up. If there was a God I have to say that our meeting was orchestrated with impeccable timing. And He must have singled us out for special treatment because two weeks later He went into overdrive. Ten minutes from the end of a football match arranged by Simon Ralph the producer, between cast and crew and the Bovington Camp army team, God saw fit to have my right leg broken in two places. They say He moves in mysterious ways. Well, there was nothing mysterious about this miracle of opportunity. Having been laid up in my little cottage in the woods for two days, it was clear that I was incapable of looking after myself.

'Where's your suitcase?'

'Er? Upstairs in the bedroom … why?'

'You're moving in with me.'

If I could I would have danced round the room. Sex and afternoon telly. Every actor's dream. As if this wasn't deep joy of the highest calibre, there was more to come. Because of my leg, Bill Douglas thought it best that upon my return to the film set I would be shot in positions of repose or leaning against things, barn walls, carts, young actresses, etc, because the plaster on my leg had to be hidden. Therefore I was filmed from the waist up. They say there is no gain without pain. Never was a truer word spoken. Wonderful sex, close-ups and afternoon telly. What a life. Happy days.

'Would you like your cocoa now, Keith?' Sue shouted up the stairs. I was in bed with my leg in plaster. Sue downstairs with her husband watching TV.

'Yes please.'

My cock was up quicker than she could mount the stairs. I think I lit up in her an abandoned sense of fun.

The brigadier would go up to London for monthly meetings with the government on issues of national security, where I know they would discuss people, particularly left-wing people. He was the face of the army at these meetings. I knew for a fact they had discussed Ian Bone, my mate from Class War, because the brigadier knew that I knew him.

Bearing all this in mind, I knew that the brigadier was not stupid and that it wouldn't have taken him too long to work out that this fruity young actor was malingering with intent in his house. Once I even discussed with him the role of the army if someone attempted a right-wing coup. The brigadier said emphatically that the army wouldn't be able to help bring about a coup of that nature because the sergeant and corporal ranks wouldn't have it. That it was them who ran the army, not the officers.

At the end of the summer, one of the last scenes we shot was a scene involving me, Phil Davis and another young actor. Bill was one for holding shots as long as possible, and this one was to take in the whole army across a field in the background in Tolpuddle. Trouble is, this scene was meant to be winter, which meant we'd have to shoot the second half of it in winter, so the cast had to wear greatcoats – except the serious and urgent young actor who insisted on sticking to his Stanislavski principles and answering the door of his cottage in a vest 'because he would have been in bed'. What a twat. We tried to reason with him but to no avail. Next we were to film in Australia before returning to complete the scene.

Meanwhile, Alison suggested we take a holiday. In January 1986 we set off with a couple of backpacks for China.

It was an incredible trip. China in 1986 was almost completely feudal. Pre-Tiananmen Square the Communist leadership exercised an iron grip. To be English meant nothing to them. If you had said 'Bobby Moore' it would have meant nothing. The one thing that singled us out was our Polaroid camera. We were suddenly these strange God-like people who could perform a miracle similar to making fire. Everywhere we went peasants would see their image appearing on the little black square and look at us in wonder.

We had to catch a ferry in an industrial town that was the Manchester of China. It was like a scene from *Apocalypse Now*, with planks laid across mud flats to reach the boat. The timetable said the ferry didn't leave until 6am so we walked into town to try to buy food and water for the three-day journey down the Yangtze River.

It was like a town in Dickensian times, the streets covered in straw with chickens running round and kids chasing them with sticks. We came across what we thought was street theatre. There was a lot of chanting and singing going on, with rows of seats and what seemed like a Q and A taking place. A woman was handing out rice wine and my eyes lit up.

'Come on, let's join in.'

'They might not want us to.'

'Bollocks. Course they do.'

We sat down and an old woman handed us some rice wine. Despite tasting like it had been drained through an old pair of fishy knickers, it had a potency similar to unrefined heroin. Suddenly the singing and chanting had us in a trance and we were paralytic.

'Hey.' I tapped Alison on the arm repetitively. 'Alishon.'

'What ishit.'

'I think this ish a funeral.'

It had dawned on me that what was going on was some kind of wake and that we were now part of a professional mourning show. People started to get up and pin fake money to a flag. Willing my legs to move and haul me to upright, I stood up and felt round in my pockets.

'What are you doing?' Alison looked worried.

'Well, I think ish only right that we make an offering to the er God of er dead people.'

In my hand lay a little skull keyring. If pressed, the eyes would light up red. Always ready to turn to my talent for mime, I demonstrated with great melodrama that my skull keyring would go via me up to heaven. My gift was indeed greeted with great clapping because it came from a 'round eye'. Now everyone looked at Alison.

'Why are they looking at me?' She prodded me accusingly.

'They're waiting for you to make an offering.'

She went quiet and then stood up on the bench. The street went into hushed awe. She started to sing, her lower lip trembling and her voice quiet and tremulous.

'The Looord's my Shepheeerd, I'llll not waaant.'

The place erupted with joy and applause. As for me, I was on the floor, dissolved in tears after witnessing the most moving scene of my life. Then the feast began in earnest and out came a variety of sparrow's giblets and deep-fried cat fur, all of which I doused liberally with rice wine to extinguish the taste. They sent us off to the ferry with a bottle of the stuff, which just about kept me from murdering the people responsible for the loudspeaker announcements every few hours extolling the virtues of the Communist State and celebrating the power and glory of the Republic.

On the next leg of the journey I snapped. We'd booked a sleeper compartment on a train back to Beijing, not realising we'd have to share it with some high-ranking general of the Red Army. At 5am the loud-speaker in our couchette crackled into life, no doubt telling me what a fine chap Chairman Mao was. The general below us got up and went to the bathroom, leaving me flailing round above like a madman looking for something to ram into the speaker. I saw his toothbrush lying on the bunk below and used it to stab the speaker with repeated jerking moments. The speaker went dead, then came a sickening cracking sound.

'Oh shit.'

Alison, who had been listening silently to this process under a sheet, now spoke. 'What's happened?'

'It's Chairman Mao's toothbrush. I've snapped it in two.'

'Christ, Keith … what are you trying to do? Get us arrested?'

She went back under the sheet and pretended to be asleep. This was clearly my mess and I had to get out of it.

Slipping down from the bunk I replaced the toothbrush, then returned to bed. I must have gone back to sleep because some time later I was woken by a light shining in my eyes and a small man doing an inordinate amount of shouting.

It was quite a relief to get on a plane in Beijing bound for Australia and the luxury of a four-star hotel to finish filming *Comrades*. Alison went straight home to London and three weeks later found out that she was pregnant with our son Alfie, who I deduced must have been conceived on the banks of the Yangtze.

When we returned to Dorset to shoot the last scenes of *Comrades* in winter, the serious and urgent young actor who had insisted on being shot in a vest was now standing in six-foot snowdrifts turning blue with cold. To our great amusement he had to be covered in several layers of goose fat just to keep him alive.

Throughout this time I kept up my affair with Sue, but I think we both knew it would have to end once the filming was over.

Chapter 23

MY AFFAIR WITH Sue Roderick Jones and my increasingly roguish behaviour was the emotional backdrop to writing *The Yob* with Danny Peacock. But the philosophy behind *The Yob* was not a reference to my own behaviour, it was a bit more thoughtful than that.

The Comic Strip had now gone to the BBC and they asked me to write a one-off film for the new series. I wanted to use *The Yob* as a medium to take a good look at this new 'pop video' culture while having a pop of my own at how fashion-conscious London was becoming. My relationship with pop music had come out of punk. I saw this obsession with style and fashion and suddenly I was looking at 'Rio' by Duran Duran and thinking, what is this shit? We were listening to crap about the brave new world of filmmaking (which was in fact the brave new world of technology, trickery of editing, etc) and I wanted to get across the superficiality of it.

The Yob has been described as a film that captured the zeitgeist of the eighties. Unfortunately Danny was also writing an adventure movie called *Jackson Pace*, and was only interested in where the next gag was coming from. Therefore I spent far more time writing *The Yob* while he wrote his movie. Of course he and others had ideas of who was going to play The Yob but in my mind, no one else was going to play him but me …

In 1986 UB40 were the band of the moment, a cultural melting pot typifying a 'hang loose' vibe that inner-city Britain had spawned, based around reggae and pop culture, home-grown weed and home-made tunes. They had taken the best of black and white British working-class music and put it together, but more than that they just were brilliant people.

They really were the best example I've ever come across of 'the whole being more than the sum of its parts'. They did as much to introduce the white working class in England to reggae as Bob Marley did. And that's a fact. When they formed none of them could play. Not one. They taught themselves together at the same time. But in Ali Campbell they had, I think, one of the world's truly great voices.

The Comic Strip loved the script and we boarded a train to Birmingham to pitch the idea to the band, who were understandably suspicious of white middle-class 'comedy'. These were not people you messed about with. Ali and Brian, the heart of the band, asked, 'So what's this about then?'

'Right, well, er, it's called *The Yob* and I want UB40 in it because I think you're fucking genius.'

'Yes, but what's it actually about?'

'Well, it's complicated.'

Ali and Brian sat down and looked at us. 'Come on then. We've got all night.'

Someone in the studio racked out a line of cocaine and we all tucked in. It was my first ever. Up to the age of thirty-four it had been strictly booze but now a whole new realm of possibilities opened up. It was like my happiness had just got in a lift and gone up another twenty floors and was now standing at the top of the skyscraper looking down on the world and saying, 'Yes, fucking great. I've made it to the top.'

Cocaine also introduced me to the hours between 4am and 10am, and the word 'tomorrow' suddenly meant 'the day after that', such was the reallocation of hours in the day from twenty-four to forty-eight in order to adequately house 'the Bender'.

An hour later we'd acted out every scene in the film. The band agreed to do it on the strength of our performance and the fact that we'd bothered to make the effort to go and see them.

'Not like the usual southern wankers who want us to appear on their television shows.'

'What's *that*?' I cried in horror while Alison cooed at it.

'It's my Alfie,' she said.

'It's Winston fucking Churchill.'

'He's beautiful.'

'He's the aging process in reverse. Tell you what, why don't we just skip the life bit and create an old man.'

Alfie was born in the same hospital as Lily, a year or so later in September 1986. That is where the similarity ends. While Lil had been out faster than a draft, Alfie looked as if he was preparing himself for the new millennium.

It was a long and difficult birth, and though I'm sure I was there throughout, there's not much coming back in the way of memory, apart from when he came out – that's hard to forget. Although Lily was green and covered in shit, at least she looked like a new-born baby. After about three and a half days of labour they managed to shoehorn Alfie out and handed us this thing that had more in common with a deflated crisp packet than a child.

As well as the uncanny physical resemblance, the application that Alfie showed fighting birth was akin to that of our great leader fighting the Nazis. Where Lil had porcelain skin, dark eyes and a mass of dark hair, Alf was completely bald and creased up. He was so wrinkled that it took six months for him to get back from one hundred and fifty years old to nought.

But once I picked him up, all that was forgotten. My son. *My* fucking *son*. I was determined that the love I felt for him meant that the father-son relationship we shared was not going to mirror the one I had with my own dad.

I was now responsible for three kids, two of my own and a step-daughter. Me and Alison fitted the kids into our lifestyle (still in the hippy seventies liberal way), rather than changing our lifestyle to fit round them. Despite the fact that my career was on the way up, there were still periods of unemployment between acting jobs and we never had any money. Alison was bringing up the kids and whatever came my way I felt it my duty to piss against the wall. Not intentionally, it just happened.

We went into production on *The Yob* soon after and I won the casting war and persuaded the powers-that-be that I was playing the lead. My fascination with charlie led me to play the character of video director as a vainglorious coke-snorting bore (no reflection of myself, of course). Lia Williams was cast as my girlfriend. She was tall, gorgeous and blonde. I'd like to think it was me who gave her her first ever television break.

The film came in at one hour and ten minutes and the producers were so delighted with the end result that we campaigned for it to have a cinema release before its television showing. It was an ideal opportunity for me to make the break into movies. Any actor would be lying if he said this wasn't the endgame. The ultimate recognition – years of watching Pacino and Bogart and knowing or at least dreaming that given the chance I could do it better. At the same time, although I was driven by ego, ambition itself never drove me. Yes, I wanted movie fame but not at any cost. My primary need, to express my opinions, would always come first.

The bad news was that due to internal wranglings, Nick Powell and Bob Wooley, the bigwigs at Scala Films, decided not to give *The Yob* a movie billing. Urgent action had to be taken. The next evening I went to the Scala office and stole the film.

A couple of calls to well-placed friends in the business and I organised a private showing in a Soho screening room. I stocked up with booze at the off-licence and set up a bar at the back. The taste-makers and opinion-formers of Soho started to pour in, as did a healthy smattering of East End gangsters.

A couple of dangerous-looking geezers turned up, looked round the Soho screening room and sniffed the perfumed air of middle-class media privilege. They were here to cause some mayhem and nothing could have pleased me more. I stopped them at the door with my clipboard.

'Names please, lads.' I kept up the act.

This being an impromptu screening, I was doing my guest list in reverse by writing people's names down as they arrived, like an anti-VIP list.

'Johnny Rocka and Paul Dennis.'

I'd met Paul Dennis a few weeks before in the VIP room of this new

Powis Square, 1980. I have no idea what I was thinking

Mum and dad in the 'poop deck'

Lily and Alfie share a bath, 1988

'Lily was changing from an angelic little girl into, well, into me'

With Lily and Alfie, 1993

Nira and I get married

Lily, Damien, Nora and Alfie on the steps of the church with me and Nira

The NME – it doesn't get any better than that

Glastonbury 2000: 'Jarvis Cocker sang "Saturday Night" by Whigfield'

© Mirrorpix

© Mirrorpix

With Noel Gallagher

© Amelia Troubridge

'Fat Les and heinous behaviour in the Groucho Club were secondary in my friendship with Damien'

With Lily at the 2007 Brit Awards

As the Sheriff of Nottingham

Left to right: Charles
Fontaine, me, Ali Campbell and
Brian Travis at my 50th

All grown up? You decide

club, the Limelight. Pissed out of my head and completely penniless I'd wandered in there and seemed to be the only VIP in the entire place. Various people flowed in and sat down so I'd lurched over towards them.

'Don't suppose anyone wants to buy me a drink.'

The non-VIPs in the VIP room politely declined my appeal and went back to their strawberry daquiris. Through my alcoholic fug a face appeared. It was Paul Dennis. He grabbed my hand and shook it vigorously.

'All right, mate. Just wanted to say hello, mate. I really rate you.'

'Oh great. Can you buy me a drink?'

'Course, mate.'

Paul grinned. He was tall, maybe six three, well built and very good-looking – straight out of the John Binden mould. All cockney wide-boy charm and aggression bubbling below the surface. And he had massive hands. He was the kind of man you wanted on your side in a fight. Correction, the kind of man you wanted on your side full stop.

We sat down with our drinks (well, I fell down). He grinned again.

'This is my club night. Come down any time.'

Turned out he was running his own night at the Limelight. It was about this time that the concept of one-night clubs was born. The likes of Rusty Egan, Paul and Johnny Rocka were going into established clubs and taking over for a night, hosting regular parties. This new breed of club entrepreneurs were always from places like Rickmansworth. They had a new-romantic look about them but their soul belonged on the north bank at Chelsea. Paul was utterly fearless. His clique used to have a death wish. Once they nicked a car and drove it down the artificial ski slope at Hillingdon. Their idea of fun was to see how far they could get in Europe without a passport.

But why we bonded was that Paul had an idea of the bigger picture in life. He responded to things that were funny and challenging and appreciated the 'have a go' attitude. (Proved to me once and for all when he dressed up as King Arthur under several tons of chainmail for the *Pepsi Chart Show* appearance of my 2002 World Cup song 'Who Invented Fish And Chips'.)

Anyway, this particular night the two of us went back to Bury Place and annoyed Alison until seven in the morning yammering away about nothing. We became firm friends.

I want to say a word or two here about the nightclub culture of the time. There were two major changes, which were interconnected. The first was opening hours. You have to remember that up to this point I'd been used to pubs closing at ten thirty. In central London there were no bars open after eleven until the late eighties. Even the Groucho Club closed at midnight.

The second change was the emergence of these one-off club nights, and it was the Wag club that started the change in 1987. Before then, no one used to go to clubs in the West End. They were for tourists or people from Watford. No one from, say, South London would come in. In 1987 I used to drink and watch gigs in the Rock Garden in Covent Garden, which was then a proper live music venue where I saw The Police and The Pretenders. Even that used to shut at midnight. Everything changed for me when these club nights started to spring up all over the West End, such as at the Wag and the Mud Club. Unfortunately for Alison, it gave me another excuse to stay out all night.

Most normal people live within their means and go and get drunk maybe once, twice a week, whatever they can afford. I went out every night, and dutifully spent whatever was in my pocket at the time. Whether it be twenty quid or two hundred, it was always me at the end of the night asking if anyone could spot me a tenner to get home.

When you get drunk, something happens called 'spontaneity' and people whose grave you would quite easily spit on suddenly become your best friends. You buy them drinks, you tell you were wrong to hate them, and buy them more drinks. In the morning you're cleaned out, and why? No reason. What is it about human nature that makes you need not to hate whoever you hate just because you're drunk?

One of my greatest faults (there are many) is to be generous. Perhaps to assuage the guilt that accompanies some of my other faults, or maybe just because I've never attached any importance to money, it has always slipped through my fingers. It also came from watching my father's frugality. In hoarding it and protecting it 'for a rainy day' he turned our family life into one rainy day after another, sacrificing fun for security.

His generation, the war generation, did it unconsciously. It wasn't his fault, but this was part of my rebellion against him.

That said, Alison and I were grafters. If we didn't have cash, we'd come up with a scheme to make some. First we started a sandwich business and made mountains of ham baps (well, Alison did) and sold them round the offices of Bloomsbury (well, Alison did). The ham sandwich business wasn't quite edgy enough for me, and though I never shied away from honest work, there was something girly about rocking up at an office with a wicker basket and saying: 'Sandwiches! Come and get 'em! Ham and tomato, cheese and onion or beef and mustard.'

No, much more up my particularly shady alley was the late-night booze business. In the mid-eighties there may have been Rick Astley and Terence Trent D'Arby to listen to in the pub, but there was nowhere to take them afterwards. It was virtually impossible to find a Spar that would serve you after eleven.

Despite being up to her knees in babies, Alison was still connected to the 'cool rich' set of London through Lucy Astor and Rose Boyt, and I hit upon an idea one day after buttering three hundred rounds of bread.

'Alison.'

'Mmmmm.'

She couldn't see me for the bread mountain in front of us.

'Fuck this for a lark. I know where the real money's to be made. Get on the phone to your posh mates and find us a party.'

A few hours later we'd loaded the car up with booze from our friendly Indian off-licencees. Alison had discovered that there was a well-heeled house party in Hampstead and off we went. There were fifty toffs standing in the garden on their last drop of red when we turned up, the back of the car groaning under twenty cases of Red Stripe. Alison rushed in and rushed out again with a bevy of posh totty all desperate for a drink.

'Thank God for you, Keith. We're bloody parched. The whole party is cleaned out.'

It was a great wheeze this. Every party in the capital ran out of booze by midnight. I opened the boot to reveal my bounty.

'OK, girls, how many you want? A quid a can.'

'Red Stripe? Haven't you got any Beaujolais?'

'No, I didn't manage to get across to Calais. Sorry.'

This last comment was delivered with more than a hint of sarcasm and earned me a kick from Alison.

Posh Totty shot me a look. 'This isn't a Red Stripe kind of party.'

'Well, what kind of party is it?'

She leaned into me and spoke through gritted teeth. 'It's Trudi Styler's party ... for *Sting*.'

'Well? He's supposed to be a sodding musician not an aristocrat.'

'Why didn't you get any red wine?'

'Because I'm *working class*. Now they can have fucking Red Stripe or piss off.'

They'd been at the nosebag so it was only a matter of five minutes before they were back and loading up with lager, since cocaine without booze is like rubbing your fingers with a cheese grater.

Next time, however, we were more organised and started servicing the parties of West London after striking a sale-or-return cash-and-carry service with the old black man who owned the offy on All Saints Road. The cash was rolling in and with Alison starting to get temporary work on the music videos we were able to get by.

Always looking for sales opportunities, I spotted that it was the 150th anniversary of the return of the Tolpuddle Martyrs. The TUC had organised a huge march through the village of Tolpuddle in Dorset to celebrate the homecoming of the Tolpuddle Martyrs from Australia. I knew about this not because of a desire to march (practical application of my left-wing beliefs was too much like hard work), nor because of any affiliation with the unionists, but because I'd played James Hamlet, one of the Tolpuddle Martyrs, in *Comrades*. I didn't have much time for unionists after I discovered how poor old James Hamlet was treated by his so called 'mates'. After his return to England he fell on hard times and ended up in a poor house. He was taken by his comrades to Tolpuddle where he was given a gold watch to honour his part in the uprising and then unceremoniously shipped back to the poor house. Charming, brethren, simply charming.

So for me Tolpuddle wasn't about fighting for the rights of the working-class man, it was about selling him beer and making a profit, showing the kind of entrepreneurial spirit that Thatcher would be proud of.

On the day itself, me and Neil Brown, an artist and fellow member of my old band The Tesco Bombers, set up a stall across from the village pub as coachloads of union members arrived from northern England. Anticipating our friends from the north, we'd bought hundreds of cans of bitter, which we stacked up in full view of the crowds gathering outside the pub and were selling for a very reasonable sixty pence a can.

'Get your bitter here, lads. Celebrate the Tolpuddle Martyrs in style! I was one, you know, way back. Don't I look good for my age?'

A burly miner with goalie's hands stopped, picked up a can and inspected it, while his friends loitered behind, hands deep in pockets, eyeing us suspiciously.

''Ow much?'

'Only sixty pence to you, cheaper than the pub by forty pence.'

'What? You're trying to bloody con us.'

'No, I'm not.'

'There must be summat wrong w'it.'

'Course not. I'm just making a living and doing you a favour at the same time.'

He put the can down and walked off in disgust. 'Bloody southerners.'

The plan was backfiring badly; to them I was a cockney spiv trying to do 'em. It all came down to the age-old but ever ridiculous north–south divide. Such was the extent of the chip on their shoulder that they'd rather give their hard-earned wedge to a poncy pub in a village full of rich people than to me.

'All right then, forty pence a can …'

Still no takers and an ever-increasing crowd outside the pub.

As I frequently found, the irony of politics was almost too much to bear. Here were the poor, downtrodden workers coming to celebrate the Tolpuddle Martyrs (who were such a selfish bunch of cunts they let one of their own die in a poor house), by marching through a town full of second homes while the locals lay on sunloungers sipping Pimms. I'd had enough, and with great ceremony opened all the cans and poured the bitter all over the village green, much to the chagrin of the watching workers.

'Fuck you! I'm a socialist too, you know, but I'd rather pour it away than give it to cunts like you.'

With that Neil bundled me into the van and drove me back to London.

'Keith! What have you got me into now?'

Alison slammed the door of Bury Place against me. I looked round at the queue of oddballs clutching instruments. They looked like they were waiting to audition for a talent contest …

I let myself into the flat and spoke to Alison softly through the door.

'It's going to be massive, Alison, and we'll charge them all for entering.'

'Yes, Keith, and who's going to pay the winner?'

'No one.'

Alison opened the door.

'You have to give them a prize, it's a competition.'

'No we fucking don't. They can bask in the glory of knowing that we've launched their careers in showbiz.'

So it was that our weekly talent show got under way. I conceived it as an antidote to *Saturday Night Live* hosted by Ben Elton, which of course I hated as another example of middle-class left-wing studentville. So Alison and I decided to run our own version of what a talent contest should be in the Falkland Arms. There was no business on a Saturday night in that part of Bloomsbury, so we took it over. We put an advert in the paper. Big fucking mistake. The phone didn't stop ringing and there was a never-ending stream of people outside the door.

'I don't know how you think this is going to work, Keith. But you better do something about them …'

Alison stormed off to man the phones and we decided that instead of auditions we'd make people describe the act on the phone and if we liked the sound of it they were in.

Interspersed with complete weirdos we found Les Bub, who did things with elastic bands, an erotic dancer who covered herself in cling film, and three sisters from Blackpool who credited us with launching their careers in showbiz when they ended up working the cruise ships.

We also had a regular performer called Mr Nasty and a spoken-word specialist called Phil Dirtbox, a strapping Welsh lad in bovver boots and a pork pie hat who talked in rhyming couplets while kicking your head in.

On the first Saturday we gathered a celebrity panel of judges that included Robbie Coltrane, Sting and me. The next week we had Joe Strummer and Peter Richardson.

The best act of all was Russell Bell, ex-guitarist from the Tubeway Army. He rang up and described his act.

'Well, it's me playing the theme to *The Deer Hunter* ...'

'Yeah ...' I probed.

'While cooking an omelette.'

'A what?'

'An omelette, mate.'

'On what?'

'On a Baby Belling.'

We started it with Bob Flag, who was a performer in his own one-man band, and we charged fifty pence to get in. It was of course a massive success and after three weeks we'd outgrown the Falkland Arms and had to move to a conference room in Tavistock Square. (So fuck off, Simon Cowell and your *X Factor* – we did it first.) I'd finish the show each week by singing Engelbert Humperdinck's 'Release Me' and make the audience sing along.

Turned out that Russell Bell's omelette act was a massive success and after we'd auctioned off the omelette and made even more money, he confided in me that he'd only made up his act while on the phone to me.

Like I said, me and Alison were grafters, but in a very different way to my mum and dad, who in 1988 embarked on a new work venture: the Poop Deck Restaurant in Brixham Harbour. They went on a caravan holiday there – thought it was heaven. After nearly forty years of waitressing, Mum now had her own place. Dad was the cook (he saw the saving there; why employ a chef?) and Mum the maitre d'. I took the entire Comic Strip cast there when we were filming *Supergrass*.

Dad served up ten plates of his famous roast dinner. Lamb with nine vegetables. Boiled, roast and mashed potatoes, parsnips, carrots, cabbage, swede, greens and peas. Piled high on the plate in that traditional English working-class way. Fucking hell.

'It's what the empire was built on, son,' said Dad, gladly serving Robbie Coltrane another portion. The Poop Deck was to be the culmination of all their hard work, yet I don't think they'd anticipated the extra pressure of doing it themselves. By rights, after a life spent grafting they were allowed to buy a caravan and do fuck all, but no, oh no, there was more work to be done.

Alison also began to pursue her career with vigour. I introduced her to Steve Barron, who in turn got her in with Limelight Films making music videos and more useless fucking English films about grim northerners unable to afford television. Steve and I had bumped into each other while I was promoting *The Yob* at the Val d'Isère Film Festival.*

The peripatetic lifestyle of a jobbing actor suited me fine, and while Alison started to move up the career ladder, our relationship continued to move down it. She probably passed it somewhere about the fourth rung. When Debbie Horsfield got in touch and offered me a part in her new drama *Born to Run*, it was another nail in the marital coffin.

Filming in Manchester meant hotel rooms and per diems and no distractions apart from the welcome kind. I whiled away the hours between work and work committing indiscretion after indiscretion. Not that they ever got out. When it came to my private life, it would have taken several SS interrogators with liberal doses of the truth drug to get me to give up my secrets, so intrinsic were they to my personality.

It was as if sharing my life with anyone completely would rob me of my identity, which is what women want. They want the couple to merge into one person, whereas men instinctively prefer to be detached, thus preventing themselves from being hurt. It's not very hunter-like to be too heartbroken to go out raping and pillaging, is it?

---

* Since the bars in the resort were so outrageously expensive, me and Paul Dennis started a nightclub in my hotel room called Club De Yob. On the second night there was a queue round the block as music pumped out of a little ghetto blaster. My room was like a Soho drinking club.

THE NINETIES

Chapter 24

IN 1990, MYSELF, Phil Dirtbox and the dancer Michael Clarke opened our own one nighter in Bruton Place called Beautiful Contradictions. The club was owned by Arabs. They would chop up lines on the bar at the end of the night the length of your arm. 'That's for the laydeez,' they'd chortle before chopping one up the length of your leg, 'And this is for the men.' An acceptable sexist discrimination I thought at the time. But it didn't last. Their drug-induced paranoia meant we couldn't operate our own door staff and policy, we had to use theirs. It came to a head one night when John Galliano was refused entry on the grounds that he was wearing trainers. The fact that his name was printed on them and he was in them meant nothing to them. We left after five weeks.

One night in April 1990 I was brushing my teeth in preparation for a big night at the club when Tony Wilson called.

'Keith, mate, it's Tony Wilson.'

'Who?'

'Tony.'

I couldn't hear a fucking word. The taps were running and I was brushing away.

'I can't hear you. I'm brushing my teeth.'

'Turn the tap off,' shouted Tony.

(This hadn't occurred to me. Much rather ask people to shout than stop whatever it was that I was doing.)

'I'm with New Order,' he went on. 'We want you to write the new England song.'

My head shot up from the sink so quickly I hit it on the edge of the cabinet. Alison walked past and shook her head.

'Argh, fuck! That fucking hurt.'

'Keith? Did you hear me?'

'Yeah, I heard you.'

'I'll send you a tape of the tune. We need lyrics.'

I'd known Tony, the dashing owner of Factory Records and king of the northern music scene, since the late seventies. He was, and still is, a stylish, slight, fey geezer who always wore shoulder pads. His long flowing brown hair was a hit with the ladies, as was his slick Jag.

'Er, course, Tony.'

'Great, see you at the studio.'

'Where?'

'Peter Gabriel's place in Bath.'

That conversation preceded an all-night drug and drink binge with Paul and Billy Curry (which ended with me getting a bit naughty with Billy Curry's missus in the toilets). At 6am I suggested the lads accompany me to Peter Gabriel's studio in Bath.

'Yeah, great,' they all shouted and went back to Paul's house to wait for me.

I went home to get the cassette and by the time I got back there they were all asleep (thank God). I managed to get myself on a train at Paddington and listened to the track on the way, just enough to have a few lyrics in my head when I arrived at Bath.

'Express yourself … It's one on one.'

An old lady looked up from her paper to see a stubbly red-eyed tramp (me) talking to himself as we pulled into the station. On arriving at the studio I promptly fell asleep on the sofa and didn't wake up until Monday morning, when I heard Bruno, some German producer, mixing the track. I then wrote the whole song except the 'Love's got the world in motion' chorus, which Bernard Sumner wrote.

A few weeks later Tony called again.

'Keith, get yourself to Led Zep's studio, just outside Henley … we've got five of the England team coming down to record vocals and the song's not right.'

I drove straight up and was surprised to hear a completely new arrangement. There was a new structure and chorus. Anyway, me and Tony went to pick up Bernard from his hotel and listened to the new song on the way. I had the first two or three lines of the rap, but not the rest. I got up to Bernard's room and he laid out two massive lines of coke and we did them and got back in Tony's car. Bernard puked immediately as a result of the massive line. The tune played on the stereo.

'We're singing for England – Eng-ger-land! ...' I sang, suddenly inspired.

'Eng-ger-land,' said Bernard in disgust and puked again.

'It works,' I replied, proud to have come up with it.

'He's right, Bernard, it does work,' said Tony.

Back at the studio Steve McMahon and Peter Beardsley had already arrived. We were still expecting John Barnes, Chris Waddle and Des Walker. Craig Johnston of Liverpool had come along for the crack. One by one they arrived and the plan was to get them to sing along but it soon became obvious that wasn't going to work, so in the end it was decided they should all have a bash at rapping it.*

First up, Beardo – forget it. Second, Des Walker – a black man with less sense of rhythm I've never met. Then McMahon, not much better. Suddenly a black limo pulled up and out fell Gazza. On being told what he was there for, he immediately jumped in the vocal booth.

'Give us a go – gi' us the words like.'

He delivered it in perfect rhythm. Trouble was, no one could understand a word he said, on top of the three bottles of champagne we'd all watched him drink. (This is no word of a lie – three bottles, and when England were in training for the World Cup.)

So we asked John Barnes to have a go, and the rest is history.

'I think we need an Italian word in the song,' I said to Bernard.

'Why?' he replied.

'Er, because the World Cup's in Italy.'

I came up with 'Arrivederci, it's one on one'. What I was trying to do was to combine the terrace and the club culture, which were being glued

* 'This ain't a football song, we ain't no hooligans' in the rap was the work of Craig Johnston.

together by Ecstasy. So it seemed perfectly apposite to me to add the line 'one on one', because the question people asked at the time was, 'Are you on one?', referring to whether or not you'd had an E.

Tony was right, it was a hit. Soon every schoolkid in the country knew the John Barnes Rap off by heart, and the song went to number one. Ironically, it was this rather than my acting roles that made me a household name. I wasn't that bloke off *The Yob* any more; I was that bloke who wrote the England song.

As a result I was invited out to the World Cup and went to all the games. You remember the tension. A semi-final against Germany? Hadn't we been here before? And didn't we know how it ended?

I have to say, it wasn't all as it seemed at home in England, a blaze of glory when we fell in love with the game again. For a start, the preparation seemed a little chaotic – from Gazza downing three bottles of champagne in the recording studio, to Italy, where, twenty minutes before kick-off, I was escorted through the grounds by a steward and taken to the players' dressing-room door. It was a joke. All I'd done was ask if I could get a message of good luck to Bobby and the lads. The steward, mistaking me for someone important, took me down to the dressing room so I could do it myself.

Now I think a fair bit of myself, as you know, but even I realised that the last person who should be popping his head round the door of the England dressing room just before the resumption of the most important ninety minutes of football since 1966 was Keith Allen. When I was close enough to hear Robson's voice booming from inside, I managed to make my excuses to the steward and leave.

And one more thing I have to bring up, given all the hype from the England players about how much they respected Bobby Robson and what a great manager he was. It was bullshit. I was there and saw first hand how they treated him. I was invited to their hotel with friends I was travelling with when they had a team meal after England had exited the World Cup. Bobby got up to make a speech and Gary Lineker pretended to yawn.

After his speech the players drifted away, leaving Robson sitting alone at the end of the table while Gazza, I remember very clearly, threw bread at him. This wasn't the end of it. Afterwards all the players picked him up, carried him out to the pool and threw him in. We all watched, expecting the players to help him out again. They didn't. They just threw him in, turned and walked away, leaving Sir Bob dazed and spluttering, struggling to get out of the water. I have to say I went home with a very different view of Gazza and Co than I went out there with. They were a bunch of cunts for the way they treated Robson. As far as I was concerned, Robson was a great footballing mind. He'd got us further than anyone since 1966, and was an icon in the game.

'World In Motion' captured a moment. It was that capacity in me that I lived for, sharing my love of life with the general public. What came less easily was sharing it with one other person in a personal bond like, er, marriage for example.

After doing the song I went home to see Alison. It had been clear to me for some time that it wasn't going to work out. I just wasn't ready for it, which sounds an overly simple thing to say when you've got two kids and a stepchild, but it was true. I hadn't been a bastard for the last few years out of cruelty. I was exhibiting my maleness and shifting the responsibility for ending it onto her. She didn't, and therefore it was down to me. This made me confront something for the first time in my life and take responsibility of some sort (even if it was that of a man running away).

Spiritually the relationship had ended long ago but I didn't have the courage to deal with it. Like most men, given the choice I'd let things lie, avoiding talking about the state we were in. Funnily enough, if there had been any talking done Alison would probably have fucked off long before I did.

The rigours of domesticity fundamentally clashed with my insecurity about who and what I was. To settle was not in my nature. Perhaps because of being uprooted so many times as a kid, I had an innate undertow of uncertainty about staying in one place. About being *one* person. To me being happy and settled meant one thing – you were moving again, so much better not to get settled in the first place.

So it was that I had to do the most difficult and awful thing in my life ever, which was to sit down with my wife and tell her I was leaving her. There are only two words for it – breathtakingly horrendous.

At this time Sarah, Lily and Alfie were in Spain on holiday with a fat Australian nanny, and since I didn't know what else to do I got a flight to Malaga to join them, intending to break the news to them in the kindest possible way.

On the plane the stewardess passed me, raising concerned eyebrows to see a grown man blubbering like a baby.

'Are you all right, sir?'

'Just bring me a drink, will you?'

I wasn't about to tell her the cause of my tears. The fact that they didn't stop for three hours showed I did have some feelings.

Yet, as was so often the case, things didn't quite turn out the way I planned. On arrival I saw that the nanny was patently useless and the kids running wild, so without further ado I sacked her.

'What are we going to do now, Daddy?' said Lily, her interest in me piqued by my decisive fatherly stand.

'We're going on another holiday to the South of France.'

I found that the only flights to Nice were leaving from Alicante, so I hired a car and we drove up the coast to Benidorm to wait for the flight the next morning. There was no putting it off. I had to tell them that their parents were splitting up so we chucked our bags in a B&B and drove to the beach to do it there. Except I couldn't and put it off again, deciding to do it at supper instead.

We went back to where we'd parked the car but it wasn't there.

'The cunts have towed me.'

'What's a cunt, Daddy?'

'It's a Spanish policeman, Alf. And don't tell your mother you know that word.'

We took a taxi to the local nick and I told the kids to wait for me outside. After the World Cup, let's just say the English weren't the most popular race in Europe. The look on the policemen's faces said it all.

'My car's been towed. Do you know where I can get it?'

'You park it illegally. You have to pay fine.'

'Fuck that, I didn't park illegally.'

'Then why it on the actual beach?'

Now everyone knew I didn't like walking which meant I'd always park as near to the final destination as was humanly possible. If that was the beach, then why not park on the sand?

'Whatever. I just want my car back. Please.'

They shrugged and smiled in that way that meant 'Fuck you', so without further ado I threw the keys across the counter at them.

'In that case, you find it. I don't care, it's a hire car anyway,' I said, and walked out.

They caught up with me in the garden at the front of the nick and about five of them started pushing me back inside. It was obvious they wanted to provoke me into hitting them so they could arrest me, thinking I was just another hooligan.

As one of them went to hit me, Lily, Sarah and Alfie came running up and tried to pull me away from them.

'Oi! That's my daddy! Get off him.'

'Leave him alone.'

'He hasn't done anything.'

Suddenly the police looked at me in a new light. I was a father, not just another English hooligan. They took pity on me for having three monsters to look after. They gave me my keys back and told me to go to the English consulate. I primed the kids with a story to get the car back.

'Right, kids, listen carefully, this is what happened: we parked on the beach because –'

'Because you're lazy.'

'No, Alfie, that's not it.'

'Because we had diarrhoea and you had to find us a toilet,' piped Sarah.

'Very good.'

With that I strode into the consulate and started the old 'Do you know who I am' routine, which is usually greeted with blank stares and much embarrassed rustling of papers. For once the people at the consulate knew exactly who I was, having diligently bought 'World In Motion'. In between finding my car they gave me a very bad rendition.

Now that the kids had saved me from jail and provided me with an alibi, it seemed the perfect time to tell them I was leaving them. Oh dear. They say there's never a good time, or is it that it's never the right time? We arrived in Nice and headed for a little place called Cap d'Ail, which seemed a much better venue to sit them down and drop the bombshell. But this was before Sarah got on the phone to Alison, who put her in the picture in no uncertain terms.

'Mum said Keith's left her,' Sarah shouted matter-of-factly to Lily and Alf, who turned to me accusingly.

'Dad? Have you left Mum?'

'Er, well, um.'

'Yes or no? It's a simple question.'

I went outside and shed a few tears (kids could be so cruel). It just so happened that Nira Park was also staying in Cap d'Ail at the time. Actually I knew she was there, but she on the other hand had no idea I was about to pitch up with three kids in tow.

Nira worked in the office at the Comic Strip and we'd met first when she was a runner on the Pepe Jeans commercial that for some unknown reason I'd been asked to direct. But then, since it was an advert that featured nine people laughing in a pub, I was probably the only person to do it. Nira was about twenty-two and very pretty. There is a photo of her sitting on Rik Mayall's knee when they were filming the comedy called GLC. I saw this red-headed beauty in a maid's outfit. Thereafter began the delicate ritual known as wooing. But I decided to cut the 'woo' out of wooing and simply turn up at her hotel with three kids.

'What are you doing here?' Nira walked out of the sea straight into Lily and Alfie, who gave her the evil eye.

'Oh er … I've left my wife. Er, these are her kids, my kids, I mean …'

'Who's that, Daddy?'

'That might be Dad's new friend … Nira.'

Much worse was breaking the news to my parents, who came down in full support of Alison. I moved out and straight in with Nira in Gospel Oak.

When Alison and I split, Alfie's behaviour deteriorated and he had trouble learning and paying attention in school. He was clever and worked out exactly how to wind me up and make me snap, at which point I'd smack him. Then came his trump card: he knew that a smack was followed by a cuddle as guilt enveloped me. I'd sworn never to hit my kids in the way that kids of my generation got hit by their parents. But poor Alf worked out that the smack was worth having for the cuddle that followed.

After one such occasion something else snapped inside me and we looked each other in the eye.

'I know what you're trying to do, Alf. You want me to hit you, but I'll never hit you again no matter what, and guess what, I still love you and always will.'

In my infinite wisdom I decided that what he needed was a period of quality time with his old man, in a tent, with his old man's new girlfriend … and without further ado we arrived in the South of France, where I endeavoured to teach him the fundamentals of the English language in between the fundamentals of shagging my new girlfriend. Hmmm. It soon deteriorated into a straightforward battle of wills.

'Come on, Alf, learn your alphabet.'

'No.'

'Right, you're not having any food until you've done it.'

Nira looked concerned as Alfie sloped into the tent to pretend to work.

'What are you doing?'

'Me? I'm going to starve him into intelligence.'

After a while we heard him chatting away to himself. Thinking it might be a rendition of the two-times table, we stuck our heads in to congratulate him. There he was, going through Nira's knickers, smiling inanely with one of her bras on his head.

'Hi, Dad. Is this an A, B or a C?'

Although despairing and a little concerned, part of me was secretly proud. I thought the bra on the head was a particularly nice touch.

The split wasn't so easy to deal with when Alison found someone else. Although we weren't together, the thought of her with someone else touched a raw nerve in me. I took the kids to get a pizza for a treat and they took great delight in breaking the news. Lily, especially, wanted to shock me. It was an annoyingly familiar trait. She was changing from an angelic little girl into, well, into me.

'Dad, Mum's got a new boyfriend and he's famous.'

'So am I.'

'You're not.'

'Yes I fucking am.'

Alfie shoved another piece of pizza in his mouth and pointed accusingly. 'You swore.'

Lily kept on talking. She knew how to provoke me. We were like two peas in a pod. She twiddled with the mozzarella on her pizza and tossed her head from side to side, acting all innocent when she'd probably been planning her move for days.

'Anyway. It's not about fame. That's bullshit. It's about your mum being happy.'

'Don't you want to know his name?'

'No, I do not.'

Alfie stared at me intently, fascinated, waiting for the outcome. Lily twiddled, I smoked. I wasn't going to break first.

'It's Harry Enfield,' she said triumphantly.

'Fucking cunt. I'll have him. She's only done it to get back at me.'

Alfie clapped his hand over his ears in horror at the expletives and Lily got on with feeling extreme pleasure at getting one over on Dad, who had left Mum and made her so unhappy.

'I *told* you he's more famous than you.'

Alison bought a house in Shepherd's Bush, and the superstar comedian Harry had got himself a ready-made family. The thought of him with Sarah, Lily and Alfie ripped through me. Jealousy (a confusing emotion at the best of times, a mixture of desire and fear of loss) reared up and was accompanied by an urge to fight him for my pride.

The house was a very beautiful four-bedroom terrace off the Uxbridge Road. Sarah, now a typical teenager, was in the attic, and Lily and Alfie had their own rooms. The divorce had affected Lily. When she was younger, up until the age of five, she was sweetest girl alive. She did everything for other people and was very smiley. Then as soon as I fucked off she became very hard work because Alfie was so difficult and me going meant she felt she wasn't getting the attention she deserved.

Also, the kids would talk endlessly about how funny Harry was, which didn't go down too well with me, as you can imagine.

One Sunday I went round to babysit and Alfie was stabbing the meat I'd cooked for lunch.

'What are you doing, Alf?'

'Harry said to just imagine that it's a German.'

This seemed rather odd, but then I found out that Alfie's favourite films were 633 *Squadron* and *The Dambusters*. It was then it dawned on me that Harry was obsessed with the war.

'Kids?'

'Mmmm?'

They were all lying on their fronts, watching telly.

'Does Harry have a perverse obsession with the war?'

No answer. However, Alfie wanted me to like Harry, so we pretended.

'Dad? Harry gave me this Airfix kit of a warplane, isn't it great?'

'Tell you what, Alf, why don't I help you?'

He nodded vigorously, delighted at this display of paternal generosity. Lily just eyed me suspiciously from the television. She and Sarah were now watching *Colditz*. My paranoia took hold. Harry was grooming them to spy on me. Alfie spread the Airfix instructions out in front of us.

'Right, we don't need them,' I said, tossing them over my shoulder. 'I know how to do it.'

My tongue protruded as I glued a pilot, who should by rights have been in the miniature plastic cockpit, to the undercarriage. Alfie watched curiously, a mischievous smile spreading over his face.

'But that's wrong.'

'I know. But it's funny.'

A few hours later Alfie and I had put together five planes in the wrong order, propellers stuck to wheels and guns upside-down on the engine. We left them where Harry would see them.

My juvenile reaction was the only way I could deal with Harry. Fortunately Lily and Alfie had their own way of coping. They had inherited my devilishness and made his life pretty unbearable. Suffice to say he quickly found out he had not inherited the ideal family after all.

Alison decided to sell the Shepherd's Bush house and move into Harry's disgustingly nice pile in Primrose Hill. Ever the magnanimous ex (and short of my own abode at the time), I offered to live in it and sell it for her since the market wasn't moving.

Since it was next to White City, it was perfect for BBC employees, so I advertised it internally in Television Centre. Pretty soon I'd got Alison a buyer and they were exchanging contracts. The phone rang.

'Hello, son. It's your dad.'

'I know who it is.'

'What you doing living in Alison's house then? You back together? That's nice.'

'No, Dad, we're not.'

'What about Lily and Alfie, for their sakes?'

'They're fine. I'm not dead, am I?'

'Don't be sarcastic, Keith. Here's your mother.'

I rolled my eyes, sighed and threw myself on the sofa, waiting for the charge of the clucking-chicken brigade.

'Keith!'

'Yes, I'm here. No need to shout.'

'Are you still with this Nira then?'

'Yes, Mum.'

'When are we going to meet her then?'

I'd put it off for a couple of years but the clucking and whining about Alison wasn't going to stop until they realised it was over.

'Why don't you come and stay here and I'll get her round for Sunday lunch?'

Silence at the dim end of the line. Then: 'What … at Alison's house? Is that right?'

'It's only a house, Mum,' I sighed, 'not a moral high ground.'

Chapter 25

I SUPPOSE I SHOULD touch on the Groucho Club. You've probably all heard of it by now, either because someone has 'fallen out' of it at 2am or perhaps because it was a notorious pit of decadence in the nineties.

Well, I can't talk about all that until I've told you how I first met Damien. It was of course in the Groucho, in 1993, and he lurched over and introduced himself. He was in T-shirt with some obscure slogan on it, jeans and I can't remember the shoes. He looked like a mad professor, albeit a charming northern one. He's the kind of person who becomes even more attractive once you spend time with him. Charm? He had it in truckloads. It was mad passion, mad blinding passion between us. What I liked about him was his wit, intelligence and his live-for-today philosophy. Oh, and his beautiful eyes.

'Aren't you the bloke who did that film?'

'What film?'

'That film. You know.'

'Not really. But aren't you the man who pickles sheep?'

That set the ball rolling for a long rambling discussion which transferred to the Black Hole – a filthy after-hours drinking hovel in Cambridge Circus. There were a few of those types of places, sordid and full of terrible drinkers and crack whores. People were desperate for drugs and would pay sixty quid for a gram of speed. There began the hedonist years. Where I think Damien, me and later Alex James upset many many people we probably shouldn't have.

A typical night would begin in the Colony. The Colony is a one-room club full of interesting paintings and fucked-up people. Francis Bacon was a regular, and now the new breed of art and rock and roll had moved in. The Colony is a well-kept secret, so I'm not going to give anything more away …

Alex James – who you all know from Blur – had decided that the route to drink and drugs was the road he wanted to travel at that time, and he was privy to and part of our madness. Completing the 'shambles à quatre' was Charles Fontaine, the gruff-voiced larger-than-life French chef, who had a heart of gold. Charles always reminded me of Inspector Clouseau when he can't work out 'who done it'. Constantly pissed off with everyone for no apparent reason.

One night at the Colony Club in Dean Street, me and Alex were having a line in the washroom when Alex slid the window open and looked across the roof.

'Hey look! We can get in the snooker room of the Groucho over the roof.'

I had a look.

The next minute we were out the window.

Over the roof.

In through the ladies'.

Where we met a couple of girls doing charlie, got chatting.

Think either me or Alex got a blow job off one of them.

Snooker room.

Damien, Alex, me, Charles and the other charlie of course.

3am: order four bottles of wine.

Hide under the snooker table.

Wait for the manager to close the club.

Stay locked in the snooker room till 10am.

Stagger downstairs.

Take our trousers off and stand at the bar naked from the waist down.

Tell everyone it's No Trousers Day.

Stephen Fry walks in for business breakfast.

Orders sausage.

Damien comes out with his cock on a plate.

'You ordered a sausage, sir.'

Stephen doesn't even blink. 'I said a sausage, not a chipolata.'

Yes, it really was like this all the time, and mainly because of Liam Carson, the then manager. He made the whole idea of a private club OK because he was one of us. He got me in there in 1989 with poker nights. Then the club was only a small bar downstairs and the restaurant. Liam* made it a meeting of like minds rather than any elitist bullshit. You could, and still can, always get a proper conversation there, about pretty much anything from science to art to rock climbing or pigeon fancying (mostly goes: 'Oi, mate, don't fancy your bird much).

There was one particular night in 2002 when the whole reason for the Groucho became clear. Such a marvellous meeting of oddballs and rockstars you never did see. Picture the scene, reader.

On piano – Moby trying to play 'Blue Monday' while Bernard Sumner tapped out the beat on the piano lid with a beer bottle.

On bass – Alex James, Chris Martin and Guy Berryman looking on curiously.

On vocals – Neil Tennant.

On a bender – Me.

On a stool listing 90 degrees to stern – Tony James.

On a tight corner – Damon Hill trying to be a rock star.

On a table top – Wayne Sleep doing pirouettes.

And, of course, it was while behaving badly in the mid-nineties that I befriended Pockets – or rather he followed me. The bespectacled vision that was Pockets slid from one bar to another till he settled snail-like in my study. He'd successfully kept a lid on his tendencies, though it was his obsession with wiry young men in tight trousers that alerted me to the idea that he was batting for the other side. (Pockets must have come from an extraordinarily large family – he was always waking up in bed with his cousins.)

---

* Liam died of a drugs overdose in 2005.

Chapter 26

I HAVE TO take time out from the ordered chaos of this book and give Glastonbury (and other festivals) its own chapter. My first Glastonbury Festival was 1979. I didn't know at the time that it would go on to become such a massive part of my life. It was a hippy festival then, not a young person's festival at all. The old Bath festival that I'd visited while on the run ten years earlier had to relocate after complaints from the neighbours, and it moved to Michael Eavis's farm in Pilton, Somerset – not Glastonbury at all. I went along with the lads from the Crystal Theatre of the Saint. In those days it was a small affair with one stage. The Pyramid stage then was a corrugated-iron structure under which the cows sheltered. The entire site was no more than two or three fields and you were allowed to camp with your cars round the place. The festival culminated in a moonlight pagan parade.

There were no stalls but there was wonderful hippy food and the bands weren't big names, just good bands. It was all very kiddy-orientated with swings and a train that went round the field on a track. I loved it because it seemed like a closely guarded secret. Only the West Country locals seemed to know about it. The Hells Angels handled all the security and to stop the audience storming the stage they poured cooking oil on the sloping wooden barriers. People would still try and climb up them, though. The game was to see how far up you could get before sliding back down again.

There was always a weighty number of travellers and by 1981 they were getting politicised because of the advent of Thatcher. They objected to Thatcher and the police trying to stop them gathering anywhere in large numbers and so Glastonbury became a haven.

In those early days, Arabella Churchill ran the Comedy Tent. Its first year was 1980, and Malcolm Hardee set up the performance tent with her, bringing acts from his own new comedy club in South London. I was one of the first people to perform comedy at Glastonbury and because of that I feel I have the right to call myself one of the founding fathers of the modern Glastonbury Festival. I hope I capture the spirit of it.

And probably some of the stench. In the early days there were no showers and only rudimentary toilet facilities. Safe to say, sex wasn't high on the menu for those more discerning romantics. Probably safer to wash your cock in scrumpy than trust the local water supply. But I had a secret weapon. I met Gretchen, who organised the workers' party on site (not the socialists – the litter picker-uppers). It just so happened that Gretchen also used to be the scorer at my local cricket team in London, and I really fancied her daughter. Anyhow, me and the daughter, let's call her Tulip, started snogging before she pulled away and said, 'No ... let's go somewhere ...'

She took my hand and led me to paradise. It was, after a week in the same clothes – she took me to a shed at the Eavis farm in which there was a hot-water tap halfway up the wall. We undressed and made love under warm running water. I remember it to this day. I kept this secret very close to my chest, nipping off with Tulip whenever the mood took us but telling none of the other lads about the shower.

Back then the hardcore festival posse was just me, Roger Pomphrey, Kevin, my brother, and Nellee Hooper, Dom Thrupp and a lad called Aaron. Of those, only me and Roger remain stalwart Glastonbury-goers.

In 1981 the *NME* scoffed at the festival, saying it was hippy shit. What they didn't understand was that it was also a place where lots of smashed working-class lunatics could be found, who saw it as a great one-day bender. Not only that but we were moving it forward with the comedy.

And we never paid to get in. The game was to see who could get the most people in (this was before there was even a need for a proper entrance – people just paid up) and I never felt guilty about this because I reckoned I put in as much to the festival as I took out.

The whole concept of Glastonbury for a 'situationist' performer like me was one long show. I did impromptu performances all the time. This started in earnest in 1983 when Alison and I went together and I was interviewed round our campfire by two dour overcoat-wearing journos from the *NME*. We'd just got ourselves one of the brand-new Sony Video 8 handhelds, which was a revolution in technology, and set about making our own little film. I was being interviewed because by then I was a bit of a face thanks to *Whatever You Want*.

'So, er, Keith, what do you see in all this hippy ceremony? I mean, you're involved in the punk movement, yeah?'

They just didn't get it at all.

'I see Glastonbury as a very good way for people to express themselves,' I countered. And to prove my point, Alison and I performed our own pagan ceremony for them, which involved a ring of flowers, the 'psychic circle', and Alison dancing for me and then taking off her knickers and putting them on my head. Wonderful. And touching.

They left after not being able to make out whether we were joking or not. Of course, that's the beauty of situationist performance. One situation I'd have gladly swapped was my first experience of magic mushrooms. Which happened later that same night. A woman who looked like she was on the way to Scarborough Fair by way of the insane asylum pitched up at the fire. She had a diamond tattooed in the middle of her forehead and a basket on her head.

'Mushrooms.' She smiled.

'Go on then, I'll have twelve.'

She took them out and we saw that they were individually pressed, like dried flowers, between the pages of a book. Alison and I took six each. Oh my God. I've had mushrooms many times since, but these were something else. We spent the next twelve hours crouched on all fours undergoing waves of hellish hallucinations. All the while the madwoman watched us from a distance, smiling at the effects of her potion. Alison got in the back of our van (which was full of amyl nitrate and beer – which we were selling) and tried to sleep. I went to check she was OK, only to find the madwoman caressing her brow and slowly making her way down to Alison's breasts. Poor Alison.

In 1984 there was a wind change. The festival tripled in size and was 'branded' for the first time. Stalls selling prepacked factory beefburgers appeared and a fence went up. A security firm from Manchester was brought in and there was a face-off, which resulted in a full-scale riot. A large retinue of travellers gathered outside the main gate; none of them had tickets and consequently they weren't allowed in. They saw it as their right: it was pagan spirituality and all that. So they simply stormed the entrance, which was guarded by thirty-odd burly security guards. I was watching from a safe distance, Alison and I cowering in our van as they clashed. It was like a scene from *Mad Max*.

This was the signal for all of us to get in as many people as possible without paying. Kevin put five people in a cardboard box and told security it was a fridge. It was a symbol not only of childish fun and entrepreneurial instinct, but also a sense that if Michael Eavis was taking the festival in a more commercial direction then we'd object in our own way, by not paying.

In 1985 we took Lily for the first time as I was determined to make it a family affair and found an eight-week-old baby was a great selling tool for my out-the-back-of-the-van beer and amyl nitrate business. I hadn't told Alison about the amyl nitrate bit of the business, which started as a gimmick to increase sales and came about after meeting a couple of irons in the Bottle and Basket off-licence in Hammersmith. I was in there buying wholesale booze one day, when they sidled up and tapped me on the shoulder.

'Aren't you that comedian off the telly?'

'Actor. I'm an actor.'

'Oh, whatever, same thing.'

'No it isn't.'

'Whatever, you like a party. I've got something to show you.'

Then one of them waggled his head and intimated I should follow him into the back. But the last thing I wanted was an offer of bum fun.

'Look, guys, I'll do you an autograph if you want ... but *that's all*.'

'Shame, you've got a nice arse, but this is about something else.'

In the back of the shop they showed me their wares by sticking it up my nose. (The bottle, not the cock.) It was home-made amyl nitrate. Five minutes later I came round, feeling like someone had just split the atom inside my head.

'Fuck me, that's strong.'

'We make it ourselves,' said Iron One proudly.

'I'll take everything you've got.'

So it was that my beer and amyl stall was born. I didn't see what was wrong with taking baby Lily along with me as a sales tool, rather like the homeless lads do with dogs. Cute puppy guarantees punters will stop and stroke it and therefore give you money. Lil sat next to the stall gurgling in a pushchair while I cranked up the sales patter and knocked out the lager. While Alison was hanging out backstage with the movers and shakers of the music business, sensibly using the opportunity to network and advance her career, I was getting mindless with the hippies.

'Roll up, roll up! A quid a can plus a free sniff of amyl.'

A couple of Welsh lads stopped.

'Come on, lads, Iron's Amyl, free with a lager.'

'What's that then, boyo?'

'It's like your own personal warhead delivered up your nose … Go on, buy a beer and I'll show you.'

They took two cans each, which entitled them both to two amyl hits. A few days later they got up.

'Fuck me that's strong,' said one, shaking his head.

'Give me the 'ole bottle, will you?'

'Ten quid it's yours.'

It wasn't long before Lily and I were surrounded by a pile of semi-conscious revellers on all fours picking up bits of their shattered minds.

1986 was the first year there had been serious mud at Glastonbury, and after kitting out Lily in wellies and waterproofs I discovered another way of making money and amusing myself in the process. In those days the only shops were at the top of the hill above the Pyramid stage. After two days of rain and thousands of feet tramping up and down to get to the stalls, the hill had become a mudslide.

I stationed myself at the bottom of the hill and started selling my beer, but after watching a few people fall arse over tit in front of me, an idea started to form in my mind.

'Roll up, roll up! A quid to win a fiver. You give me a quid, I give you a snort of amyl, you run up the hill without falling over and you win a fiver.'

I knew it was virtually impossible to get up the hill without falling, but it was like lambs to the slaughter. Soon I had a crowd of delighted revellers watching the spectacle of people covered in mud trying to claw their way up a steep hill only to fall back down.

Glastonbury put the ridiculous into sublime. The only place in the world where you can get away with selling coals to Newcastle and not only get away with it but get a hug as well. The more mud and rain the happier I was, thriving on the things that made other people uncomfortable. Chaos and confusion were my bedfellows. Years of squatting, busking and being banged up taught me that everything I needed was within rather than without. I loved the mud and the rain, embracing the Dunkirk spirit and siege mentality, but after trying to ram kiddie buggies through swamps of shit, Alison gave up and went home.

So on went the pattern – you get the drift. But there was a bit of a lull after 1986 because I was working more, and I wasn't a big enough 'face' to demand a week off every June so that I could go to a rock festival. The next great Glastonbury 'era' started in 1995.

It was in early 1995 that I got to know Joe Strummer properly. Nira and I set up a production company called Big Talk, on the basis of an idea for a series of spoken-word cassette tapes, on which interesting and notable people from the cultural world would talk about their lives in an informal setting.

The first were Jeffrey Bernard and Jonathan Meades. They had lunch and we put a tape recorder in front of them. One of the pairings was me and Joe Strummer. I interviewed him in a pub in Reading. It was obvious that we came from a similar place in terms of mentality. Joe had a wicked sense of humour, not one you'd expect of him. His cool image belies a fun, mischievous character, who loved putting the cat among the pigeons. By now in his forties, he still had the eyes and the rock-god hair and cheekbones. He was softly spoken and quiet, even shy. He came to life when surrounded by people, a gig or at his favourite place, Glastonbury.

In 1995 Oasis were headlining Glastonbury and I still didn't know who they were. I never went to Glastonbury to see a band. For me it was about the people. And Glastonbury 1995 saw me, Lily and Alfie, Damien Hirst, Angus Fairhurst, Nira, her best friend Nora and Damien's girl-friend Maia and their son Connor hire some vans and set up camp backstage. I was desperate to show my best mate Damien how great the community of festival life was. The campfire had expanded, so had the people.

But I was soon to discover that Damien didn't really like festivals in the same way as me, or Joe (Strummer). Damien and Joe hadn't yet met but they were about to. Like me, Joe had seen something in the festival lifestyle and he was also being informed by the traveller lifestyle, a sense of going from festival to festival. Next on the festival itinerary was Womad and I knew Joe was going to be there.

The night before Womad, me and Damien had been up all night. At the time Damien was living in a mews flat in Chelsea. It was nine in the morning, there was no booze left, so I took control.

'Right. I'm going to hire a van. Don't go to sleep.' I went down to a rental place in West London, picked up a transit and drove it to Portobello Road, where I found an old organ in a junk shop. As per the rules of the game, we had to get into Womad without a ticket, so I hit upon the idea of pretending that we were delivering an organ. We drove to Womad with this organ and were stopped at the gate by security.

'Tickets and passes, please.'

'Er, we're delivering this organ to the Mtumbi African drum band.'

'Right, well, you can't drive your van in. Park it over there. We'll give you a lift with it.'

So me, Damien and the broken organ were not only in but delivered right into backstage camping by the organisers. There we found Joe Strummer and his wife Luce surrounded by carefully positioned trucks and awnings, giving the impression of a multi-coloured tented village. Also there was Sean Ryder's girlfriend, Chrissie Hynde and her American boyfriend, and this butler-type figure called Dave Girvan – who was to become Pockets. Cumbia music belted out of a huge customised ghetto blaster. Damien was flagging so I introduced him to Joe and went off to find some drugs.

Oh dear. It was the first time any of them had GHB.

The astute Damien could see where this was heading and declined to have any. We were joined by John Govett – a spitting image of Richard Ashcroft and the nicest man you could ever meet. We all sat round the fire. On GHB you lose time, space and reason. Everyone looks like they are made out of a grid. You feel like you've been away for hours and it's only about thirty seconds. Don't try it at home, kids.

Joe said to Damien, 'You need a name.'

'I've got one. It's Damien.'

'No, man, I mean a real campfire fuckin' name.'

'Tell you what, let's all have campfire names,' I joined in.

We were all lost in thought. After some time it was decided. Joe spoke.

'He's Damien Pickles.'

We all looked at Damien. Hmmm.

'You're the punk warlord,' we told Joe.

'And I'm the lion,' I said.

Chrissie Hynde's boyfriend Norman had a weird hat so he became Psycho Norman.

'What about me?' Dave piped up. He was wearing this fisherman's jacket and since we arrived he'd been pulling all kinds of things out of his seemingly unlimited pockets. Fishing hooks, Rizla, plasters, fishing hooks – if you'd needed a steam iron, he'd have found it.

'Well, it's obvious,' we all said. 'You're Pockets.'

And so Pockets was born. A full description of him can be found at any local police station.

Damien collapsed even without the benefit of GHB and had to be taken back to London in a roll of carpet. Thus began a two-day bender on GHB which left John Govett needing AA, NA (and anything else with A in it), Damien hotfooting it back to the RCA, me needing the RAC (the van had broken down) and Pockets needing the RSPCA.

I realised then that Damien was uncomfortable at festivals because he wasn't in control. I understood. To truly enjoy festivals you have to be able to abandon yourself to the moment. It reminds me of being a child: if you're tired you go to sleep, any time and anywhere. What I love about Glastonbury is the freedom of not knowing what's going to happen next. I thrive on that uncertainty. The whole festival experience is one huge voyage, an adventure. Also I love to see the effect that festivals have on people. I loved observing. Joe was also a great people person. What was interesting about Joe was that he never strayed far from the campfire because he knew that people would gravitate towards him, and he liked to watch people who didn't know each other, different types of people. Observing and being with different types of people, this was integral to Joe. He hated judging anyone – rich or poor. It was live and let live with Joe.

Still, even though Damien had fled vowing never to return, I knew he would. I also knew that an important meeting had taken place. Joe and Damien.

1995 was the beginnings of the campfire scene, and Womad was the first time I'd seen any of Joe's camping doodah. Which consisted of bits of string, a collection of flags, some gaffer tape, mouldy tarpaulins, neon spray paint and Cumbia music. Little did I know that these were the rudiments of the world-famous Strummer campfire, of which two of the cornerstones were me and Pockets. I didn't know it yet but Pockets was an institution as well. When not being a GHB-guzzling youth botherer, he was also a qualified potter.

Joe and Luce moved to Devon the following year and they became very close friends with Damien and Maia. (It was me and Damien who got Joe back out on the road. He had just recorded 'Yalla Yalla' and played us the song in the back of a taxi after we'd left Damien's Turner Prize exhibition. It was a great track but he wasn't sure about it. We harangued him to get a band and get back out there. I'm pleased to say that he did go on tour soon after.)

So, in 1996, the modern campfire era of Glastonbury was born, when all the ingredients came together. The last ingredient was the Manchester posse. Joe had met them at a Black Grape concert in Manchester, where, through Sean Ryder and Kermit, Joe and Luce met the hangers-on. They introduced themselves to Joe and told him how much they loved The Clash. They were all working-class hard men who have been moved by what Joe sung about. Joe invited them all to Glastonbury and they came. Basically they never left again.

So it was that Big Danny, Fonzo, Cresser, Winker, Bez, Fat Neck, Scully and Tommy Dunn arrived. They brought the kind of 'dirty drug end of urban chaos' and it was brilliant. They took it upon themselves to run the campfire as a protected area and with it the whole ethos of scally life, currency fraud, touting and all, none of which you'd think would sit pretty with Joe. But it was out of Joe's loyalty to them, his fans – and his respect meant so much to *them* that you could see his philosophy getting through. They ditched their prejudices and practices and took on Joe's community philosophy instead. Suddenly hardened Manchester scallies were going round with binliners keeping the place clean. They developed a respect for their environment and a social responsibility they'd never had before.

The campfire also fulfilled my need to perform. First in 2000, when I launched my now famous karaoke contest – not in backstage VIP but out in the people, at the Future Forests stall. I got Jarvis Cocker on Ant Genn's shoulders and he sang 'Saturday Night' by Whigfield (really rather well, actually).

In 2002 I spent the entire weekend sitting by the campfire barely able to move. In need of a costume for the karaoke, I had emerged complete in a pink and lime-green Adidas shellsuit (size small) and a leather biker's hat.

'Hello,' I said to the gathered crowd of popstars and *NME* reporters. 'I'm Dai Honky Tonk. I'm a gay. I drive taxis in Llanelli.'

It just so happened that Matt Lucas and David Walliams were in the audience. (Let me remind you of the year – 2002 – of my 'only gay in the village' act. Now work the rest out for yourself …)

Trouble was, in the process of 'being in character' I'd reduced Joe's spiritual campfire into a Benny Hill sketch and Joe lay under his truck fuming with me and refused to come out. Meanwhile, Lily was also fuming because she could see the seams of her pink and lime-green tracksuit bursting because her MDMA-stoked buffoon father was wearing it, and Zoe (my girlfriend) was fuming because every time she tried to ask me anything I just blew raspberries. (Still a little growing up to do, I hear you say …)

But the most 'out there' festival experience I've ever had was the last that Joe and I did together in July 2002. The Mount Fuji Rock Festival in Japan. Masa, the organiser of the event, had hung out at our campfire when I did Dai Honky Tonk and had loved the atmosphere. He was so eager to bring that atmosphere to his own festival that he simply imported the entire campfire to Mount Fuji. Quite literally he paid for me and Joe, Luce, Eliza (Luce's daughter), Pockets, Dermot, Maia, Norman, Zoe and a few others to go out there for a week – our only 'job' was to set up the campfire, as it was at Glastonbury, and sit there and get bollocksed. Thereby, I presume, showing the Japanese how it was done.

Joe took all the flags and his camping doodah and we set up a fucking brilliant campfire, sweltering in the July humidity, creating a kind of neon anarchy. It was very important to Joe that we all go out there, and many times since I have asked myself why. Certainly sitting round that fire with him, hour after hour, I realised that there was no place in the world he'd rather be than at his camp. I think the Japanese were a little perplexed by us. Being an island people like us, they are very proud. Unlike us, they also know how to tidy up and hold their drink. After a particularly wild performance by the Chemical Brothers, I watched twenty thousand Japanese ravers pick up all their rubbish, putting all their ciggie dimps in portable ashtrays that hung round their necks, then put their rubbish into various recycling bins. They then went off to bed in their tents, lights were out by eleven, and they emerged bright and early the next morning to start another day.

I could see them looking at us, slowly losing all our powers of reason round our extraordinary campfire, as they went off to do their teeth at 9am. We, of course, hadn't been to bed in days and were gibbering and sweaty. A crowd of fresh-faced Japs stared at me as I attempted to hold a conversation with an empty karaoke booth. Had this all been an elaborate joke by Masa?

A few hours later Joe had picked up a piece of string, I'd picked up a dicky tummy, Dermot had picked up a wallet containing several hundred quid and Pockets had picked up a muscular young Kiwi named Quentin.

It was the most amazing experience, topped off when, at the end of the festival, the Japanese packed up and left, leaving Me, Joe, Dermot, Pockets and a geezer called Kenny, who'd been in Japan for the World Cup and still hadn't managed to find his way home, alone in the field, surrounded by thousands of hectares of Japanese rainforest and the most massive spiders you ever saw.

Zoe, who'd given up and gone to bed around twenty-four hours earlier, came back to find us in order to make sure we didn't miss the flight home. What she found was five grown men with eyes like pork chops, red-raw sunburn and five-day-old clothes crouching round a kiddie cassette player listening to something that was obviously hilarious because we were crying with laughter.

'Why are you crying?'

'Shut up and listen,' urged Joe to Zoe. 'It's really important.'

He pressed play again. And the Roger Miller track crackled through the kiddie speaker.

'You can't rollerskate in a buffalo herd, no you can't rollerskate in a buffalo herd ...'

We all collapsed in hysterics again, and continued to sing all the lyrics. It was a very important time to share with Joe, especially with what happened later that year.

Chapter 27

IN 1995 I got a call from my agent.

'Will you go and see Richard Eyre and David Hare at the National?'

So off I went. Like all actors I saw the National as a place where proper acting took place and I always aspired to end up there. Richard and David interviewed me with a view to being part of a trilogy of plays called *Murmuring Judges*. It was to be in the Olivier, the largest of the stages, and a notoriously imposing and difficult space to play.

'How would you feel about playing a space like the Olivier?' said Richard.

'Well,' I considered. 'When you've walked onstage in front of thousands of Stranglers fans at Wembley Arena in a leather posing-pouch and a leather cap, I think it will be a piece of piss.'

I went on to explain how I'd opened for The Clash and Dexys Midnight Runners and was very familiar with ritual torture and humiliation.

I got the part and it was a brilliant experience. It was where I met the great actor Michael Bryant. He was very round and short, with a twinkle in his eye. He used to do rehearsals with an earpiece in so he could listen to the test match. When he died, his wife sent me a very moving letter.

Michael was playing the part of Badger in the Christmas production of *Toad of Toad Hall* and during some 'character work' in rehearsal was famously asked by the director, 'What do you think Badger looks like?'

Michael took off his glasses and stared at the director before replying. 'Like Michael Bryant, of course.'

My worst disgrace during *Murmuring Judges* was not what I did on stage, but what I did off it. At the same time I'd fulfilled a dream of being in a *Carry On* and was filming *Carry On Columbus*. I really wanted to attend the wrap party so I excused myself from duty on stage in *Murmuring Judges*, called Andrew, the understudy, and told him that he was going to be on the next night.

At the wrap party of *Carry On Columbus* I managed to piss off the Dreamboys, who were the hired entertainment, by stealing their thunder and walking out naked to collect glasses. Maureen Lipman and her female co-stars in the film were sitting on the floor of the bar at Pinewood waiting for the Dreamboys when I came out naked and bent over right in front of them – not a pretty sight.

'Oh yes, very clever,' said the manager of the Dreamboys, pissed off because their entire tanfastic risqué routine was about keeping their pants on.

The next day I was hauled in front of the director and the producer of *Mumuring Judges*.

'You've let the cast down. They all feel very bad about this.'

This was not true. The cast were fine about it, particularly my understudy Andrew, who finally had a chance to star in the role he'd prepared so hard for, and my co-stars told me how much they'd enjoyed a change. I know it isn't done in the theatre to take a night off willy nilly (particularly when I'd been so publicly flouting my naked manhood at Pinewood when I should have been on stage at the National), but at least I'd warned my understudy so he had time to prepare and deliver a great performance.

'Keith!' my agent shouted down the phone, tutting and sighing.

Sounds of motorbikes, laughter. 'What do you want?'

'You've got an audition for *Evita*.'

I was scrambling up a hill in Devon with Alex James on the back. We were drunk, it was early. We were staying with Damien in a farmhouse he was renting while his new place was being done up.

'For *what*?'

'You know. *Evita* the movie – with Madonna. So for God's sake pull yourself together and get yourself back to London. Oh, and don't forget to learn the song.'

'The *what*?'

'It's a musical, Keith, remember? So learn a song to sing at the audition.'

'What, me? Sing? Are you having a laugh?'

'Well, try. This could be a big break for you. You're up against Jonathan Pryce.'

'Oh not that old piece of fucking cardboard.'

'Yes, *that* piece of cardboard happens to be having singing lessons.'

I imagined Dear Johnnie Pryce, probably at that very moment studiously hitting the high notes, while I was staggering around hitting a very different kind of high note – a rolled-up tenner to be precise.

'Alex, can you teach me how to sing?'

'What's it worth?'

'My eternal friendship.'

'OK.'

There started the most bizarre course of singing lessons known to man, the first few taking place at the top of a hill, the next in a Little Chef on the M5.

'Right, Keith. We need to find you a song you can easily impress with.'

'What about "I Am The Walrus"?'

'I don't think that's the right mood somehow, Keith. No, we'll do "I Have A Dream" by Abba.'

'Have you gone mad?'

'It's a great song, and in the right genre as *Evita*.'

'It's a girl's song.'

'Do you want this part or not?'

So it was that the entire population of the Somerset Branch of the Village Idiots Society (aka the employees of the Little Chef)* were treated to a long and gut-wrenching rendition. The staff watched open-mouthed as Alex downed the Stella and I sharpened my vocal chords.

---

* One small moan – people who run Little Chef Group, do me a fucking favour and employ some illegal immigrants, will you? Their grasp of English would be better than that of your entire staff put together.

'I belieeeve in aaangels, something good in everything I dooo. I belie –'

'No no no no no NO. Keith, stop! Do it again. This time sing from your heart, not from the fucking furball you call a tongue.'

In between songs, we tried to order some food, which proved to be more difficult than making it through an Abba chorus without vomiting.

'Excuse me, exc –'

The lolloping inbred wandered past again. No one thought to take an order, preferring instead to give us some more laminated menus.

I was still living at Nira's and got back to London to discover that my parents had called and were coming to stay. Dad took to Nira but Mum was a bit more reserved. Being the typical mother-in-law she wanted to make sure that she was 'right' for me. Christ knows how she thought she knew what was right for me; I didn't know myself.

I knew that my mates were 'right' for me, and my pet pig, a pot-bellied black called Dennis. Nira wouldn't let me have him in the house so he was sectioned to my orange VW Golf, where he took great delight in crapping in the gearbox. It dried and ceased to smell, except when you shifted from second to fourth, which opened up an inner chamber of filth and filled the car with nauseating pong.

'Jesus, Nira, did you have to?'

Dennis was snuffling his snout in between the seats covering Nira's best coat in saliva. She batted Dennis away and looked at me aghast.

'I wasn't me! It was you.'

'Me?' (I was having fun with this one.) 'It's not me. It's your arse.'

'It's Dennis! He's shat in that gearbox again, hasn't he?'

'That's right, blame Dennis.'

We were on the way to collect my parents, who were coming up to stay the weekend. It was a landmark in our relationship, a time for letting go of the past (Alison) and accepting the new (Nira).

We bundled them into the back of the VW and put Dennis in the boot where he oinked away in a fit of pique. The back seat he could handle, but being banished to the boot of his own car was too much. Clear road ahead meant one thing: fourth gear.

Nira spoke through gritted teeth. '*Don't* put it into fourth, for God's sake ...'

But it was too late: the beast under the gearstick had been awoken and emitted a hellish stench.

'Cor bloody 'ell, son, have you let off?' Dad held his nose.

'No, it's Nira.'

'Cor bloody 'ell, that's a stinker.'

Nira hit me and went bright red.

'It's not me, Eddie, it's, erm, a problem with the gearbox,' said Nira.

'What sort of problem? It doesn't smell very mechanical to me.'

'Dennis crapped in it.'

'Dennis? Who the bloody 'ell is Dennis?'

'My pig.'

'I *thought* I could hear oinking,' said Mum, relieved. 'I thought I was going mad.'

Dad shook his head. 'Blimey, son. What are you like, eh?'

Eddie and Mary had been fully expecting that the very capable, organised and efficient Nira would expunge disturbing irregularities (such as keeping a pot-bellied pig in one's car) from my life.

We pulled up at traffic lights and the four of us sat in silence, listening to the strained oinks coming from the boot as Dennis took umbrage.

'It's not right, son. It's just not right.' Eddie leaned forward and tapped Nira on the shoulder. 'I hope you're going to do something about him.'

'Like what?'

'You know. Get him to settle down.'

'Dad.'

'Well, really, keeping a pig. At your age.'

'Lots of people over forty keep pigs, Dad.'

'Not in North London, they don't.'

'That's right,' Mum chipped in.

'I have to agree,' added Nira, throwing me a look of daggers.

'Oh here we go. All of you gang up on me.'

Eddie stared out of the window at a Turkish man carefully stacking aubergines.

'Well, it's true. You're not young any more, Keith.'

'Yes I am.'

'You have to think about the future.'

'Why?'

'A pension, that's why.'

I growled and switched the car between second and fourth gear just to spite him. A fresh burst of the devil's breath filled the car.

'Oh, Eddie, I feel a bit queasy now.'

'S'OK, Mum, nearly there.'

We pulled up outside Nira's flat and she hurried them in, taking coats and making cups of tea. After lunch there was a game on and the men of the house (me and Dad) relaxed while Nira and Mum chatted in the kitchen. (Well, Nira chatted and Mum said 'Oh really' a lot, before remarking on how wonderful Alison was.)

Without looking away from the television Dad got back on his soapbox, his hands resting on his thighs, fingers splayed, legs slightly open, chin down.

'You see, son, you gotta *plan* in life, save for a rainy day.'

'I do plan. I'm having eggs and bubble for breakfast, that's why I made extra cabbage.'

Cooking is a great hobby of mine. My philosophy is to keep it simple. If it's any more complicated than Nigel Slater you might as well go to a restaurant and get someone to do it for you. I'm not a squid-ink-fucking-risotto man, I'm a Welsh-stew-with-barley type. For lunch I'd cooked lamb with roast vegetables, and swede with pancetta and garam masala spice, which I noticed Eddie didn't eat. Anything more spicy than beef gravy was shunned.

'Don't joke about it, son. You need to put something aside.'

'Bollocks.'

'Well, who's going to support ya when you're old?'

'I don't fucking know. My kids, hopefully.'

'You're too much, son. You think it's all a joke. You should do like Kevin. He's got some put away.'

'Yes I bet he has.'

All this time he'd watched the ball pinging around the pitch, as if his words were separate from his eyes or his expression or his emotions. To give me his full attention, to look me in the eyes, would be too frightening. That was human contact, a two-way street, a risk.

'I don't know, son ... this actor thing, one minute you're working, the next minute you ain't. It worries me and your mother. You want to get something regular, proper money.'

'I get proper money.'

'Proper money? For acting? Don't make me laugh.'

The phone rang and I got up to answer it, making a face behind his back.

'Hi, er, is that Keith Allen? It's Tristan Sperrin, I'm a researcher on *The Word*.'

Tristan was undoubtedly wearing a purple hooded top, wacky tartan trousers and limited-edition Nike converse, twiddling a pencil. He had probably attended a very good school indeed topped off with Bristol or Manchester Uni, was extremely young, go-getting and very very very fucking annoying.

'Yeah? What do you want?'

A kick in the head was the answer I was looking for. It was totally unreasonable but deeply satisfying to hate these gits, who'd come from a life of privilege and done nothing to buck the trend, full of self-satisfied *Viz* jokes and knowledge of 'gap year' life. They had a sprinkling of experience of poverty and politics but shunned it all in favour of life of the 'meeja' darling. It made me want to be cruel for the sake of it, to scare and terrify. It was part of the act but these kids made me feel that all was wrong with the world. He went on ...

'Yeah, um, just a quick enquiry really.'

'Well, which one is it?'

'Um, sorry?'

'Is it quick or an enquiry? Because by its nature an enquiry isn't quick, it's just an enquiry.'

'Oh, OK, got you. Well, it's just to see if you're available to come on the show tonight.'

His eager breathing told me that they were desperate, a guest had just dropped out and they were doing the ring-round to see who they could get.

'How much?'

'Er, hang on.' He put his hand over the phone and all I could hear was the sound of skin rubbing against the telephone mike.

Dad turned to look at me, making a prodding gesture at his ear.

'Who is it?'

'Oh, just a bit of work.'

'Yeah? What kind of work?'

'Just an interview.'

'An interview?'

Eddie shook his head and went back to the telly, making a kind of 'pah' noise as if to exemplify what a waste of time my 'work' was.

Meanwhile, Tristan came back.

'Um, yeah, Keith, uh, the producer said two.'

'Two? Fuck off. I'm not doing it for less than three.'

'Um, I'm not sure we can do three, um, I'll have to call you back.'

'Fine.'

What would be happening Chez Tristan was mad phoning to see who else they could get at such short notice. It didn't bother me one way or the other – who needed the hassle?

I was scratching my blackheads idly and staring at the game. A shot shaved the left-hand post and both me and Dad extended our hand towards the left-winger at exactly the same time, letting out similar yelps of frustration.

'Why did he shoot? He had a man out wide calling for it.'

'He did. He had a man free on the left wing.'

'Exactly, left fucking wing.'

'Look at him.'

'He's out there on his own, calling for it.'

'Exactly.'

We settled down, shaking our heads and tutting. The phone rang again.

'Uh, Keith? It's Tristan again, Keith.'

'I'm here.'

'We can give you three.'

'Great. And I want it in cash.'

'Cash?'

'Yeah, and I want a car to pick me up and bring me home.'

'I'll have to check about the cash.'

Dad looked round again.

'Who is it?'

'Same as last time.'

He tutted and turned away. I had a feeling that I was driving both him and Tristan mad with my brutal telephone style.

'OK, Keith, We can do one and a half in cash.'

'Fine, give me the other half in a cheque.'

'OK great. The car will be there at seven to pick you up.'

'Fine. Bye.'

Dad couldn't stand the suspense.

'What was that about?'

'Oh, I've got to go and do this interview.'

'When?'

'Tonight.'

'*Tonight?* Where?'

'Docklands.'

'You *what?* Bloody liberty. How you getting there?'

'They're sending a car.'

'A car? What, all the way? How you getting back?'

'Same way.'

'Another car? Bloody hell, how much they paying you?'

'Three.'

'*Three hundred quid?* Is that all?'

'Not three hundred. Three thousand, Dad.'

Dad dropped his can of beer and jumped up to look at me, his face and eyes wide.

'You what? *Three thousand quid?* For an interview?'

I laughed out loud. Suddenly my job didn't seem so bad to him. Money like this was a 'windfall', the kind of money you might stick away in a pension plan or save up over the course of a couple of years. To Eddie it was preposterous. He'd worked hard all his life for peanuts.

'You get them on the phone and tell 'em I'll come down and do it for five hundred.'

*

Nira was still working at the Comic Strip and I was starting to spend more time at the Groucho than at home, which was starting to put a strain on our relationship. I think she was having an affair with a producer at the Comic Strip. So while I was partying the night away at the Groucho, she was doing some extra 'producing' at work. And as they say in Dear Deirdre columns, 'One thing led to another ...'

I think the thing that sealed her affair was my own dalliance with her best mate. Me and the lady concerned – who shall remain nameless, let's call her Petal – started having the odd fuck in the Groucho. It's not big or clever, I know. But you have to consider the state of me at the time. London was afloat on a sea of second-rate cocaine and the good ship Allen was bobbing along atop, welcoming all aboard. It was never meant to hurt Nira or split us up, but Nira, being a woman, found out after something was left about the house (a pair of purple panties if I remember). I was recording a radio play at the time with Frances de la Tour and Margi Clarke at a studio in Soho. Nira burst through the door and started screaming, 'You've been fucking my best mate, you bastard. Don't try to deny it.'

Margi and Frances looked at each other and then at me in disgust. Nira left in tears, vowing revenge. But not on me, oh no. The next week Nira asked Petal to meet her in the Groucho for a 'drink'. Unbeknown to Petal, all Nira's friends accompanied her to the club. Therefore Petal arrived for a nice glass of Chardonnay only to be confronted by something akin to the Spanish Inquisition. Nira and her mates all sitting in a line on the comfy purple sofas, taking it in turns to destroy and humiliate Petal.

My audition for *Evita* loomed large. After a couple more singing lessons (booze-ups) with Alex it was D-day. It was only in the actual audition that everybody finally understood what a huge error had been made even considering me for the part. The director sat open-mouthed as I rasped my way through the song like a transvestite with a sore throat.

'Ha hem. Er, *thank you*, Keith. We'll, er, let you know ...'

He smiled and spoke behind his hand as I left. I'm sure I saw him mouth: 'What the fuck was *that*?'

I have to say that I agreed.

The point of this story is to highlight the indifference to work that I felt in a phase of my life when I was more interested in my new friends Damien and Alex, but also to highlight my objection to going for roles that just didn't *feel* right, therefore making sure, by hook or by crook, that I didn't get them.

But one job I definitely *did* want was for the new BBC flagship drama *Martin Chuzzlewit*, which was one of the more obscure Dickens books and I'd never read it. (Neither had most of the cast.) My agent asked me to go to a meeting so I went along to meet the director, labouring under the misapprehension that I was up for the part of Martin Chuzzlewit. As I bullshitted away about why I was the right person to play Martin, their jaws slowly hit the floor.

'No, Keith, you're here to talk about the character of Jonas Chuzzlewit.'

Ah. Now we were all on the same page of the same book (albeit my version was written in fucking Chinese). They asked me to come back the next day, and I went off and read the critical part of the book. As soon as I'd done so, I knew exactly what to say.

I went in the next day. 'If you were to give someone Dickens's description of Jonas, and then organise an identity parade and put me in it, and tell that person to pick out Jonas Chuzzlewit, I bet you they'd point to me.'

They all looked at each other and Pedder James, the director, considered for a moment and then said, 'You know what? I think you're right.'

I got the part. This was great news. It meant I was being taken seriously at last. This was proper acting. We had a read-through and I met the likes of John Mills, Paul Schofield, Julian Fellowes and Tom Wilkinson. These were all major players, and then of course there was the very delightful Julia Sawalha.

We were located all over the Black Country. I knew that Julia was going out with Dexter Fletcher and because he was a nice bloke and a great actor I'd no intention of going after Julia, but I could tell her relationship was over. Me and Julia were getting on very well on set and towards the end of the week we all went out for a company meal, where Julia let it be known that she fancied a very good-looking waiter. So I thought, hang on, and excused myself from the table.

I cornered this good-looking waiter and asked him to give her a note with her Irish coffee. When she got the note she was very excited, thinking of course that it was from the waiter. She opened the note and read it. *Dear lady, I am gay and I very much fancy the man sitting next to you. Can you get me his number?*

The man sitting next to her was me. So in one fell swoop I'd made him look bad and me look good. We went back to the hotel and had a few drinks and I told her the truth about the letter. I think this worked because now she knew I fancied her. Half an hour later we were in bed fucking like stoats.

This became a full-blown affair and mine and Nira's relationship became confused. I think you could describe it as a separation of convenience. Whether we were separated for good or not was very muddy.

A film set is an intense environment, a ready-made family. It requires no long-term commitment, no pledges of loyalty and, above all, no promises. A community of souls, away from home, the outside world unable to affect us, cosy and cosseted by an army of production assistants, make-up ladies and wardrobe dollies. Actors want to be loved, and put a group of them in a field together and it's like a pass-the-parcel of mutual love-making. If you have a co-star who happens to fuck you in the film, the natural sequence is to actually fuck.

'Keith?'

'Mmmm.'

'Do you think it's a good idea? I mean, us sleeping together and working together.'

Julia was making hummus and I was watching *Match of the Day*.

'Er, that's the only reason we're sleeping together.'

'Don't say that. It's horrible.'

'Well it's true, it's what actors do.'

We got back to London and it continued for a bit. I moved out of Nira's and in with a friend, Mary Lou, in Oxford and Cambridge Mansions, the same block I'd lived in with Cracky all those years before. But Nira carried on doing my washing. Julia would be seething when I pulled on a freshly laundered jumper from Nira's house, smelling of fabric conditioner and devotion. Things petered out with Julia after about six months. I was taking a lot of drugs, and when they wore off I found that Julia and I didn't have much to say to each other. Nira and I both realised that our respective affairs weren't nearly as good as what we had together and took up where we left off.

In spite of how I'd pissed off the producer of *Murmuring Judges*, I can't have pissed off the National too much because in 1996 they called again.

'Keith,' said my agent, tutting again. 'Trevor Nunn and Roger Michell want to see you at the National.'

So along I trooped. It was *The Homecoming*, and this time I'd done a little preparation (or so I thought). Terence Rigby, who had played the part of Joey in the original production, leant me a VHS and I'd watched it with the part of Lenny in mind. Now Lenny is the lead character. I, however, was up for the part of Teddy (see Martin Chuzzlewit – you will see a pattern emerging here). Roger, the director, informed me that I was up for the part of the long-lost son, Teddy, who had to sit and watch while his beloved wife fucks his brother. (Some of you might say this is divine retribution for my own sins.)

I have to admit I was scared of getting the part – which I of course did. A Pinter play. This was a different league. I was in the realm of serious fucking acting and serious fucking actors. David Bradley, Michael Sheen, Eddie Marsan and the ice-queen Lindsay Duncan. On the first day of rehearsal, when Roger Michell told us that Harold would be coming in twice a week, I nearly shat my pants.

I'd never been a great one for sticking religiously to the text, which is a prerequisite with Harold's work. It's beautiful poetry, based on rhythms, and if you get one word wrong and the rhythm goes, it ruins it.

Roger set up a league table of line fuck-ups and of course I was top. Harold was due to come in for the first time the following day and I was in serious bother. I was getting my entrances and exits right, which *I thought* was a start, but a lot of my 'knick-knack acting' was being hampered by my insistence at carrying my script round (because I hadn't learnt it). I could see Lindsay Duncan's face getting longer and longer as I struggled to pick my coffee cup up while holding my script and a fag.

'Keith? You're supposed to have a sip of coffee between those lines,' said Roger.

'Hang on, I'll just put my script down ... that's it.'

'Oh my God,' said Lindsay, dropping her head into her hands.

It was obvious to her that she was acting with a half-formed chancer whose comedic and improvisation skills carried no weight in this production and certainly not in this rehearsal room.

The next morning we did a full run-through in front of the great man himself. Afterwards we went off to get a coffee and pulled up chairs in front of Harold. There was a long Pinteresque pause. He took off his glasses and put them on the table.

'Ahem.' He cleared his throat. 'Well. There are certain parts of this play I don't recognise.'

All those parts, of course, included me.

'Don't get me wrong,' he went on. 'I found them quite amusing.'

He looked at me for the first time, before continuing. 'But, that said, *not mine.*'

I got the picture. I had to learn very quickly about the discipline of the text and pull my finger out. I knew this was a revolutionary production, with a groundbreaking three-dimensional set.

The first night was upon us and Roger Michell took me for a walk along the South Bank. He told me he genuinely believed I could deliver a great performance, but that I had to believe in myself. That night I delivered all my lines perfectly. In that show I learnt more about acting than I could possibly know, and not by acting, but by watching.

Like in Glasgow, because of the 3D set, I never left the stage, but unlike Glasgow, I loved being on stage the whole time, and decided that acting (rather like drumming, see above) is as much about what you don't do as what you do. For example, having to sit and watch my 'brother' shag my 'wife' onstage, and just act through watching, was an eye-opener. I was 'in the zone' and loved it.

At the opening-night party I took Damien Hirst and Maia along and noticed that Trevor Nunn, who had studiously ignored me up to that moment, was over in a flash, congratulating me on a wonderful performance. He swivelled round to address Damien.

'Ah, Damien, so good to meet you. I have one of your spin paintings.'

'Oh yeah? Which one?'

The answer was something like 'squirly hoops touch my nuts peace and love'.

'How much did you pay for it?' said Damien, without hesitating.

'Oh er,' said Trevor, looking away.

'Go on, how much?'

'Twenty-seven grand.'

'Oh right. Well, that one was done by Keith's son Alfie and my son Connor.'

Trevor smiled loosely and went off looking white. A funny joke – you say. The funny joke was that it was absolutely true.

Chapter 28

NIRA AND I WERE now officially back together and decided to take the kids skiing in a show of familial unity. I had taken to skiing with gusto after trying it at the 1989 Val d'Isère Film Festival while plugging *The Yob*. Paul Dennis and I had decided to teach ourselves. We took a lift to the very top of the mountain, put the skis on (after much cursing and swearing) and pointed them downhill.

'Bloody lovely this, ain't it, Keith?'

Paul Dennis surveyed the vista from behind a massive pair of very expensive goggles and a ridiculous bobble hat. He looked like Franz Klammer on E. Especially after the burning cigarette, which he hadn't noticed was burning, melted his top-of-the-range ski gloves.

'For fuck's sake! Look at that. Ruined they are.'

He examined his gloves while I fell out of my bindings again.

'For fuck's sake.' I lay on the floor and reached in my pocket for a smoke. 'This skiing lark's not all it's cracked up to be, is it?'

In order to smoke I had to remove my gloves, which meant I had to remove my goggles in order to see properly, which meant removing my hat, which in turn meant I had to fucking undo my sodding coat. This process meant reversing the entire fucking shenanigans I'd just been through to get the clobber on. It was then I realised that skiing is just one long series of adjustments with a bit of exercise in between.

Eventually we were ready to move off. In this period of adjustments, cool French skiers had been disembarking from the lift and scooting off, obviously wondering what we were doing sitting right at the exit from the chairlift having a fag. We must have looked like a right pair of twats. Paul this cockney hard man dressed head to foot in the latest gear but who every time he tried to move fell over, much to my mirth. Then there was me in borrowed salopettes and an anorak from Millet's looking like I'd just wandered out of the Peak District National Park.

'Come on, Paul. Let's have a go ...'

I pointed my skis downhill once more. It looked steep, very steep. It had looked less steep from the safety of the chairlift on the way up when puffing vigorously on a Marlboro. Full of bravado we'd said things like: 'Yeah, easy.'

'I mean, 'ow hard can it be, eh? Just point the fucking sticks downhill and fucking go.'

Now it was Paul who was the doubting Thomas.

'Er, don't you think we should have had a bit of ski school first?'

'Don't be so bloody ridiculous. If you think I'm standing in a line being told to bend my fucking knees by some French poof you've got another thing coming. Snowploughs have engines. Now, come on.'

I launched myself off the edge and remember little else until much much later. Probably after about three hours of inching my way down backwards, sideways, arse over tit and head first, I met up again with Paul, who by the looks of him had a similarly fractured experience. (The fracture was the gap between fear and terror, which alternated on the way down.) God knows how, but we'd managed to avoid the other kind of fracture after mistakenly picking the most lethal black run to come down on our first ever time on skis.

'It's harder than it looks this skiing thing, ain't it?' remarked Paul.

We were firmly installed in après-ski at the bar at the foot of the nursery slopes.

'I think it had something to do with attempting a ninety-degree drop without first knowing how to attach a ski to a fucking binding.' I pulled shakily on a cigarette while Paul stared at the wall in delayed shock.

'Ski school tomorrow then?' Paul lifted a pint to his lips, grateful he still *had* lips.

We both nodded, preferring not to mention our complete U-turn on the issue. The idea of standing in a girly line sticking your arse out and skiing like a spastic was preferable to sliding down sheer black ice using your bollocks for brakes.

After grasping the initial principles in the first lesson, I thought save the money and do the rest myself. Therefore my style developed all on its own, but was highly effective in getting me down any slope very fast. The closest relative to my skiing style would be the pencil. Rod straight, little flexibility, but ever so practical and effective.

So anyway, back to 1996, and I was hooked on skiing. Nira and I took the kids to Madonna de Campiglio in Italy. Thus it was that after an exhausting day on the slopes teaching the kids to ski, Nira, Lily, Alfie, Sarah and me sat in front of a humungous pile of chips, basking in the glow of family life.

The kids had got used to Nira by now, and Lily, as ever wanting to get involved in something she had no right to get involved in, had cornered me at breakfast, again perfecting the art of looking casual while asking the most awkward of questions.

'Dad. Why don't you and Nira get married?'

It was just the two of us, and Lily bit into her toast innocently.

'Because I don't believe in it.'

'But it's lovely, Dad. And me and Sarah can be bridesmaids.'

I dismissed it, but it got me thinking, and that evening, over dinner, Lily decided to have a bit more to do with it.

'Dad, why don't you ask Nira to marry you?' Lily had a mischievous twinkle in her eye and kicked me under the table.

'Why the fuck should we?'

'Because Alfie wants to be a page boy, don't you, Alfie?'

'No.'

'Good boy, Alf.' I gave him another handful of chips.

Nira looked at me for a moment. I'd fucked up once and nearly lost her. It wasn't going to happen again. In a flash it was out of my mouth.

'Oh OK then … Nira, will you marry me?'

'Yes.'

*

There were twenty-five of us for the stag do and we went in a coach from London. Damien's house was being renovated and I'd decided on no women – of any description. I hated all that stripper nonsense.

It was my idea of heaven to spend three days round a campfire in the company of your mates, everyone telling stories (about me). Jarvis Cocker was the DJ and Charles Fontaine, the chef, was in charge of cooking and served a whole lamb. (Which of course stayed the same size while the mounds of charlie went down.) Damien made everybody a stetson hat, personalised for each individual character. We even had a pyrotechnician who strapped fireworks to his asbestos suit. It rained solidly, which added to the Glastonbury campfire feel.

Simon Brown reduced us all to a state of catatonia with a story about his grandfather's watch. Now, you know that the coke has taken hold when grown men start talking about their grandparents. Just like you do when young men start talking about the crisis in East Timor at the arse end of a long night in the Groucho Club. (Why is it that the interest in world politics is directly proportional to the ingestion of class A drugs?)

'So my grandpa gave me this watch ...' Simon went on.

We all stared into the fire, hoping for death. Then Joe Strummer piped up. 'Let me see it.'

Simon willingly took it off and handed it to Joe, who stared at it and nodded. You could tell he was deeply affected. Then he threw it in the fire.

'Never be ruled by time, man.'

Simon couldn't speak. It was truly a very very funny moment. But I suppose you had to be there. Damien handed me the bottle of wine. We'd been awake for three days. Around us were the bodies of twelve men, all in various states of decay.

'What the fuck do you want to get married for?' Damien sat cross-legged in front of me like the Great Buddha looking for answers.

'Because.'

'Don't fucking do it. It's stupid.'

'I'm ready for it.'

'Ready for what?'

'Goats.'

The conversation had been going round and round for days. We'd lost track of time, of space, of reason … One of the corpses moved and sat up. If we'd been even the slightest bit able to move we'd have run away.

'What the fuck time is it?' Charles's stomach gurgled strangely as he made a grab for the fag packet beside me. 'Fucking 'ell. 'Ow long was I asleep?'

'About three minutes.'

'Fuck off. It was hours.'

'Honest. It was three minutes.'

'Fuck off it wasn't. I'm fucking starving. Is there any food?'

Charles got up and searched round under Jarvis Cocker's head and found the sausages. Alex James was flat out on his front with his arms tucked down his pants, cheek to the floor, enjoying some kind of famous dream. Charles yanked the frying pan from under his feet.

'Am goin to mek the motheur of all fry-ups for your famous fucking friends, Keeth.'

With that he opened the fire and added another log. A Moroccan yurt is an ideal venue to house twelve drunken men on a seventy-two-hour stag do (we had two yurts between us). Yurts were designed for leathery, homeless goatherds to shelter from harsh mountain weather for two or three days – which exactly fitted my required brief (and the description of my mates). Damien had bought them and erected them in the middle of a field above the farmhouse. The circular tent has a fire in the middle and a hole at the top to fit a chimney through. This gives the warmth, and the shape of the tent engenders a great feeling of togetherness as twenty people can easily sit and sleep in there. So there we stayed in our hermetically sealed drug yurts for days on end driven slowly crazy by the M25 of all conversations.

'Eh, Keeth.' Charles was cooking bacon, black pudding, egg, mushroom and wine in a sizzling pan.

'So why are you getting fucking married again?'

'So I don't have to put up with you any more.'

Around the tent men were slowly waking, coughing, lighting up and slipping outside for a pee. Alex sat up and grinned inanely. Alex, a tall man with a girly flick in his hair, but very pretty to look at, had a habit of grinning like this. He was thoroughly nice in the English way. All good manners and sloe gin. Or perhaps a gin and tonic.

'Shit … how long have I been asleep?'

'Three days.'

'Fuck off I haven't.'

'You fucking have.'

Me and Damien were having fun with the sleeping gag. Except you had to be able to stay up while everyone else dozed off in order to play it. I finished the last bottle and looked round for more.

By now I'd come to the conclusion that even endless chats about 'feelings' with a wife was preferable to the crap I'd been listening to for the last seventy-two hours. It was like being in a knitting circle or Alcoholics Anonymous. Time to put a stop to the conversation once and for all.

'I'm getting married because I fucked it up the first time.'

'That's no reason to fuck it up a second time.'

''E iz right, Keeeth. You will fuck it up again.'

I got married in December 1997, and in May 1998, me and Alex were playing snooker in the Groucho Club and discussing the impending World Cup. The official FA song was shit as usual. A few weeks earlier I'd taken Alex to watch Fulham because I had written a football song for Mohamed Al Fayed called 'We're Not Real Madrid'. There was a fan at Craven Cottage who banged a big drum. Back at Groucho's Alex replayed the drum beat in his head and mentioned how it would make a great beat for a football song.

So it was that an idea was born.

'Why don't we do the unofficial World Cup song?' I said.

'Fucking great idea.'

We went round to see Guy Pratt, who was the bass player with Pink Floyd and a great musician who had a studio. At that point all we had was the blueprint of a traditional football song in our heads, as well as a drum beat. Alex started it.

'Where on earth are you from? We're from Eng-land.'

I went on. 'Where you come from do you put the kettle on?'

So that was that then. Well, not quite. We decided to work the melody round the established terrace chant: 'Da la laaaa, da la laaaa, da la la la la la' and then we called Andy Kane, a well-built, good-looking chap you wouldn't recognise but who is in fact the voice behind every boy band in the country.

We retired to the Star in Portobello to try and find a name for the band. We were all stumped, when my phone rang and a woman I won't name called me about doing a TV show. When I put the phone down Alex says, 'Who was that?'

So I told him. To which he replied, 'Oh no, not that fat les.'

That was it. The band Fat Les was born. Damien wasn't involved in it until we asked him to do the artwork. At which point of course he became very important to the band.

We worked into the night and ordered a takeaway. When the pizzas turned up I remember thinking, Oh no, I wish we'd had a vindaloo. Like a bolt of lightning it came to me! Our unofficial World Cup song should be about vindaloo – our nation's favourite dish. I thought about the implications of vindaloo – the oompah of the song was custom-made for the standard English right-wing lout, so putting in the standard dish of their standard enemy the Indians seemed to me absolutely perfect.

I played the tune to Alfie as we drove to Devon to see Damien. I was making a special effort to bond with Alf – by going away, just the two of us.

'Thing is, Alf, the song just needs a bit extra in the chorus …' I thought out loud.

Alf was on a completely different topic altogether. 'No, Dad, it was you, Mum, your dad and Nan …'

'That's it, Alf! You're a genius.'

I turned and smiled at his cheeky face. The beauty of kids is that they constantly surprise you. Particularly Alfie. Both Lil and Alf were normally fucked up by our divorce, but Alfie had his own problems to contend with on top of that, so I took every opportunity to make it up to him. Well, maybe not *every* opportunity. The two of us would go on long weekends together and while we were in the car we'd make up characters in a fictitious radio show. I was Bosun Checkyourprice and Alf was Powder Monkey. We would make up songs and raps with class lyrics like: 'Nothing could be finer than sweetpantyliner …'

'Vindaloo' went to number two in the charts behind the sappy idiocy of the middle-class 'Three Lions' and its collection of unfunny comedians. (With the exception of Frank Skinner. Oh, that just leaves Dave Baddiel – well, there you go then. Sorry, I couldn't help it. I've held back in the rest of the book. I had to get one in.) Fat Les became the country's favourite band and we were to be featured in the Cool Britannia issue of *Vanity Fair*. On the day of the photo shoot Damien, Alex and I plotted up in the Groucho early and started drinking and by the time the crew arrived we were already drunk and on the hunt for charlie.

A guy called Toby Young was supposed to be organising the shoot. I could tell that our near oblivion was alarming him and he hastily produced three contracts for us to sign.

'Could you sign the release forms, please, fellas.'

Little beads of sweat were forming on his upper lip.

'Not unless you get us some charlie.'

'And grow some hair.'

'And a moustache.'

'And cut your toenails.'

This was not the answer he was looking for and it was clear that poor old Toby was a bit green. *Vanity Fair* had booked a top photographer who was becoming stressed and flouncing about queenily while we just giggled. The whole photo shoot was costing a fortune and not only were we drunk, we were obnoxious.

He rushed off to call a dealer and after about five failed attempts he started to cry.

'Please. Just sign the forms, please.'

'No.'

'This is costing a fortune.'

'It will cost more if you don't get some.'

An hour later he went off and reappeared with huge sweat rings on his shirt. He handed over the drugs and we gracefully proceeded with the shoot. For the record, I'm not proud of our actions, but in the light of Toby's ensuing 'kiss and tell' pamphlets it is with great glee that I take this opportunity to return the favour. But Fat Les and heinous behaviour in the Groucho Club were secondary in my friendship with Damien. We had bonded over kids. When Damien and Maia had been expecting their first kid (Connor), my visits there with Alfie had helped both Damien and me.

Alfie was developing into a chaotic child who drove us to distraction. At first he was simply hyperactive and disruptive. Then he started getting expelled from every school we sent him to. Harry Enfield didn't help when he told Alison to send Alf to his own boarding school. But that didn't last long (neither, by the way, did their relationship once Alfie started being violent). But, just as an aside, Harry and Alison split after Harry kicked the bathroom door in while Alison and her mate were in there doing a line of coke.

Alfie was diagnosed with ADHD (Attention Deficit Hyperactive Disorder) and the doctors recommended we put him on a drug called Ritalin, which I was dead against.

'Why are you giving him drugs? I don't want him on drugs.'

Alison looked at me and laughed. 'OK then, Keith. *You* try and live with him.'

'Fine, I will.'

A few days with Alfie and I knew what she meant. I took him to Devon to stay with Damien and saw for myself what he was like. His attention span was a few minutes at best, and trying to interest him in his homework was impossible. But Damien was brilliant with him, creative and laid-back. He taught him to draw and the three of us went fishing together. Damien would cook fantastic meals while Alfie pored over his maths homework in the half-built kitchen.

Deep in the sports pages I looked over at Alfie, who was busy cutting into his new Arsenal shirt with a pair of kitchen scissors.

'Alfie! Stop doing that and bring your homework here.'

He grudgingly slid off the bench and sidled over to me. Head hanging and arms floppy, he presented the blank paper. Our eyes met for a second.

'Now bring me the newspaper you were doodling on.'

He dragged himself back to the table and brought back the paper. On the front was a picture of Boris Yeltsin, now complete with handlebar moustache.

'What's five times five, Alf?'

'Dunno.'

'Perhaps if you spent more time on your maths homework and less time drawing moustaches on the Russian president you might know.'

I immersed myself in the sports table. All the while I could feel Alfie still standing there, refusing to budge. I didn't know what to do next to make him interested in anything.

'Alfie, do you want to learn how to make soufflé?' Damien was chopping and dicing and before long the two of them were arm-deep in egg and cheese. It was the longest Alfie had concentrated on anything since we'd arrived. Damien's easy way with my kids gave him the confidence he needed to be a father.

Their bond also encouraged me to stick at it with Alf. This book is the proof of the pudding that father-son relationships are the hardest of all. But my experiences were too raw to stop trying hard with Alfie. I didn't want him to be an outsider at school like I was because I was always moving about – like Alf was – from school to school. By 1998 we'd finally found a school that Alfie settled in: the Steiner School in North London. They emphasised group responsibility and there he started to form friendships he still has today.

I noticed that Alfie was a chubby kid and that he never felt confident enough to join in with other kids at school so I pulled my finger out and we used to keep fit together. We would run to the gym, do some gym work and run back (well, he'd run, I'd stagger, wheezing).

Around the same time my mum and dad came up to stay with Nira and me in our new house in Fairmead Road, which Nira had lovingly done up. They arrived with a bottle of good wine and Dad handed me a wine rack he'd made.

'Is that for me?'

'Yes, son. I knocked it up in the garage for you.'

'Still knocking things up in the garage then, Dad?'

'Careful, son. We don't want talk like that in front of Nira.'

She and my mother were sitting in awkward silence. My attempts to lighten the mood had fallen stunningly and inappropriately short.

'So, Nira, you got a degree?'

'Yes.'

Eddie looked at me accusingly, as if it was my fault.

'See, son? She's clever. Got a degree, not like you.'

At the time I was filming the pilot of *You Are Here*, the most influential comedy programme never seen. Apart from me it featured Paul Kaye, Matt Lucas and David Walliams. So I made my excuses and left Mum and Dad with Nira and Alfie. I don't know where Lily was. Probably shopping with her mother. Later on, halfway through a shot, I get a call from Nira.

'Keith. It's me. I've just told your parents to fuck off.'

'You what?' I could feel the colour draining out of my face.

I don't need to tell you, reader, that my parents a) didn't appreciate being sworn at, b) didn't appreciate being sworn at by Nira (who was still a poor second in their eyes to Alison), and c) well, fuck it, they must have deserved it.

'Sorry, but it was your dad.'

'What did he do?'

Whatever it was – I couldn't imagine Nira telling him to fuck off.

'I couldn't have him speaking to Alf like that.'

'Like what?' I was getting more and more irate.

'He told Alfie he wasn't responsible. That he could never have a dog because he wouldn't be able to look after it.'

That was all I needed. I raced home from the set immediately and confronted my father. It felt like, after all these years, it was finally time. After a childhood being told I wasn't responsible, I was not going to let him speak to my son like that.

'Get out,' I fumed.

Dad looked at me in shock. 'You what, son?'

'I said get out. And don't ever speak to my son like that again.'

'What do you know?'

'I know that Alfie's my fucking son and I won't have anyone tell him he's not responsible. Like you did to me.'

I didn't have to wait long for the follow-up. Still not looking at me, he said, 'That's because you weren't, son. You could have made something of your life.'

'I have made something of my fucking life. I'm famous. I'm an actor. People pay me a lot of money.'

Dad looked stunned. 'All right son, there's no need to shout.'

'All my life I've lived with the fact that you're disappointed with me. I'm not like you. You're a fucking disciplinarian, you live for order and structure. Well I don't, and I don't care that I don't. I know you're ashamed of me but I don't give a toss.'

He stared at me, then his lip started to quiver. 'How can you speak like that to your poor old dad?'

'Just get out.'

I went to the shop and bought some fags. I was shaking. Everything was raw. I could feel everything. Nira chased me down the street.

'You've got to go back in.'

'No way.'

'If you don't go back in – they'll leave and you won't speak again.'

She was right. I had to go back and sort it out. But I wanted to leave him in there steaming for a bit longer. I'd finally stood up to him.

When I got back, Mum was washing up and Dad was deep in thought.

'Sorry, Dad,' I said immediately.

Mine was the first move, but he returned the move and we met in the middle of the room and gave each other a big manly hug.

'Me too, son.'

We went to the pub and he told me that he never thought his opinion had meant anything to me. It was as if he was suddenly proud that although he'd been a negative influence, he'd been an influence all the same. He was proud that what he thought mattered to me. After a watershed akin to parting the Red Sea, our relationship moved on to another level. Neither of us talkers, we developed a language without words, him sorry and me forgiving – a mutual acceptance. A very manly form of communication.

THE NOUGHTIES

Chapter 29

2001. NEW YEAR. My house on Fairmead Road felt like a house of ghosts of people who should have been there. Nira worked hard at making it a family home in waiting. The kitchen was all hanging pans and fashionable butcher's blocks. A huge dining table made for entertaining was surrounded by sleek minimalist cabinets containing Mexican knick-knacks and souvenirs from our holidays together. Up the stairs hung a series of photographs of our respective lives before we knew each other. Our mothers and fathers, friends and kids. Our wedding photos sat in the middle, surrounded by this happy tale of two lives before we'd met. The photo missing was the happy tale of our life right here right now. I'm afraid that it didn't exist.

What I objected to was other people's perceptions of marriage, which seemed to revolve round money and 'living the dream' of mortgage, kids and Habitat décor, of catchment areas and good schools. It was that cunt 'aspiration' again, and in the heart of newly trendy Tufnell Park we were surrounded by its dedicated followers. All people talked about were 'little Johnny's school grades'.

All that mattered to me was community and people living together and not valuing material wealth. Blairism seemed to be developing us into a nation of selfish coffee-drinking middle classes with the working classes getting pushed out of their own shitty areas to even shittier areas. Community? That was a joke in the smart streets around us, where the moneyed folks leapt from their Volvos avoiding the passing youths from the local estate. The comfort of living comfortably made me uncomfortable.

'Happy new year.'

Smoke filled the kitchen. In the far corner, through the smoke, a human form was visible. (Well, it professed to be human.) Thank God, someone to talk to. The new year was already a few days old but the party hadn't stopped yet.

'What year is it?' The form spoke.

'2001, you prick.'

The form moved through the smoke and sat down at the table. It was Pockets.

'Oh God. Why are you still here?'

'Because you love me. I'm your best friend.'

'No you are fucking not. You're a pain in the tits. Do the washing up.'

'Only if you say you love me.'

Pockets was in the habit of turning up at the houses of his more fabulous friends and staying three years, leaving again with only a plastic bag full of memories and old bits of cardboard on which people such as Joe Strummer wrote things like, 'Pockets is a legend.'

Pockets put on another of his mix tapes. The dawn was peeping through the designer shutters; the cool green shades of the kitchen deserved better than two drunks sipping the night away.

'Where's Nira?'

'How the fuck should I know?'

'She's your wife.'

Pockets opened the fridge and studied it critically before settling on a carton of tomato juice. He put together a mean Bloody Mary.

'Listen to the lyrics of this song … it's about me. It's called "Dave Girvan". It's by this band The Duffle Coats.'

'Pockets. Shut the fuck up and go and buy me some fags.'

'It's true. And Joe's written about me.'

Pockets was standing against the morning sun, in silhouette. His profile (if you could call it that) put me in mind of a horrible car crash involving Dangermouse's sidekick Penfold and Worzel Gummidge.

Straw-coloured and straw-like hair sat precariously on top of a round face complete with round glasses, not much sign of a chin and a fag end burning unnoticed.

His shirt had seen better days (most of them in the previous week), and his jeans had an interesting collection of red, brown and black stains around the thigh areas. Where he came from nobody knew, and where he was going was even less certain.

'So, er, you and Nira?'

'The marriage is over.'

'Great. Er, I mean, does that mean I can move in?'

'Don't be so bloody rude.'

The lock made an ominous clicking sound and Pockets leapt behind the door with as much grace as an overweight gerbil attempting to mounts its little plastic wheel. He put his finger to his lips and a bauble of vodka snot came out of his nose. There was no hope. Nira walked in, nose in the air, horrified at the heady mixture of chemical and ash that hung in it.

'Hello, Pockets.'

He didn't respond. Only kept looking at me in terror. She avoided my eyes and went upstairs. There wasn't anything to say. A few moments later she left with a suitcase.

'You can come out now. She's gone.'

Pockets stayed and his company, although a little like socialising with a half-empty bottle of meths, was better than having to cook, clean or buy my own fags. Nira moved into a flat in Notting Hill which she rented while we sorted out the split. Eventually my parents fathomed something was amiss. My mobile was ringing illegally and the barman at the Groucho shot me a look.

'Son? It's your mother here. Why haven't we seen you and Nira and the kids?'

'I can't talk now, Mum. I'm in the, er, cinema.'

'Why is there all that talking then in the background? Is that Nira?'

'We've split up.'

'You bloody what? Oh no, Keith. What on earth for? She's such a nice girl.'

'It just wasn't working.'

'What do you *mean*, not working?'

'I mean it wasn't working.'

'Oh I don't understand you, Keith. Speak to your father … I'll put him on.'

After ten years of begrudging Nira taking Alison's place, they'd finally accepted her and now worshipped her. It was incomprehensible to Mum and Dad that it was over.

The next day I woke up in my room at the Groucho, showered and got back into bed in order to proceed with the business of the day, which involved another three hours' kip followed by three phone calls. The first to Pockets, to bring fresh clothes, the second to Nira, to check whether we were still divorcing, which apparently we were, and a third to my mates in Manchester, Tommy and Fat Neck, who would win a fight with some very hard nails.

They were brilliant scamsters, and had recently got Fat Neck onto the pitch at Old Trafford to have his photo taken in the team line-up.

'All right, Keef? 'Ow are yoh? Me and Scully wanted to ask a little favour of yoh.'

Tommy, 'Neck' and Scully were the kind of men that one did favours for. You didn't argue with them.

I smoked and listened as Tommy went on.

'We was wondering if you could get our birds into that Groucho Club tomorroh. They're coming to London for a bit of shopping like.'

'No problem, lads. Tell them they can stay at mine.'

'What about your missus?'

'There is no missus. Only Pockets. He'll let them in.'

'Brilliant, Keef. Top one. We'll see you right, don't worry.'

It was vital to keep on their good side if you ever wanted to have a good time in Manchester. Working-class lads who would give you the world as long as you showed them respect. I examined my stomach in the mirror on the way to get a lighter. If I breathed in, I still looked under forty. I breathed out and fell back into bed.

The phone went. It was Phill Savidge.

'Hi, Keith. Fancy a round of golf?'

'Why not?'

Phill was a music PR man who in the golden era of Britpop had gone round in a kimono and make-up. He also played off six and was the best golfer any of the lads had ever seen.

'But that's not the reason I'm calling. I'm sending you over a play called *Glastonbury*. I presume you're at the Groucho.'

'Why would you presume that?'

'Because I've just spoken to Pockets and "she" said you didn't go home last night. She sounded very put out.'

'Jesus Christ. It's worse than having a wife.'

The play arrived, and since the life of an out-of-work actor is one essentially devoted to the pursuit of pleasure, the rest of the afternoon passed reading. At the end of it my energy had returned. I called Pockets immediately.

'You don't care about me. You didn't even tell me you weren't coming back,' she moaned.

'Shut the fuck up and ask Phill Savidge to get me a meeting with this writer.'

Pockets knew that the banter between us was affectionate, but others were horrified when they heard the way we spoke, thinking he was some kind of mug for taking it. If they didn't understand the humour, that was their problem.

The play had potential. It captured that spirit of rampant and often hopeless hedonism that you felt after three days of solid drug-taking. All friendships made at Glastonbury were intense, beautiful and temporary. Until the next year, but then again only for three days. Phill called again.

'Phill, listen. I want to buy the rights to this play. Tell her, will you?'

'She won't sell. I know her. She's heard about your reputation and anyway she's living in Spain.'

'Shut up, Phill. Get me on the next plane and get me a phone number. I haven't been this excited about a project for ten years.'

I left the writer a message and after a few hours she called back.

'I want to buy your play.'

Silence.

'At least let me come out there and talk to you about it. I won't scare you, I promise.'

Silence. Then: 'OK, you can come if you want. But don't expect me to change my mind.'

She agreed to meet me from Gibraltar airport the next morning. Everything was organised so there was nothing else to do but go to a party and stay up all night.

At six the next morning: 'Pockets, you oaf! Where's my passport?'

'It's not my fault you can't find it. Ask Nira.'

'Nira's in Notting Hill.'

By the time we found it, in the back of a pair of jeans in the washing pile, I was late and got to Gatwick ten minutes after my flight left. No sleep and surging despondency messed with my emotions. There was no other option but to book myself on the next flight, to Malaga. Worse still, I couldn't find Zoe's number which meant she'd be meeting the plane in Gibraltar without me on it.

The journey out was long and painful. I had no idea what the reception would be, if there was one at all. At Malaga there was the prospect of a drive into the middle of the Andalucian countryside without any clue where to go apart from a scrambled address that Pockets managed to obtain. Around midnight, suffering from excessive sleep deprivation, swerving to avoid sheep down a narrow road somewhere near Cadiz, I arrived.

'What the fuck are you doing here?'

'I said I'd come so here I am.'

'But you left me waiting at Gibraltar airport for hours this morning, it's past midnight and how the fuck did you find this place?'

'I'll tell you in the morning. Can I just go to bed?'

She and her mate Jane looked at each other, aghast to see me and more aghast at my temerity. They were out there living the bohemian life and trying to write. The house was on the beach, with hardly any furniture and a fire that was smouldering away uselessly. A little dog tried to bite me.

'You're not going to bed. You can come to the bar with us. It's still early.'

This was the worst ever news. They took me to a rustic beach bar right on Trafalgar Point and delighted in a sightseeing tour despite it being the middle of the night.

'This is where Nelson defeated the Spanish fleet, right off this point.'

'Oh really.' I yawned.

'It's the southernmost tip of Europe, don't you know?'

'I do now.'

A couple of hours later they showed no sign of stopping, enjoying the novelty value of putting me through the hell of tequila slammers and drunk locals. A toothless peasant came over grinning hopelessly and bearing a cloudy bottle of liquor, intimating that we should down it.

'Eh, Paco, this is Keith Allen, the infamous hell-raiser.'

At that moment the only thing I was capable of raising was a duvet over my head.

'Can I go to bed now?'

'Bed? Now? I thought you were Keith Allen. The least you can do is prove it.'

The next morning I got up early and went on to the beach to collect some dry firewood. It was my mission to get the fire going. There were several large pieces of driftwood so I lashed them together and hauled them back to the house with the stupid little dog yapping at my feet. Zoe was impressed with my efforts and grateful for a proper fire. We found out that we shared both a hatred of most theatre and a love of Harold Pinter.

'So will you sell me the rights?' I asked, hoping to get something out of this trip.

'I wouldn't have done. I really wouldn't. But you came all the way out here on the back of a three-day bender so you must like the play.'

We agreed to find the funding to take the play on tour and then back to the Roundhouse in London. We would hire a big-top tent that would be erected in parks in the centre of the major cities and would be a mini Glastonbury Festival. The experience would be as far away from traditional theatre as one could possibly get.

It wasn't the plan to end up in bed with her. My plan was to remain single and enjoy myself. Trouble is that that has never been easy to do. Women sort of happen. It started casually. A night here and there. One night in London, while discussing the machinations of act one scene one and the structure of act two and enjoying a post-coital cigarette, she laid it on me.

'Why don't you direct the play?'

'Me?'

'Why not? You know *Glastonbury* better than anyone else.'

While I was pondering, the phone rang.

'Yes.'

'Keith. It's Harold Pinter.'

I mouthed 'Harold Pinter' to Zoe who mouthed back '*the* Harold Pinter?' at me. At the same time she had been trying to get out of bed and slipped. She landed with a huge crash, knocking over my wedding photos in the process.

'Keith? What the hell's going on?'

'Oh nothing, Harold. Just a naked woman falling out of my bed.'

'Of course, of course. That's life.'

'Well that's *my* life, Harold.'

'Now, Keith, I'm doing a new production of *The Room* and *Celebration* to run at the Almeida and then to take to the Pinter Festival in New York. Are you available?'

'No, sorry, I'm washing my hair.'

Harold chuckled. 'See you at rehearsals.'

Zoe came with me to New York for the Pinter Festival. Although it had been my intention to remain single for a while, I realised that I'd never been single for any substantial length of time and was probably incapable of it. But I was in love again and this time it was for ever. (It always is at the time, isn't it?)

On the first night of *The Room/Celebration*, Zoe was supposed to be watching from the stalls. Instead she mistakenly wandered into the Opera House next door, impressed that I was making my American acting debut in front of three thousand rich old ladies in ball gowns. She thought this might be an avant-garde production, until she realised she was watching *Swan Lake*.

After the performance there was a party on the top floor of the Lincoln Center and Harold proceeded to get us all very drunk, including himself.

Danny Dyer, a young cockney actor, was stealing the show as the waiter, delivering the lines as if he was selling 'lovely jubbly strawbs and rasps' down the market stall. At the party, he pushed through the crowd and collared Harold, shoving his girlfriend Davinia into his line of vision.

''Arold. This is my girlfriend Davinia. She's an actress. She finks you're the fackin' bisnis.'

Davinia leaned forward, all perfume, hair and expensive clothes. 'I just wanted to say that I think you're a brilliant writer.'

I cringed for her. It wasn't her fault; you just assumed he already knew.

'I'm an actress and I'd LOVE to work with you.'

Harold looked her up and down before responding. 'You're not an actress, my dear. You're a waitress.'

He turned back to Lady Antonia and his wine. It was left to me to take the edge off the comment.

'Ha ha.' I chuckled limply. 'That's Harold's humour for you ...'

Davinia was welling up and Danny stood staring at Harold with his mouth open. There really was nothing to say. Later that night I watched Danny packing his stuff and threatening to leave before the morning. Davinia was inconsolable as Danny shouted the odds. 'No one speaks to my girlfriend like that. Not even arguably the world's greatest living playwright.'

He shoved another pair of designer jeans into his luggage while Davinia wept into her expensive luggage, forcing several pairs of Prada shoes into a Louis Vuitton holdall.

'All right, all right. Just stop packing and leave it to me.'

Back in my room, fuelled by a need to make the peace and save the production, I picked up the phone, but in my drunken eagerness to be the peacemaker I overlooked the fact that it was three o'clock in the morning. Zoe woke up and looked at me inquisitively.

'Who are you phoning?'

'Harold. I'm going to make him apologise to Davinia.'

'I may be drunk but I'm not drunk enough to think that's a good idea.'

As I dialled his room she kept making frantic scything gestures across her neck as if to indicate a violent death.

'Yes.'

It was Lady Antonia Fraser, clearly confused as to why her phone was ringing in the middle of the night.

'Antonia. It's Keith. Can I speak to Harold please?'

Long silence.

'Keith. No one phones a mother at three in the morning unless it is to inform her that one of her children has died.'

'Oh, er, sorry, but it's very, very important I speak with Harold.'

A pause. Harold came on the line. He didn't speak, but simply breathed. I barrelled on.

'Harold, listen, it's Keith. Danny's really upset. He's threatening to quit. You have to apologise.'

Another agonising silence.

'Never *ever* call me in the middle of the night again.'

The line went dead. I poured a large drink, reckoning my career as a Pinter favourite was now over. Still, speaking my mind has always been more important to me than anything else.

The next morning Danny woke to find a note under his door apologising to him and Davinia. Peace was restored.

On my return from New York I got a call from the *Daily Sport*, asking if I'd like my own weekly column. Not half, was my reply. Thing is, I think they were expecting me to spill the beans on my bad behaviour (and that of my friends). Now I was in a good place, a good relationship. And people had begun to remark on how happy and content I appeared. Well, I was, and I wanted to use this new me to help others. Namely the *Daily Sport* readers.

'I think we should start it with a comment on the heroin trade in Afghanistan,' I said thoughtfully, reclining on my sofa while Zoe tapped away at her computer. We'd decided to do the column together. Well, I'd do the pearls of wisdom and she'd do the funnies. She was very funny.

'Er, are you sure the *Daily Sport* want left-wing intellectualising, Keith?' she replied, fingers poised. 'Or just tits and arse.'

'Forget that shit.' I put my fag out firmly. 'I want to educate these people, take them in another direction.'

This was true. After 9/11, I was the first person to point out in a

British tabloid newspaper the link between terrorism and the heroin trade in Afghanistan. All from my humble column in the *Daily Sport*. Of course, what the *Sport* readers wanted was for me to delve into the depths of Jordan's arse looking for dirt. What they got was week after week of high-minded moral philosophy. Bring Back National Service, Ideas for Dealing with Juvenile Recidivists … I was on a roll.

'Keith, er, ahem, well, you're sacked,' said the voice on the phone. It was the subeditor at the *Daily Sport*.

'What?'

It turned out that after seven weeks of taking not a blind bit of notice of what was actually in the column, which was conveniently hidden on page 10, sandwiched between a large pair of tits and a plethora of Dial-A-Fuck phone lines, someone at the *Sport* had finally read it. Oh dear.

Safe to say they weren't best pleased with my passionate politicising. They wanted Keith Allen the reprobate.

'Well, tell them *he* is no more,' I shouted down the phone.

I threw my mobile across the room and walked out with great drama and went to the pub.

'So where are you going to live?' Nira asked, presenting me with the divorce forms that handed my half of our house over to her. My only requests were the sofa and television.

'On a boat.'

'A boat.'

'Yeah. I've always wanted to live on a Dutch barge.'

She left the room shaking her head, while my dreams were filled with old rusty hulls and large bulkheads. Perhaps it was the navy baby in me.

'Where do I buy a Dutch barge?'

'The internet,' Zoe replied matter-of-factly.

'The what?'

Technology and me had never mixed. The idea of learning anything from anyone else still filled me with terror. The idea of failing brought up all sorts of problems in my complicated psyche.

Zoe brought her laptop out and presented it to me. My good eye scrunched up and peered at the keyboard. My head jerked away from it like a dog realising that the fly it is attempting to catch is actually a wasp.

'What do you want *me* to do with it?'

'I'll teach you how to get on to the internet. Then you can find a Dutch barge.'

The problem with computers is that you are always one click away from the answer but also one click away from fucking everything up. Once fucked up it seems that only someone's 'mate on the other side of London' has the technological know-how to sort it out.

I had a go and after much shouting and cursing and prodding it with my stubbies, shouting things like 'fuck you', 'cunting thing' and 'useless shitting machine', Zoe grabbed the computer, made a few taps and arrived at the Dutch barge website.

The first entry read, '*Kaapsedraai*, a DIY nightmare or the beginning of a lifelong love affair …' and described a hundred-foot 1910 cargo barge used in the war to transport guns for the Germans. A sense of being part of history fired my imagination.

'That's it! That's the one.'

'Don't you think you should look through the rest of the ads?'

'No! That's the one! I can feel it. Where is it?'

'Rotterdam.'

'Let's go! Book a flight, we'll leave in the morning.'

'But there isn't even a picture. How do you know you'll like it when you get there?'

'I just know. Is there a phone number?'

I picked up the phone to someone called Rod. After three or four attempts someone finally picked up. A large cough was audible at the other end.

'Yeah?'

'Is that Rod?'

'Last time I checked, hur hur.'

'Listen, er, Rod. Your boat, I want it.'

He coughed again and started up with a series of jokes that he chuckled away at.

'Oh, er, hur hur hur, well, you see, hur hur hur, she's not really for sale any more. I've had an offer.'

'Don't sell it to anyone until you've talked to me. I'm coming over.'

''Fraid it's not convenient this weekend.'

With that the hapless Rod signed off but the spirit of *Kaapsedraai* was in me and I was swept along on a tide of romance, imagining myself sailing the canals of Europe wearing a hardy sailing smock and an even hardier smile. The taxi dropped us at the port in front of two thousand Dutch barges. Zoe looked at me, exasperated.

'How will we know which one it is?'

My eyes searched rows and rows until it settled on something brown and beautiful, sitting barely above the waterline, its bulk concealed underwater leaving a graceful profile. On top was a huge oak mast.

'That one.'

It was love at first sight until a hatch opened and Rod emerged from below, all grey matted hair and spliff with two old dogs for company, brain shot after forty years of sustained dope-smoking.

'Oh er hi, hur hur hur … thing is, Keith, I've changed my mind and once I change my mind … well, let's just say immovable objects and all that … hur hur hur.'

A tour revealed the full scale of the work needed, with the vast cargo hull resembling the chest cavity of a rotting antelope. It took about two minutes to pay Rod off and take ownership, his resistance having decidedly more in common with rollerskates than immovable objects.

The next problem was getting her back to England. I made some calls while shuddering in front of Rod's tiny woodburning stove, designed to heat old women's drawers rather than a hundred feet of steel-hulled barge.

'Pockets.'

'What do you want?'

'Stop snorting your way through the underpants of North London and get on a plane.'

'What about signing on?'

'Don't worry, you'll be back next week.'

He was joined on the crew by Arthur, an inane village-idiot-type West Country builder whose stock in trade was boats. His line was: 'Yeah, I can do that, no problem. Plumbing system? No problem.'

How was I to know that the closest he'd come to a U-bend was when he'd had his head in the pan after twenty pints?

Pablo, my old friend and bongo-drum player, joined us for musical light relief and we all waited in a local bar playing Dutch marching-band music for Tom the skipper to arrive. Tom appeared through a cloud of spliff smoke like Clint Eastwood in *Unforgiven*, dark and swarthy with hands that had seen a few too many arguments between fender and portside.

'You, Keef,' puffed the cockney gypsy. He didn't say much but laid out the sea charts and put a dirty yellow finger on our position. Through slitty eyes he examined me.

'You want to make a run for it over the North Sea?'

'Do I ever.'

'Fing is, Keef, we 'ave to do it in a force three otherwise she'll go over.'

Pablo and Pockets looked at each other and turned white, the adventure seeming a little more precarious than they had mettle for. The boat was flat-bottomed, which meant any more than force four and she'd sink like a stone.

We were to set sail the next morning but not before a mammoth drinking session. Sleeping on a few planks in sleeping bags in a freezing steel hull and waking with a hangover wasn't the ideal preparation for a voyage. I kicked a mound of moulding flesh that I assumed was Pockets. It replied by poking a reptilian head out.

''Allo there. Remember me?'

'Obviously not. What are you?'

'The name's Roy. You said you'd pay me to help Arthur.'

At the other end of the plank Arthur grumbled into life, dirt smeared all over his face from fixing the engine the day before.

'Arthur? Is this something to do with you?'

Arthur squinted at Roy, now busily packing his sleeping bag away, having miraculously pulled a washbag from somewhere.

'Nope. Looks like a pervert to me.'

Pockets ambled in from upstairs holding a bottle of wine, swigging liberally and pointing accusingly at Roy.

'Who's that? I'm supposed to be the butt of all jokes round here,' before sniffing round the empty vodka bottles. 'Shall we go to the pub?'

'You've just been to the fucking pub. Now get cooking breakfast. I'm the captain. We sail at midday.'

We set off. Overcome by the romance of the sea I reached for the captain's log. In times of extreme pressure the captain of a diseased and pustulent crew would seek solace in making a record of the occasion, which could be consulted on future voyages or in times of crisis.

I lit a pipe and picked up a pen.

Captain's Log. February 7th 2002. 'We slipped out of port under the cover of dark, wind favourable, dawn lighting up the underbelly of the sky ... making good progress across the shipping lanes of the Rotterdam estuary and the Zuider Zee ... when ... wait ... Tom? Tom! That's a fucking super tanker ...'

Before we knew it the boat was rocked by a huge wave. We had been hit portside by the wake of an oil tanker and were now being fast approached starboard by the *Hellespont Fairfax*, a monster ship that would either swallow us herself or let her wave do it.

Pablo turned white and everything not tethered down flew into the air and shattered. Then the second wave hit. The washing machine flew off its shelf and nearly decapitated Roy. On deck Tom struggled manfully to keep her out of the path of the ship.

'We've strayed into a shipping lane, Keef.'

'I can fucking see that, Tom.'

Pablo grabbed a life jacket and held on, wibbling things like: 'We're all going to fucking die.'

Arthur shouted at Pockets and Roy to tether everything down, only Tom remained calm and impassive, spliff still dangling from the corner of his mouth. Then the engine stopped.

'The engine's out, Keef.'

'Yes I fucking know it is! What the fuck are you going to do about it?'

Tom just looked calmly out to sea, as if accepting his destiny. As we drifted further out into the estuary, ships the size of the Empire State Building increased in number. My dream had turned into a nightmare. We were in serious trouble.

Tom sent out a radio signal for help, but no one was in the area to help a bunch of ill-equipped tossers. As my crew regretted the day they'd ever set eyes on me, on the horizon appeared salvation. A floating Spar supermarket tug that carried fuel and food supplies was sailing towards us. We waved it down frantically and got a tow to safety in the port of Willemstad, a little fortified town that would need decidedly more fortification now that Pockets had arrived to pillage its bars of young tender flesh.

Chapter 30

WE SPENT THE next three weeks there carrying out repairs to the engine and getting the bulk of the renovation done and leading the townsfolk astray with a series of fancy-dress parties and Dutch party songs. Then Zoe came to stay and took one look at us all, filthy, oil-stained and gibbering, and checked into a nearby hotel.

'I hate to remind you, Keith, but you have a play to direct.'

With that we went home and started to prepare for touring *Glastonbury*. Without going into too much detail, it was an absolute fucking nightmare.

In fact, I will go into detail, because it's an indictment of the state of this country that when people try and do something different, i.e. put on theatre that means something to a generation of people alienated by the theatre, they are stopped by the very people who should be doing the most to support them. The local councils. I accuse three in particular. The councils of Cardiff, Manchester and Brighton all conspired to close the production for the simple reason that they were scared. They didn't know what it was.

What it was: a big-top tent, seating five hundred, covered in coconut matting, no seats, so the audience sat on the floor and were free to get up and go to the bar or the loo during the performance. Outside we had Glastonbury portaloos and stalls. The show would open with a band every night and we never revealed who it would be – so it could be New Order or a local band, that was the beauty of it. We didn't sell the show on the band, it was part of the experience. The band would come on and play as if they were part of the 'show' before walking off stage after less than three minutes, and the play would begin.

Our first date on the tour was Cardiff and we were due to pitch the big top in the park next to the Welsh College of Drama in the middle of town. We very specifically chose inner-city parks because of the proximity to students and people who didn't usually go to the theatre. On arriving in Cardiff we found we had been moved from our location and stuck in a field miles from the centre. The council had got scared, seen the amount of publicity the show was getting – Damien was designing the set and New Order had agreed to play in Manchester – and expected a rave. They had no hard evidence for this whatsoever. We correctly applied for a theatre licence. By moving our location they'd effectively shafted us. We'd relied on the location to get a walk-up crowd, and we had none.

On top of this we were caught in the worst hurricane Wales had seen for twenty years. The field was waterlogged and the cast demoralised. While Zoe battled with the council, I tried to rehearse in – ironically – truly Glastonbury-like conditions. On top of all that, we opened the same night as Wales played Italy at the Millennium Stadium, and beat them. Oh dear.

The next day the reviewers trashed it. We hadn't invited the broadsheets to review the show because it wasn't about that, it was never for a middle-aged broadsheet audience. It was a living piece of theatre for people who didn't go to the theatre. The reviewers came anyway, pissed off not to be invited, and trooped en masse all the way from London to sit on the floor of a tent in the rain with the sole intent of trashing it.

A few hours later we got a call from Manchester council, our next destination. They announced that they were cancelling the licence. With it went all our hopes for the success of the tour. They told us that an article in the *Manchester Evening News* had leaked that New Order were playing at our show. Despite our protestations that they were doing a three-minute guest slot (legally allowed under the rules of a theatre licence), they insisted on cancelling. This meant we had to return all tickets from a sold-out week and remain in Cardiff for another week. I don't need to tell you the state of the cast. Zoe managed to raise enough money to save us and ensure we got the show to Birmingham, where more bad weather meant small houses. We were out of money and mentally exhausted.

Worse news was still to come. Brighton council called and, now nervous about the show, despite no hard evidence, decided that we couldn't put the tent in the middle of town, it wasn't safe. Here we were taking the rap for Fatboy Slim's disastrously popular gig the previous year.

'Maybe it's time to call it a day,' I said.

'No way,' said Zoe. 'We have to get this show to Brighton.'

I was doing my best to keep the cast up. Paul Broughton, Kate Ford, Kieran O'Brien and Chris Coghill were with me when we heard the news about Brighton, sheltering from the rain in the Moroccan yurt that doubled as our dressing room.

It seemed like a million-in-one chance. The council were not only disputing the site, but the licence as well. The money had run out. I wanted to quit there and then, and had it been up to me, would have done. But it was Zoe's call.

With a superhuman effort we secured a site and a licence for Brighton Racecourse, and despite opening four nights late, we played triumphantly to two packed houses – five hundred people each night. We were vindicated. The fuckers in charge of local councils in this country – who would much rather we all lay on our sofas and vegetated watching reality TV – were defeated. *Glastonbury* the play rose like a phoenix from the ashes that weekend. And despite the nightmare, the debt and all of us losing money, it had been worth it.

The call came through to me while Pablo and I were in the studio producing my daughter Lily's first pop album. Pabs was the technical maestro, laying down the beats and operating the desk, and I chipped in with the tunes and melodies. Lily would wander in occasionally, sit down and build up a spliff.

'Right, what do you want me to do?'

'Well, some singing might be a start.'

'Oh all right then.'

She got up and dragged herself to the vocal booth, the typical seventeen-year-old draped in the latest casual fashion, mountains of gold and a leather Adidas jacket.

'Lily.' My paternal concern kicked in. 'Is that a skirt or a belt?'

'Yeah, like *you* care, Dad. The last time you looked at me you thought I was your latest girlfriend.'

'Just shut up and start singing.'

Once the mouth opened, the argumentative youth who reminded one too much of the person who stole your phone, was transformed into an angel. Lily had a voice that could shatter hearts.

'Dad.'

'Yes, Lily.'

'You know Kevin.'

'Who?'

'Your other son. And Grace, your other daughter.'

'What about them?'

I didn't like where this was going. Lily, as you know, had the knack of bringing up awkward topics at inopportune moments. It being her great delight to make me feel uncomfortable, just to see what I did.

'Don't you want to see them?'

'No, Lily.'

'Why not?'

'Because.'

'Because what? Aren't you curious about them?'

'No.'

'Why not? They're your kids.'

'No they're not. They never have been.'

I saw my kids as Lily and Alfie. They were my kids who I loved with all my heart. The others, I didn't *not* love, but they weren't my kids.

Lily tutted and sloped off, seeing she wasn't getting anywhere, leaving the studio after her rudimentary fifteen-minute stay.

'Gotta go, Dad. There's a party in Hackney innit.'

Pabs started loading her vocal tracks and was interrupted by his mobile. He didn't answer it. It kept ringing so we turned it off. Then mine started ringing. It was ten at night. We turned off all the phones. Then the studio phone rang.

'Keith, it's Amanda. I've got some bad news. Joe's dead.'

Pablo dropped his guitar and covered his face. Pabs had been in Joe Strummer's latest band The Mescaleros but had left two years earlier.

'I haven't seen him. I didn't say goodbye.'

Luckily I did. Two nights previously Joe and his wife Luce had been drinking in the Groucho. But that didn't make the shock any less profound. He was exactly the same age as me.

At the funeral, while hundreds of well-wishers crammed into Willesden Crematorium, I nervously fingered the poem that Luce had asked me to read. It was the last lyrics Joe had ever written, for the Mandela concert in South Africa. It was a huge honour and my voice quivered as the room stopped shuffling and listened. There wasn't a sound except for the sound of sadness and grief. No words came out. All I could see was Joe in the coffin.

I'd taken Alfie to say a last goodbye to Joe in the funeral parlour at Taunton. Alf tucked a packet of blue Rizla in Joe's top pocket. The room looked like Joe's life, decorated in colourful flags and punk memorabilia by Pockets and Dermot, who were both crying in the corner. Dermot, a big hard geezer from Manchester, was inconsolable.

'He was a real friend; all the rest are just acquaintances.'

It was Joe in the box. It was *Joe*. But he was dead. He looked dead but he also looked like Joe. Dressed in his favourite black. In the background a ghetto blaster played his favourite music.

At the funeral I gave my speech and people started clapping. It was all a blur.

'Well done, Dad.'

Alfie lurched up to me in a borrowed suit and new shoes that his sister had bought him. My eyes filled up. It was too much to take in. Lily and Alfie stared at me, worried. Lily put her arm through mine.

'You OK, Dad?'

At that moment a sense of my own mortality drifted in.

'I was just thinking of how fucked up life is. Eh kids?'

They rolled their eyes.

'Well yours is Dad, yeah.'

I was so fucking proud of my kids, but wondered what effect the chaos of my life had on them. It had made them very worldly and that was something to be proud of, and they knew how much I loved them. But there must have been other effects …

Lily was on the phone for the fourth time that day. It was 11 September 2004, Alfie's eighteenth, and me and Zoe were on our way to the Groucho.

'You are coming, aren't you, Dad?'

'Yes, Lily, I'm on my way.'

This uncharacteristic diligence on Lily's part should have alerted me that she was up to something. We arrived at Groucho's to find the party in full swing, which involved lots of moody teenagers skinning up in corners and no one dancing. As the night wore on, Alfie got more drunk and more loving.

'I love you, Dad.'

'I love you, Alf.'

'Nah, man. I mean I really love you, yeah.'

'Yes, Alf.'

I'd noticed another kid staring at me for some time. He was tall and good-looking, wearing a baseball cap, smart shirt and jeans. Then I got a feeling something was definitely up. Lily walked in the room grinning from ear to ear accompanied by Grace, my daughter. I'd met Grace a couple of times before – she'd called me and asked if we could go for a drink. I got the impression that she was fine about it all. She was the spitting image of her mother, and now she was a twenty-one-year-old woman, pretty and bright. She may not have been 'fine about it all' but that is what I liked to believe. Anyway, to say that I wasn't exactly expecting to see her at Alfie's party is an understatement. I pulled Lily aside.

'Why is Grace here?'

'Because Alfie wanted her here. She's his half sister.'

'OK, that's cool.'

It was definitely time to leave and I said my goodbyes and headed to the exit.

'Keith.'

I turned around. It was the good-looking tall boy in the baseball cap. He moved and stood in my way, staring at me with some urgency.

'I'm Kevin.' He grabbed my hand and started to shake it. The eyes … 'Your son.'

I knew I'd seen his eyes before: they were my own. Lily came to join him, so did Grace, all watching me. Lily stared at me precociously. Grace just smiled nervously.

'Hi, Dad.'

'Oh er, hi, Grace.'

Grace looked at me expectantly, waiting for something.

'Aren't you going to say anything?'

'Like what?'

I laughed nervously and hugged her. Over her shoulder Lily stared provocatively, watching for my reaction and wondering what firework to let off next. Lily had orchestrated all this. She is a very emotional person, some would say a drama queen. She did it without considering its effects, just because she wanted everything 'to be all right' and was yearning for a big family moment – for us to be one big happy family. I suppose I'd ruined all that for her by leaving Alison when she was five. So, standing there confronted by a son I'd never met before and another daughter who was virtually a stranger, I didn't feel it was my place to be angry with Lily. Just with myself.

Kevin continued to stare. I laughed nervously. I could see he was desperate for some acknowledgment from me.

'Oh, er, can we, er, talk?' he said.

'Yeah definitely, but not now, it's not a good time,' I countered.

He nodded and we hugged. It was brief, awkward. But it was a start.

I have to admit that I ran. Being cold-called like that left me high and dry. We drove back to Oxford to Zoe's place and I didn't say one word for the entire journey. What was I thinking? Well, yeah, some guilt about the past, but not much. I was far more concerned about what the future was going to be. I was scared that they wanted me to be the 'father' thing all of a sudden. I wouldn't be able to give them the emotional stuff they needed, if that was what they wanted.

I was also worried about Alfie and what he would think. He was my boy. Would Alf feel threatened by Kevin's presence? A few weeks later, Grace contacted me to tell me that Kevin was in custody. Grace had stayed in contact with him after the party and now felt the need to tell me that he was in trouble and could I help him. He was in court the next week, so I went along and sat in the crowd so he could see I was there. It must have been important for him because even though he was remanded in custody again, he wrote me a letter.

I think it started: *Dear Dad* … Well, I was never going to be that. But the letter went on to say how he'd liked seeing me there and would I go and visit him inside. I went along because I had to tell him the truth. Which was that I didn't feel the love for him that I felt for Alfie. He told me he respected that and he just wanted me to acknowledge him as my son. Which I did.

I did what I could for him. I got him a job at Harrods selling designer clothes, and I also paid for the mother of his two children to bury her father.

Many years ago I said to my brother we have to be friends first, brothers second. OK, I'm not very good at families, but that's because I believe that families fuck you up. I think you have to get on with being who you are instead of being part of a family. The human being is part herd animal, part individualist. Which is why I've always found gay politics so interesting. The families they belong to are created, not inherited. Are they any less valid? Of course not. But the idea of The Family as an institution per se, I don't believe in or respect.

The more children who reared their heads, the more money I had to earn, even if it meant taking jobs I didn't want. Work took me to Mumbai to film some shameless reality show. The banality and celebrity-driven talentlessness of modern life nearly finished me off. It seemed the whole point of taking me to Mumbai was to edit me in between Caprice's tits and Julie Goodyear's bingo wings.

But Mumbai was the biggest head trip for years. I bought a little piano thing that you blew into, and kept cast and crew amused for hours by making up songs. Walking through the shit-stained streets I was amazed to see whole families living on traffic islands. However poor they were, the Indian women kept their space beautifully clean and tidy, while their babies picked up any old shit and put it in their mouths.

Dennis Waterman was also on the job and suggested a round of golf on an exclusive well-groomed course that could have housed the entire slum neighbourhood next door. Suddenly an Indian came running out of the clubhouse with my phone, shouting, 'Phone call for Mr Allen. They said very urgent.'

He urged me to put the phone to my ear.

'Keith, it's Kevin.'

I feared the worst. My brother's voice meant it was something to do with my parents.

'What's happened?'

'It's Mum. You better get on the next plane. They don't think she'll last the night.'

Before I left for India, Mum had gone in for a major heart operation. I nearly didn't go and see her before I left, being too lazy to drive all the way to Cambridgeshire. Luckily I did go. Thousands of miles away in Mumbai, faced with the prospect of my mother's death, it seemed the best, most wonderful decision I'd ever made. I hailed a trishaw.

'Take me to a shrine. And let me stop at a shop for some cigarettes.'

It was seven months since I'd last smoked. Now it was time to reach out for instant comfort. At the shrine I cried and said goodbye to Mum.

So many fuck-ups in our relationship, so many complications and wrong turns, so much lack of understanding, blame and regret. Yet I knew she loved me and did what was best for me.

The crew had run round trying to get me out of India as fast as possible. The plane touched down and I switched my mobile on as the stewardesses glared at me.

'Kev? What's the news?'

'She's still with us.'

In the car on the way to the hospital, prepared for the worst, the words 'Keith Allen, what a cunt you are sometimes' went round in my head, followed by: 'Yeah, but I'm not a bad person.'

There's no point in trying to conform. I can only be who I am. I exist in the public space, to perform. This is where I live and there's no point in fighting it.

Mum pulled through. The look on Dad's face said it all as he choked back tears of joy.

He couldn't imagine life without her. I'd spent my whole life swimming against the tide that my father and my mother had swum with, together.

Afterword

EVERYONE IS FULL of self-doubt, me included. It's an integral part of being. On reflection, I think that this self-doubt is exploited by our society and its institutions, which seem more concerned with putting you down than building you up.

Believe it or not, I'm a shy person and my behaviour is a double-bluff. I did once say to my ex-wife that given the way I live my life, if I ever stopped and looked at myself from the outside, or examined what was underneath, the whole house of cards would come down. For years I hid behind a veneer of not caring. For example, kind of gloriously not ever wanting to do a stand-up comedy 'act'. This was to disguise my fear of failure. Never organising myself was another protection. Sometimes I got away with it by living in the joyousness of constant invention, but the fact remains that the greatest fear any performer or actor has is the fear of being found out – and so it was with me.

I know this to be true, therefore I have to keep going. Keep moving, both physically and mentally, forward – without any backward or side-ways glances. I know that both teachers of acting and therapists say that in order to reconstruct you they have to strip you down first. For much of my life I've been like a train with no brakes hurtling along at high speed. It didn't matter about the speed so long as I didn't think about the fact there were no brakes. If I had, then the whole fucking train would come off the rails.

But I'm quite happy as I am, and also happy with the fruits of my philosophy in life up to now.

Obviously there is a good deal of it left to live. What happens next, I know not. In fact, a good title for this book would have been: *One Thing Led to Another* … Which is why I love festivals so much, because that's what they're all about: nothing planned, just opportunities. You could say that I see my life as one long festival.

A great friend, a famous and talented man, once said to me, 'I wish I had the balls to live like you do,' and I think he meant the way I have no qualms about moving on, leaving everything and just going, not feeling any overwhelming responsibility.

I'm an outsider. That doesn't mean I'm lonely or alone. I'm not. I have wonderful friendships and I cherish those I love. It's just that I'm outside of it all, looking in. It's the best place for me to be to have some sort of effect on the world.

I live in a community of outsiders: boat people. We're different. I didn't set out to be one; it just happened. My boat was the first home I owned. I was forty-seven when I bought it. I have never felt more at ease or at home anywhere in the world. My neighbours are from all walks of life – a policeman, a National Trust photographer, BT engineer, novelist, carpenter, glassblower – and not a weirdo among them, but there is something about them, and if you've never been a 'live-aboard' you won't sense it. If you have, you'll know. It's a sort of stubbornness, a deep-rooted refusal to do it the proper way. It's not a community in a romantic sense. It's a community of individuals exercising their right to be different. I don't want to be locked into the pain of bricks and mortar and mortgages and debt. I don't want to live somewhere that has been designed as far away from nature as it's possible to be. I like it when rainwater leaks into the boat. I like the way it rocks on the water. I love the fact I can move any time I want to. I love it because the cunts can't get me on the treadmill called home-ownership.

Years ago in an interview I said, 'If everyone was an anarchist, I would become a bank manager.' I really am like that. I *am* full of self-doubt, but creating this book has rid me of some of it.

If I hadn't met Alison and married her, we wouldn't have two of the most wonderful children parents could wish for. We married because it was the right thing to do at the time; we parted for the right reasons too.

We both knew it wouldn't last – I said it first, that's all. Of course, I feel terrible about the pain it caused, but mostly I celebrate all that's happened. Gracie was brought up in a loving environment, and we speak. Kevin I feel bad about … that I'm working on.

A couple of years ago I was coming back along the Thames with Zoe on board when a rope wrapped itself round the propeller and I had no power. No power means no steering, you are sliding along the tide. My mate Tom was on a small cruiser yacht and threw us a line. He tried his best but his stern was being dragged under (my boat is a hundred feet long). He came alongside and Zoe jumped ship, and Tom and I radioed the Port of London Authority for help. If your life is not threatened you can't send out a 'mayday', so the PLA operative in his wisdom said he'd try and get a boat to me at the first light. It was two o'clock in the morning; the wind was gusting up to 70mph and I was at the mercy of the tide.

'You fucking idiot. I won't fucking be here at first light – I won't have a boat left.'

'That's the earliest we can do it, sir.'

Luckily, the wind was blowing on to the tide, which meant we were sort of holding our position in the middle of the Thames, but it also meant the waves were pretty big, and being flat-bottomed she went through terrible rolls. I was frantic, panicking.

'This is my life – everything I fucking own is here!'

Everything … I put on my life-jacket and stood on deck, feeling utterly hopeless, unable to do anything about my predicament, and then something strange happened. I thought, hang on a minute, I've got a life-jacket, Tom is standing by… if it sinks, Tom can fish me out of the water. I'm not going to die. What am I worried about?

I made my way to the bow of the wildly rolling *Kaapsedraai* and sat down. What was I going to lose? All my possessions? So what? The things that meant most to me, I could save: two letters Lily wrote to me when she was about fourteen, Alfie's first pair of trainers and a diary of his holiday with me and Nira when he was about six, and a couple of paintings given to me by friends. If she was going to founder, I would have time to get them. It was a wonderful moment: in a howling gale, about to lose everything I owned, without a care in the world.

I wish I could say I'd engineered the moment. But I hadn't; I'd arrived at it by a combination of instinct, wilfulness and making some terrible mistakes and some wise decisions, with some other force, I know not what, pushing me. Sitting at the front of that boat seemed to define me, and I smiled, because I liked the feeling.

I was rescued by a small tug. Its skipper had overheard the conversation with the PLA and came out and threw me a line, then towed me onto a pontoon where we were able to cut the rope off the propeller. They charged me £100. Good value, I think.

I know deep down I'm a good person. And I know that you must fuck who you want when you want but understand that it comes at a price. And remember, readers, cocaine is administered by Catholic countries and heroin is administered by Muslim countries. If you base your belief system on this, whether your belief system is moral or spiritual, you will have to conclude that it's wise not to believe the hype.

Good luck and good hunting.

PS Obviously I haven't mentioned most of my sexual liaisons. I haven't because too many people would be hurt, but I wish I had the skill to be able to describe in detail the night I first made love to Janet Street-Porter, once on her snooker table, and then on the bed upstairs in her fabulously appointed flat near Clerkenwell. I don't have the words to do justice to that night, but the earth did move for me, and for Janet too, I believe, though maybe that was due more to the fact that hers was a hospital bed on wheels than to my legendary technique.

I think it's too negative to write about people I loathe. Nothing good can come of it. So if you were expecting plenty of that sort of stuff, I hope you're not too disappointed, but I will leave you with this: AA Gill – what a cunt!